CITY OF WRITERS

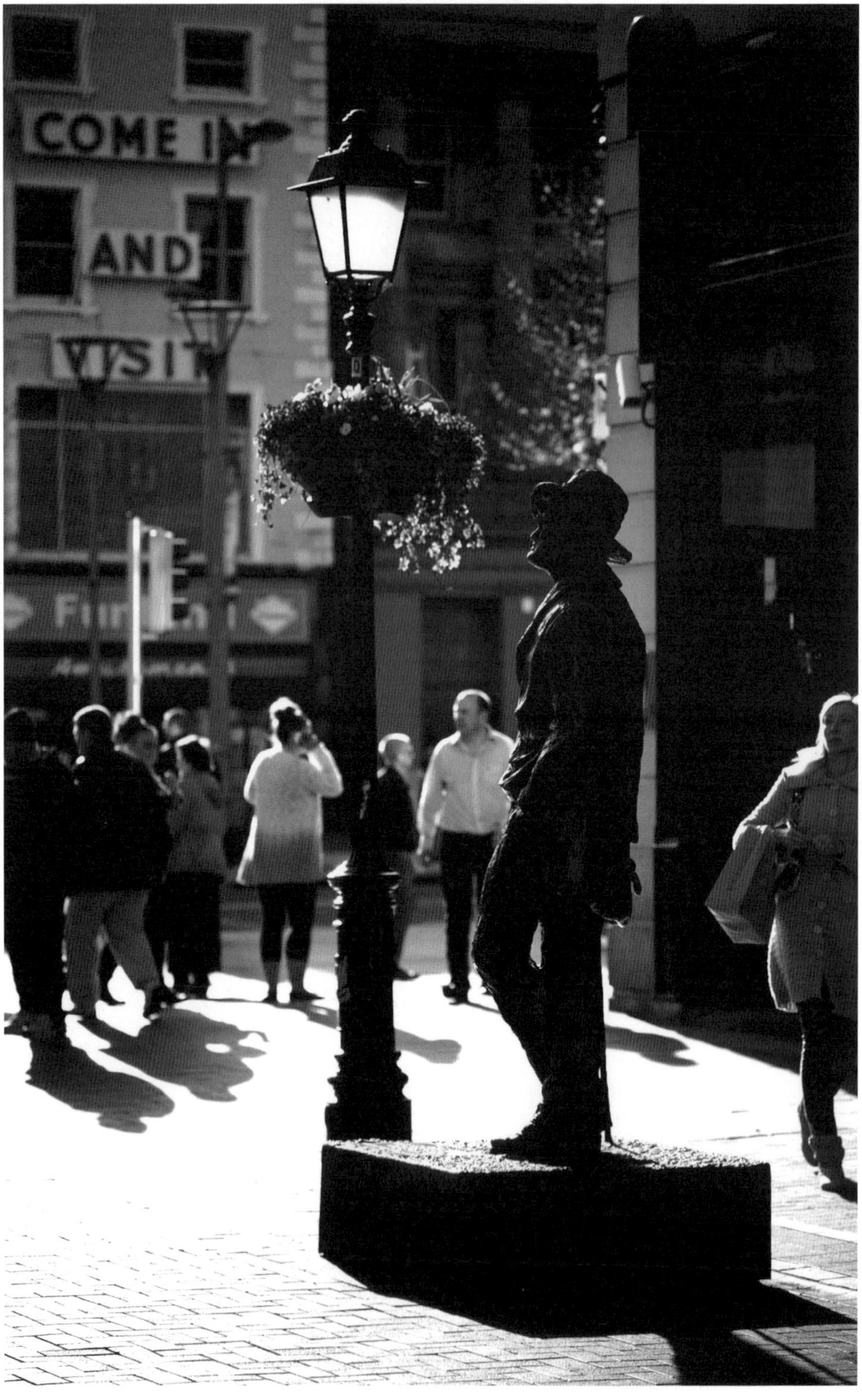
COME
AND

Best Wishes
- Brendan Lynch

CITY OF WRITERS

*From Behan to Wilde –
The Lives and Homes of Dublin Authors*

Brendan Lynch

The Liffey Press

the liffey press

Published by
The Liffey Press Ltd
Raheny Shopping Centre, Second Floor
Raheny, Dublin 5, Ireland
www.theliffeypress.com

© 2013 Brendan Lynch

A catalogue record of this book is
available from the British Library.

ISBN 978-1-908308-45-0

All rights reserved. No part of this publication may be reproduced or transmitted in any form or by any means, including photocopying and recording, without written permission of the publisher. Such written permission must also be obtained before any part of this publication is stored in a retrieval system of any nature. Requests for permission should be directed to The Liffey Press, Raheny Shopping Centre, Second Floor, Raheny, Dublin 5, Ireland.

Printed in Spain by GraphyCems

Contents

Foreword, Peter Costello	vii
About the Author	viii
Introduction and Acknowledgements	ix
Samuel Beckett, *6 Clare Street*	3
Brendan Behan, *15 Herbert Street*	9
Maeve Binchy, *1 Pembroke Road*	15
Dion Boucicault, *47 Lower Gardiner Street*	21
Elizabeth Bowen, *15 Herbert Place*	27
Christy Brown, *54 Stannaway Road, Kimmage*	33
William Carleton, *Francis Street*	39
Austin Clarke, *15 Mountjoy Street*	45
Padraic Colum, *Railway Cottage, Eden Road, Glasthule*	51
James Patrick (J.P.) Donleavy, *38 Trinity College, Dublin*	57
Ernie Gebler, *Theatre De Luxe Cinema, Camden Street*	63
Oliver St. John Gogarty, *5 Parnell Square East*	69
Patrick Lafcadio Hearn, *73 Upper Leeson Street*	75
James Joyce, *41 Brighton Square, Rathgar*	81
Patrick Kavanagh, *62 Pembroke Road*	87
Ben Kiely, *119 Morehampton Road, Donnybrook*	93
Mary Lavin, *11 Upper Lad Lane*	99

Joseph Sheridan le Fanu, *70 Merrion Square* — 105

Charles Lever, *34 Amiens Street* — 111

Samuel Lover, *60 Grafton Street* — 117

Patricia Lynch, *39 The Rise, Glasnevin* — 123

James Clarence Mangan, *3 Fishamble Street* — 129

Charles Robert Maturin, *37 York Street* — 135

George Moore, *4 Upper Ely Place* — 141

Thomas Moore, *12 Aungier Street* — 147

Sydney Lady Morgan, *39 Kildare Street* — 153

Seán O'Casey, *422 North Circular Road* — 159

Frank O'Connor, *Court Apartments, Wilton Place* — 165

Sean O'Faolain, *43 Parkgate Street* — 171

Liam O'Flaherty, *Court Apartments, Wilton Place* — 177

Brian O'Nolan/Flann O'Brien, *25 Herbert Place* — 183

James Plunkett, *20 Bath Street, Irishtown* — 189

George Russell (AE), *17 Rathgar Avenue* — 195

George Bernard Shaw, *33 Synge Street* — 201

James Stephens, *5 Thomas Court, Thomas Street* — 207

Bram Stoker, *15 Marino Crescent, Clontarf* — 213

Jonathan Swift, *St Patrick's Cathedral* — 219

John Millington Synge, *4 Orwell Park, Rathgar* — 225

Wilde Family, *1 Merrion Square* — 231

W.B. Yeats, *82 Merrion Square* — 237

Parsons Bookshop, *Baggot Street Bridge* — 243

Some Literary Walks, Pubs and Cemeteries — 248

Recommended Reading — 276

Bibliography — 280

Foreword

Since the days of Jonathan Swift Dublin has been a city teeming with writers of all kinds. Some were men and women of their day who are now forgotten to all except the literary historian. Others are among the great names of literature: Swift, Addison, Sheridan le Fanu, Lady Morgan, Oscar Wilde, Yeats, Synge, James Joyce, Sean O'Casey, James Plunkett, Maeve Binchy, Roddy Doyle . . . the list goes on.

Brendan Lynch, a lively enthusiast for all things literary, has tracked down their homes and haunts, which were many and varied, from grand mansions and stately houses down to cottages and single rooms. In this book he takes the reader on a tour of the city to visit these places and hear of some of the adventures, and misadventures of those who, over the centuries, have made Dublin an internationally recognised 'City of Literature'. It's an inspirational tour.

– Peter Costello, author of *James Joyce: The Years of Growth*

About the Author

Brendan Lynch is a former racing cyclist and driver. A supporter of pacifist philosopher Bertrand Russell, he was imprisoned in London for 1960s Campaign for Nuclear Disarmament activities.

He has written seven books and contributed to national and international media from the *Irish Times* to *The Observer*, *The Times* and *The European*. His first book, *Green Dust*, won the Guild of Motoring Writers' Pierre Dreyfus Award.

A consultant for *The Encyclopaedia of Ireland*, Brendan's features on Irish writers encouraged the establishment of Dublin's George Bernard Shaw Museum and the James Joyce Cultural Centre. *City of Writers* is his third book on literary Dublin.

Also by Brendan Lynch (see www.brendanlynch.ie)

Green Dust: Ireland's Unique Motor Racing History
Triumph of the Red Devil: The Gordon Bennett Cup Race 1903
There Might Be a Drop of Rain Yet: A Memoir
Parsons Bookshop: At the Heart of Bohemian Dublin 1949-1989
Yesterday We Were in America: Alcock and Brown, First to Fly the Atlantic Non-Stop
Prodigals and Geniuses. The Writers and Artists of Dublin's Baggotonia

Introduction and Acknowledgements

Ireland's latest export, I arrived at London's Euston station on the morning of 7 November 1961. Books, expensive to buy in those days, filled half of my suitcase. After wading through the 'No Blacks – No Irish' accommodation adverts, I found a bedsit on Earl's Court's Warwick Road.

The genteel landlady noticed the literature. 'I believe you can't cross a street in Dublin without bumping into a poet or a writer! Did you hear of Robert Gibbings – he lived next door until a few years ago?'

The Corkman who had written and illustrated *Lovely is the Lee* and *Trumpets from Montparnasse*. *The* Robert Gibbings!

The landlady enthused: 'Many writers lived in the area. Another of your compatriots, Oscar Wilde, stayed in Courtfield Gardens between trials in 1895. G.K. Chesterton lived in Warwick Gardens – and Leigh Hunt just across the road in Edwardes Square!'

As time dissipated my alien's gloom, I set out to retrace the footsteps of childhood heroes Oliver Goldsmith, Samuel Johnson and Charles Lamb. My former neighbour Leigh Hunt had done exactly the same.

He wrote in 1847: 'I once had duties to perform which kept me out late at night, and severely taxed my health and spirits. My path lay through a neighbourhood in which Dryden lived: and though nothing could be more commonplace, and I used to be tired to the heart and soul of me, I never hesitated to go a little out of my way, purely that I might pass through Gerrard Street, and so give myself the shadow of a pleasant thought.'

Hunt's frequent detours brought him closer to his literary idols: 'I seem to have made friends with them in their own houses: to have walked and talked, and suffered and enjoyed with them.' An opinion endorsed by Thomas Moore and fellow-poet Samuel Rogers, who emulated Hunt's homage to Dryden's home.

Pilgrimages had been made for centuries to the homes and churches of saints. From the seventeenth century, English literary shrines attracted similar interest. John Milton's house became a tourist attraction, followed by the homes of Samuel Johnson and Charles Dickens. In 1867, the Society of Arts erected its first blue plaque at Lord Byron's birthplace. From saints to sinners – as up to recently many Irish literati were considered – the homes of Dublin's writers are now similarly signposted.

Young James and Stanislaus Joyce walked to the house of Oscar Wilde. Visiting the homes of writers, following in their footsteps, provides a rare sense of immediacy. A tangible feeling of the life they led, the surroundings which shaped them, an insight into their work. James Stephens, who had stolen bread to survive, dreamed here of becoming a writer. There, equally deprived James Clarence Mangan shuffled in his oversize cloak. Young George Bernard Shaw wiped his shoes on that foot-scraper. On this canal bank, James Joyce first expounded his theories of art.

Laden with books and encouragement, aspiring Patrick Kavanagh and Frank O'Connor descended those suicidal steps from George Russell's house. Here, George Moore wrote under paintings by his friend, Eduard Manet. Across the street, Oliver St. John Gogarty was kidnapped. This Grafton Street hamburger emporium housed *Envoy*'s office and Des MacNamara's salon. Where housepainter Brendan Behan first met Pike Theatre owners, Alan and Carolyn Simpson, who later propelled him to international fame.

Literary history illuminates every corner of the city. Experiencing these sites adds a new dimension to Dublin, its thoroughfares assume a significance which they will never lose. A quarter of a century after my London footfall, I returned home. I lost little time in retracing the footsteps of Wilde, Beckett, Behan and Bowen. This book is my tribute to them and a guide for those who wish to enlarge their knowledge of our many writers.

I started with a list of twenty. It soon grew to forty. Such is the multitude of authors associated with our modest metropolis, I could have included as many again. Little wonder that award-winning Colum McCann – another Dubliner! – described Dublin as 'the world's greatest literary city'. My apologies to those who would like to have seen Jonah Barrington, Maeve Brennan, George Berkeley, Edmund Burke, William Congreve, John Denham, Michael Farrell, Samuel Ferguson, Anna Maria Hall, Felicia Hemans, James Liddy, Edward Martyn, Robert Noonan, Martin O'Cadhain, Julia O'Faolain, Thomas Parnell, Lennox Robinson, Richard Brinsley Sheridan, Annie M. P. Smithson, Richard Steele, poets Katherine Tynan, Richard D'Alton Williams and once celebrated Mary Tighe, and other personal favourites.

Readers may be familiar with Brendan Behan's 'My Great Red Racing Bike' story about cycling to Dun Laoghaire to redecorate a house. All went well until Brendan found a carpet of yellowing newspapers: 'For me to raise a piece of old linoleum was like opening the door of a library. I promised myself that I would only read a little bit, that I would just glance at the papers before I threw them into the snow outside, but when I raised the linoleum and saw the head-line: "Viceroy's visit to Grangegorman. Vicereine waves green linen handkerchief, scenes of mad enthusiasm," I was lost and read it inch by inch...'

Beware! Like Brendan's commission, this celebratory volume may take longer to conclude than you imagine. It is highly likely – and this is the intention – that it will lead you down pleasant and enriching paths to the works of the writers themselves. And, maybe, to such atmospheric and neglected treasures as Marsh's Library, which was frequented from 1701 by generations of writers from William Carleton and James Clarence Mangan to Bram Stoker and James Joyce.

Prepare to be entertained and thrilled! Before you know where you are, you will be indulging in Lady Morgan's gossip, reliving 1904 Dublin in *Ulysses,* or its literary scandals in George Moore's memoirs. Savouring Wildean wit or wandering the hills and woods with James Stephens' *Crock of Gold* philosophers. Hyperventilating to the Gothic fantasies of le Fanu and Stoker, marvelling at the incendiary O'Casey and Swift, bathing in the lyricism of Yeats and James Clarence Mangan, or reflecting outside Parsons Bookshop where, as Mary Lavin noted: 'One met as many interesting writers on the floor of the shop as on the shelves!' To whet your appetite, I have suggested seven walks and a Recommended Reading list. Also, details of literary hostelries in which to read or recover.

What treasures await! What a wonder one small city could have produced such riches – some of the greatest literature in the English language. And by writers from such diverse backgrounds, tutored and untutored. Was it because, as Joyce wrote, Dublin was the city 'where the air without is impregnated with rainbow moisture, life essence celestial'? Or as critic Harold Bloom wrote, hailing the Literary Revival as one of the most productive periods in the history of literature: 'The rest of the world discovered what the Irish peasants had long known: that the people of Ireland are natural storytellers.'

Introduction and Acknowledgements

Poet Gabriel Rosenstock insisted that, Greek and Latin aside, Irish is the oldest written literary language in Europe. Are our authors more entertaining because the Gaelic language bequeathed a delivery which is colour and music compared to 'proper' English? The late Maeve Binchy had her own theory: 'I think the Irish are lucky in that we never had the Victorian concept of waiting until you have something to say before you say it! We value good talkers much more than good listeners, and we love telling stories. This fluent delight in telling what happened is easily translated into writing down our thoughts.'

Harold Bloom noted: 'English drama, after Shakespeare, comes alive only in Anglo-Irish writers: Congreve, Sheridan, Goldsmith are part of a cavalcade that proceeds through Shaw and Wilde, Synge and O'Casey, before its apotheosis in Beckett.'

The earlier writers covered here hailed almost exclusively from the immigrant Huguenot or ruling Protestant class, including Jonathan Swift, Charles Lever, Samuel Lover, Charles Maturin and Joseph Sheridan le Fanu. The modern Irish novel emerged in the early nineteenth century, in the work of Maria Edgeworth, Lady Morgan and Samuel Lover. A. Norman Jeffares described Thomas Moore's *Irish Melodies* (1808-1834) as 'the first successful manifestation of cultural nationalism: the turbulent present shimmers obliquely through the glorious past, which lights up a putative future'.

The Irish Literary Revival of the late nineteenth century intensified interest in Ireland's Gaelic heritage. Its leading protagonist, W.B. Yeats, became his country's first Nobel Prize-winner in 1923, an achievement repeated two years later by playwright and polemicist, George Bernard Shaw. Ireland's literary reputation was further enhanced by Europe's premier Modernist writer James Joyce and by subsequent Nobel Laureates, Samuel Beckett and Seamus Heaney.

'Seven wealthy towns compete for Homer dead, through which the living poet begged for bread.' Ireland now features multiple festivals celebrating writers from John Millington Synge to James Joyce. It was not always so. Riots greeted Synge's *Playboy of the Western World*. Joyce and Brendan Behan were derided until their work was hailed abroad. Forced to flee their country, many writers had to learn survival skills unnecessary in more civilised Europe. Like 'The soldiers and chiefs of the Irish Brigade', their bodies are scattered across the Continent from London to Trieste, Paris to Zurich.

Mid-twentieth century writers were reviled, their books banned. Packed by zealots, the Censorship Board ensured that John Broderick, Austin Clarke and John McGahern followed Sean O'Casey to England. In my time, books by J.P. Donleavy, Ernest Gebler, Edna O'Brien and twenty other Irish authors were proscribed. Censorship deprived many of their livelihoods. Also, the casts of the Gaiety and Pike theatres, when religious prosecution ended *The Ginger Man* and *The Rose Tattoo* plays.

Thanks to the fearless campaigning of *Envoy's* John Ryan and *The Bell's* Sean O'Faolain and Peadar O'Donnell, censorship itself was eventually banned. These editors richly deserve commemoration. As do the indefatigable Ken Monaghan and David Norris, for transforming a North Great George's Street tenement into the James Joyce Cultural Centre. Like Gerry O'Flaherty and the late John Ryan, Joyceans before it became profitable.

Joyce would hardly recognise modern Dublin. Property developers have obliterated much of its physical history. The envy of Europe, once grand Sackville Street has been reduced to a parade of hamburger and gambling joints. Presided over by a meaningless spike and equally alien shrubbery, Dublin is probably the only European capital without a fountain on its main thoroughfare. Would it be an imaginative leap too far for the City Council to honour James Joyce by restoring Eamonn O'Doherty's *Anna Livia* monument to O'Connell Street, so that once again we can hear the waters that gave our city life?

North Earl Street features a sculpture of Joyce, who is commemorated by a bust in Stephen's Green. The Green also features Henry Moore's 'Knife Edge' tribute to W.B. Yeats, and equally outstanding busts of James Clarence Mangan, James Joyce and Joyce's friend and WWI victim, Tom Kettle. Merrion Square Park boasts a bust of George Russell and, opposite his former home, a sculpture of a reclining Oscar Wilde. Three Liffey bridges have been named after writers – the Beckett, Joyce and O'Casey Bridges.

St Patrick's Park, in the shadow of the cathedral, hosts a parade of plaques to twelve Irish writers: Samuel Beckett, Brendan Behan, Austin Clarke, Eilis Dillon, James Joyce, James Clarence Mangan, Sean O' Casey, George Bernard Shaw, J.M. Synge, Oscar Wilde, W.B. Yeats, and St Patrick's former dean, Jonathan Swift. Brendan Behan, whose plaque has twice been stolen, is commemorated by a sculpture seat on the Royal Canal in Drumcondra. The Grand Canal at Mespil Lock features a similar tribute to his nemesis, Patrick Kavanagh. Statues of Oliver Goldsmith and Edmund Burke adorn the entrance to Trinity College, close to the bronze figure of poet, Thomas Moore.

Great writers frequently stimulate equally memorable biographies and commentaries. A. Norman Jeffares and Peter van de Kamp compiled a three-volume anthology, *Irish Literature*, which includes work by many of this book's subjects. A treasury of nineteenth century writing, it was hailed by Conor Cruise O'Brien as 'a living, breathing recreation of the circumstances that shaped us and shaped Ireland today'.

Curiosity about James Joyce will inevitably lead to Richard Ellmann's masterful biography, Peter Costello's study of Joyce's youth, Stanislaus Joyce's *Dublin Diary* and the eminently readable recent record by Gordon Bowker. Victorian Dublin comes alive in the massively annotated and illustrated *Dubliners* by John Wyse Jackson and Bernard McGinley. Conversely, what Senator David Norris described as 'the grim and deadly earnestness of the Joycean critics' can deter readers from opening *Ulysses*. David and Joyce's nephew, the late Ken Monaghan, deserve medals for liberating the writer from such kill-joys. And Stephen Joyce, who insisted at a Copenhagen conference that his grandfather's books can be 'read, and enjoyed by virtually anybody without scholarly guides, theories, and intricate explanations'.

Richard Ellmann also wrote on Oscar Wilde and W.B. Yeats. The latter has been magnificently served by Roy Foster's two-volume biography. In addition to his lives of Brendan Behan and Oliver St. John Gogarty, Ulick O'Connor penned the *All the Olympians* account of the Irish Literary revival, which comes alive in George Moore's forthright *Hail and Farewell* memoir. Mary Colum's *Life and the Dream* provides an immediate insight into the succeeding generation.

Antoinette Quinn and the poet's brother, Peter, wrote movingly on Patrick Kavanagh. Anthony Cronin penned biographies of Samuel Beckett and Brian O'Nolan and wrote on 1950s Dublin. A period detailed in the books of J.P. Donleavy, *Envoy* editor John Ryan and artist Nevill Johnson. Vivien Igoe, Elizabeth Healy and the late Caroline Walsh provided guides to the homes of Dublin and Irish writers. Painstaking efforts replicated by Ray Bateson's comprehensive record of Irish writers' graves, *The End*.

Once again, I must thank the helpful staff of Dublin's National Library for their consistently courteous and patient assistance. Also, Aisling Kirwan, Librarian, Ringsend Library, Hugh Comerford, Senior Librarian, Dublin and Irish Local Studies Collections, and the staff of both the Gilbert Library, Pearse Street and the City Libraries' Ilac Centre branch (where helpful staff are now being replaced by machines). Mount Jerome's Stephen Darker also provided valuable assistance, as did Brian Siggins and Gail Wolfe of the Ballsbridge, Donnybrook and Sandymount Historical Society. Foreword writer Peter Costello was a fountain of much appreciated advice.

Introduction and Acknowledgements

The evergreen J.P. Donleavy, Brian Bourke and Peter Keogh, and the much-missed Nevill Johnson, James Liddy, Des MacNamara, Skylla MacNamara, Ethel Mannin, Ewart Milne, Ken Monaghan and John Ryan provided first-hand information on the eventful and censored 1950s. Also, Seamus de Burca, Hugh and Maureen Charlton, and the late Mary King, May O'Flaherty and Patsy Ronan of Parsons Bookshop.

Sadly, their colleague Carmel Leahy died since the publication of my book on the shop. As did Parsons facilitator, Father Aidan Lehane, rare journalists Paddy Downey, Con Houlihan and Sean Kilfeather, artist Reginald Gray, harpist Maureen Hurley, poet Pearse Hutchinson, solicitor Enda Marren, the inimitable Maeve Binchy, Dardis Clarke, stout defender of his father's work, Mount Jerome's Don Holder, Des and Skylla MacNamara, Joycean Professor Martha Black of Brooklyn College and Caroline Walsh of the *Irish Times*. Salutations to each of them who mined so fruitfully for our benefit.

Many thanks to Tom Gilligan of The Duke for his support of this book. Also to Redmond Doran of Davy Byrne's, the equally energising Noel Lewis and Dympna O'Halloran, John and Dympna McMahon, Peadar and Treasa MacManus (Dublin's most cultured couple!) and technical genius Coleman McMahon. And to the enterprising Dromineer Literary Festival quintette, Eleanor Hooker, Pat Kelly, Deborah Powell and Donal and Marie Whelan.

Homage also to novelists Colum McCann and J.P. Donleavy for their generous endorsements. And to Adrian Kenny, publisher John Calder, Tony Byrne, Ailesh Gaynor, Diana Serbe-Viola of New York, Pat Murray and Tom Shannon of Lincoln Place. Also, to my late friends, Cirilo Catequista and Michael Gilmartin, and my indefatigable former wife, Marlene Lynch, who encouraged my early writing.

Thanks also for their support to Sonya Dixon and Lean McMahon, An Walls, Stephen and Edward of Stokes Books, Dermot of the

Secret Book Store, Peter McDonnell of the Monaghan Association and two rare professionals, bookbinder Tom Duffy and Barry Breslin of Paceprint.

A final thanks to my wife, Margie, whose sparkle and good care have enabled six books since we met. To David Givens of The Liffey Press for his enthusiasm for this project, a publisher of impeccable taste! And to GraphyCems of Pamplona for their superb print quality.

The last of my trilogy on literary Dublin, *City of Writers* is illuminated by ace photographer, Johnny Bambury. His studies have done justice to our writers' haunts and greatly enhanced this tribute. Fellow-Northsider Dubliner Brendan Behan would have been proud of him!

QUOTATIONS AND EXTRACTS

The author and publishers are very grateful to the authors of the many books listed in the bibliography for the insights they provided into literary Dublin. We have quoted from a number of these and are thankful for permission to do so. We apologise to those for whom we were unable to trace the copyright holders, and we would be happy to correct any omissions in future editions of this book.

Quotations from poems by Patrick Kavanagh reproduced by kind permission of the Trustees of the Estate of the late Katherine B. Kavanagh through the Jonathan Williams Literary Agency, reprinted from *Collected Poems*, edited by Antoinette Quinn (Allen Lane, 2004). Quotations from poems by John Montague are reproduced by kind permission of the author and The Gallery Press. Permission to quote from 'Unmarried Mothers' from Austin Clarke's *Collected Poems* edited by R. Dardis Clarke published by Carcanet/The Bridge Press (2007) granted by R. Dardis Clarke.

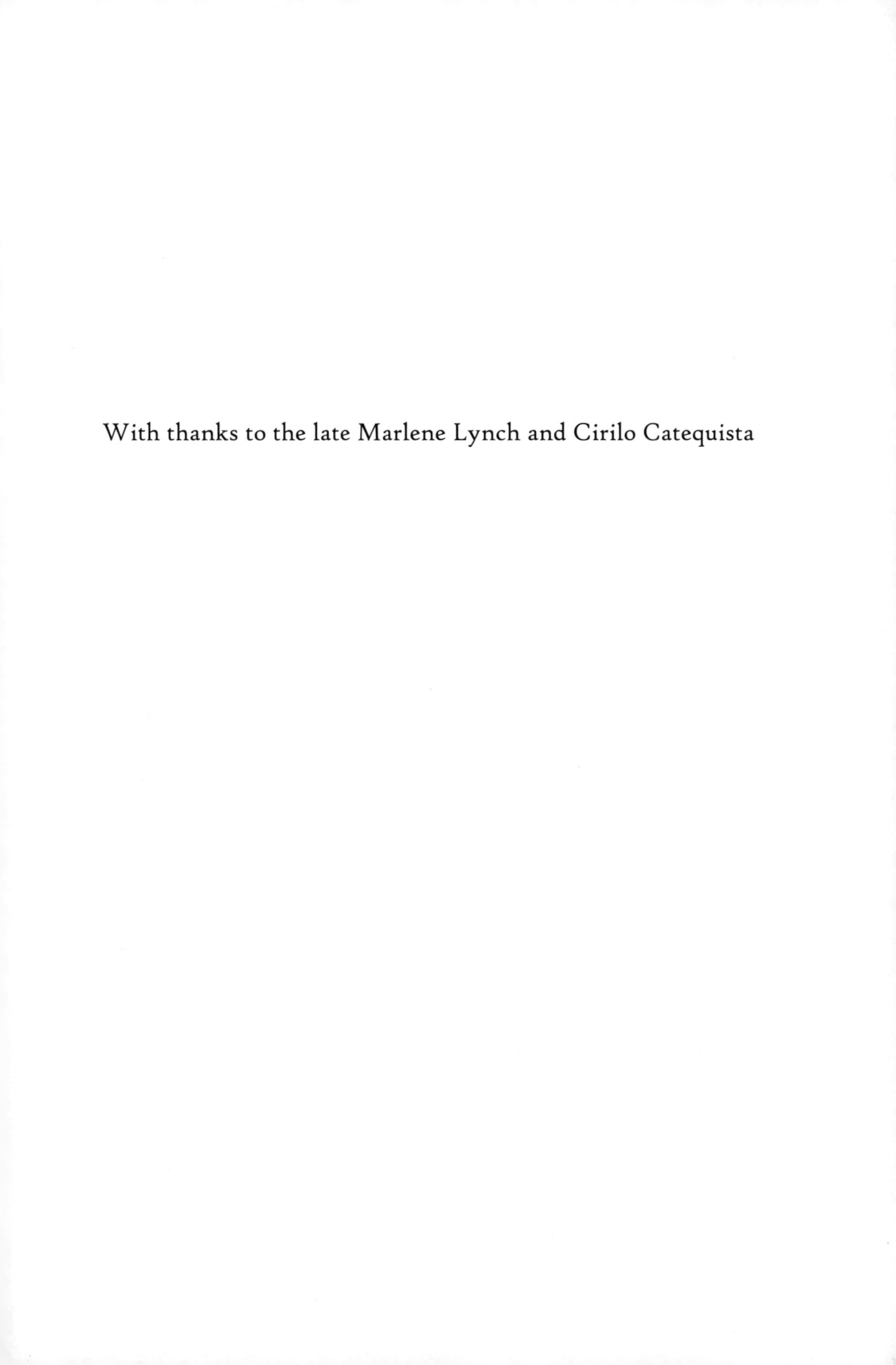

With thanks to the late Marlene Lynch and Cirilo Catequista

James Joyce once wrote that it would be a good puzzle to cross Dublin without passing a pub. An equivalent puzzle would be to tread through Dublin without encountering a writer. An even more intricate puzzle would be to find a pub that didn't have a writer ensconced in the corner, or at least the story of such a time. Dublin is the world's greatest literary city, and Brendan Lynch does a marvellous job of showing us the who what where when how and why of a place that is built on the intricacies of language. This book is a doorway into the stories of the past, and a key, then, into the future. – Colum McCann

I have seen strange places ... which have been rendered interesting by great men and their works: and I never found myself the worse for seeing them, but the better. I seem to have made friends with them in their own houses: to have walked and talked, and suffered and enjoyed with them. – Leigh Hunt

I think the Irish are lucky in that we never had the Victorian concept of waiting until you have something to say before you say it! We value good talkers much more than good listeners, and we love telling stories. – Maeve Binchy

Photographs of author homes and city landmarks
by Johnny Bambury (www.johnnybambury.ie)

CITY OF WRITERS

Grand Canal's Huband Bridge from Flann O'Brien's home

6 Clare Street

SAMUEL BECKETT
(1906-1989)

6 Clare Street

Birth was the death of him.

Samuel Beckett wrote his first book at 6 Clare Street, his father's quantity surveying office. The area played a pivotal role in his life. He studied French, Italian, and English from 1923 to 1927 in adjacent Trinity College, for whom he also played cricket. In 1931, he resigned his college lectureship, writing in the *Dublin Magazine*:

> *Spend the years of learning squandering*
> *Courage for the years of wandering*
> *Through a world politely turning*
> *From the loutishness of learning.*

Beckett was born on 13 April 1906 to middle-class Protestant parents in Cooldrinagh, Kerrymount Avenue, Foxrock. Skirting his mother's exhortations to find a proper occupation, he committed himself to making a living from his pen. He wrote essays and poems in the top floor of number 6, opposite Greene's Bookshop. Alone above the traffic, in a wilderness of chimneys and skylights, he defied rejection slips and practised his own dictum: 'Try Again. Fail again. Fail better.' He completed the short story collection, *More Pricks than Kicks* and much of the novel, *Murphy*. He co-wrote and acted in a Peacock Theatre play, *Le Kid*.

Beckett described his attic in *Murphy*: 'The ceiling and the outer wall were one, a superb surge of white, pitched at the perfect angle of farthest trajectory, pierced by a small frosted skylight, ideal for closing against the sun by day and opening by night to the stars. The bed, so low and gone in the springs that even unfreighted the middle grazed the ground, was wedged lengthways into the cleft of the floor and ceiling...'

Clare Street also catered for Beckett's twin interests in art and drink. The nearby National Gallery provided refuge on wet days, its paintings would resurface in his work. Kennedy's Westland Row public house guaranteed equally stimulating diversion. Beckett drank among dockers, railwaymen and characters on the dole where, happily; 'The aesthetes and the impotent were far away. In such pleasant surroundings, the proximity of suffering humanity coping, often majestically, with the cruelty of life, became tolerable and provided, moreover, an almost theatrical illusion temporarily blunting the pain of realization.'

Family friction and his country's insularity undermined Beckett physically and mentally. Dublin offered a 'lingering dissolution'. He escaped to Paris via London. Thomas MacGreevy introduced him to James Joyce, whose work he defended in his essay, 'Dante... Bruno... Vico... Joyce'. The pair became friends and Beckett acted as Joyce's unpaid secretary. He contributed essays and reviews to literary magazines and, in 1933, published *More Pricks than Kicks*, which was banned in Ireland. Two years later, he wrote a volume of poems,

Echo's Bones and Other Precipitates, which was followed by *Murphy*. He formed close friendships with artists Alberto Giacometti and Marcel Duchamp. Paris became home.

The 32-year-old Dubliner narrowly escaped death in 1938. He was stabbed by a local villain on the Rue de la Grande Chaumière, where artist Paul Henry had once lived. James Joyce arranged a private hospital room for him. Beckett refused to press charges, but he never forgot the randomness of the event. He faced greater peril in the war, as a courier for the French Resistance with his girlfriend, Suzanne Deschevaux-Dumesnil. Hiding as a farm labourer in the southern village of Roussilon, he wrote his second novel, *Watt*. Personally decorated by General de Gaulle for his Resistance work, his firsthand insight into the absurdity and cruelty of war shaped his subsequent work.

Beckett's experiences did not make him anti-German. Publisher John Calder had fond memories of post-war visits: 'He would sit at my piano and play from memory music he had learned before the war. He had spent time in Germany in the thirties and went there again in the seventies and, he always had a deep love of early romantic German culture in the writings of Goethe and the music of Schubert and Beethoven.'

Watt was the last novel Beckett composed in English. Henceforth he wrote almost exclusively in French, which allowed him greater economy of expression. On a final 1945 Dublin visit, he had a revelation on Dun Laoghaire's East Pier about the future direction of his writing: 'I realized that Joyce had gone as far as one could in the direction of knowing more, in control of one's material. He was always adding to it; you only have to look at his proofs to see that. I realized that my own way was in impoverishment, in lack of knowledge and in taking away, in subtracting rather than in adding.'

Beckett published three further novels in the early 1950s. But it was the 1953 tragi-comedy, *Waiting for Godot* which established him as one of the leaders of the Theatre of the Absurd. Two tramps, Vladimir and Estragon, meet on a country road: 'Why are we here, that is the question. And we are blessed in this, that we happen to know the answer. Yes, in this immense confusion one thing alone is clear. We are waiting for Godot to come.'

With dialogue based on wartime conversations between Beckett and his girlfriend, the play debated the apparent meaninglessness of life and the futility of action. Beckett's interest in cycling may have prompted the title. He asked children what they were doing outside the Velodrome d'Hiver. 'En attendant Godeau,' they replied. French champion Godeau was known to Beckett.

Godot was followed four years later by *Endgame*, *Krapp's Last Tape* and *Happy Days*. Maeve Binchy observed her compatriot rehearse *Endgame* in London. Noting his ludicrous energy and that 'his accent is sibilant French with a lot of Dublin in it', she informed *Irish Times* readers: 'The main thing you'd notice is that he thinks the play is a song, or a long rhythmic poem. He can hear the rhythm, he can hear it quite clearly in his head and his work as a director is to get the actors to hear it too.'

Now regarded as one of the most influential writers of the 20th century, Beckett's plays were staged all over the world. Ironically for such a reticent man, his furrowed brow, lined face and ironic and penetrating eyes graced international media. He was awarded the Nobel Prize for Literature in 1969. Joyce's biographer, Richard Ellmann, echoed the Nobel committee's sentiment: 'He has given a voice to the decrepit and maimed and inarticulate, men and women at the end of their tether, past pose or pretence.'

Suzanne Deschevaux-Dumesnil died in July, 1989. Beckett slipped away five months later on 22 December, aged 83. He was buried beside Suzanne in Montparnasse cemetery, close to fellow-writer Guy de Maupassant and sculptor Constantin Brancusi. Paris provided an appropriate final resting place. Beckett's Huguenot forbears, known as Becquet, had been exiled from France in 1685.

The city of Beckett's birth and rejection commemorated him with a bridge across the Liffey. Like Joyce and Sean O'Casey, the characters, tramps and streets of Dublin informed much of Beckett's writing. Watt remarked: 'for all the good that frequent departures out of Ireland had done him, he might just as well have stayed there'. Concentrating on the influence of place, Eoin O'Brien's *The Beckett Country* celebrated the streets the playwright traversed in his youth and later in his mind. In his seventieth year, Beckett told its author: 'The old haunts were never more present.'

Beckett left from a land of emigrants

15 Herbert Street

BRENDAN BEHAN
(1923-1964)

15 Herbert Street

The pubs shut: a released bull,
Behan shoulders up the street
– John Montague

Beatrice Behan retained fond memories of 15 Herbert Street, where she lived with her husband, Brendan, from 1955 to 1958: 'Brendan produced some of his best work there. Many writer and artist friends lived nearby, Parsons Bookshop was just around the corner. Baggot Street had a special atmosphere and Brendan didn't have to travel far to such good pubs as Lampshades and Mooney's. It was in Lampshades, of course, that he proposed to me at the end of 1954!'

Though his allegiance was to Dublin's working-class Northside, where his family lived at 14 Russell Street, Brendan Francis Behan was born on 9 February 1923 in southside Holles Street Maternity Hospital. His father, Stephen, treated the family to nightly readings from Charles Dickens, Jonathan Swift and Emile Zola. His mother, Kathleen, sang Labour and nationalistic songs. At the age of 14, Brendan attempted to go to Spain to fight against Franco. In 1939, he was arrested in Liverpool with explosives intended for the local docks. He was imprisoned in Walton, beside the cemetery of another Dublin socialist housepainter, author Robert Tressell. On his return from two years in Borstal, he was incarcerated in Dublin for shooting at a detective.

Brendan pursued his passion for writing, encouraged by authors Sean O'Faolain and Peadar O'Donnell. Recounting his Borstal experiences, his first published feature appeared in 1942 in O'Faolain's *The Bell*. In Mountjoy, Brendan met the murderer, Bernard Kirwan, on whom he later based *The Quare Fellow* tragicomedy. Paroled in 1946, 23-year old Brendan followed his father's trade as a housepainter. He decorated the *Irish Times* facade, the Gaiety interior and Stephen's Green's railings. He also worked as a deckhand on the *Sir James* freighter of smuggler and former British double-agent, Eddie Chapman.

After imprisonment for another Garda assault, Brendan decamped to Paris in 1948. Between painting commissions, he met *Points* magazine editor, Sinbad Vail, who published two of his stories. Brendan returned home broke, but determined to succeed as a writer. J.P. Donleavy recalled: 'Behan always wore his shirt open to the navel; he never had shoelaces and the tongues of his shoes would always hang out.' Though Brendan's personality tended to obscure his writing, Donleavy regarded him as a very profound person. Lyrics in *Comhar*, *Nuabhearsaiocht* and *Envoy* boosted Brendan's confidence. One of his Irish poems (translator, Colbert Kearney) was 'A Jackeen Says Goodbye to the Blaskets':

> *In the sun the ocean will lie like a glass.*
> *No human sign, no boat to pass,*
> *Only, at the world's end, the last*
> *Golden eagle over the lonely Blasket.*

Radio Éireann produced two of Brendan's plays in 1952. *The Irish Times* serialised his thriller, *The Scarperer*. He penned a popular *Irish Press* column between 1954 and 1956, later published as *Hold Your Hour and Have Another*, illustrated by Beatrice Salkeld. The couple met at the 1954 Pike Theatre premiere of *The Quare Fellow*, the play about a prison execution which established Brendan as 'the new O'Casey' and also encouraged anti-capital punishment campaigners. The middle-height Dubliner was now a larger than life city figure. Ben Kiely recalled: 'He would carry on conversations everywhere and with everybody as he walked through a street.'

Brendan, 32, married 29-year-old Beatrice in February, 1955. They lived in 18 Waterloo Road before moving into the ground-floor apartment at 15 Herbert Street. Beatrice motivated her sometimes distracted husband. One of her sketches shows him confronting a blank sheet of paper. Brendan recalled: 'I sat down this morning after a kipper, some mushrooms, cheese, black coffee with bread and marmalade and butter, and looked out the window, thinking of the poor. While the turf was blazing itself into a white heat of fragrant caressing warmth, I digested my breakfast and reflected on the excellence of my condition.

'"The wicked," I thought happily, "prosper in a wicked world."

'But, alas, not the worst of us is free from the improving influence of a good woman. My first wife came in and said, "I thought you were doing that bit of an article today?"'

The solitude of writing tested the diabetic Brendan. Drinking sprees and a repertoire of invective resulted in his ejection from favourite pubs. He achieved the rare distinction of banning a pub manager. One morning, he saw Paddy O'Brien of McDaid's cycling down Herbert Street. He grabbed Paddy's handlebars. 'You barred me from your gaff, now I'm barring you from my street!' Neighbour John Montague recorded the writer's nocturnal return:

> *The pubs shut: a released bull,*
> *Behan shoulders up the street,*
> *Topples into our basement, roaring 'John!'*

Concerns about his bisexuality contributed to Brendan's drinking. But his generosity, gregariousness and defiance of convention ensured genuine popularity. And his Dublin wit. A literary snob asked if he understood Beckett's *Waiting for Godot*. Brendan retorted: 'I don't understand the composition of water, but I love an ould dip.' The *Irish Press* acknowledged his stature: 'The Behans never come down town. They make a royal progress. Brendan, the curls low on his forehead, like a cheerful Julius Caesar bestowing the accolade of friendship on innumerable acquaintances. Beatrice, slender, like a gentle nun.'

Beatrice provided Brendan with the stability of a home environment. After meeting her, he wrote *An Giall*, *The Hostage*, about a young soldier awaiting reprisal execution. Also, the best-selling *Borstal Boy* and books on Ireland and New York illustrated by Paul Hogarth. Beatrice shared his triumphs, including *The Quare Fellow's* 1956 London debut, which Harold Hobson celebrated in *The Sunday Times*: 'Brendan Behan takes a place in that long line of Irishmen, from Goldsmith to Beckett, who have added honour to the drama of a nation which they often hated.'

The Behans moved in 1958 to 5 Anglesea Road, Ballsbridge. Brendan's fame attracted many hangers-on. Success never changed him, but his need since childhood for an audience proved as lethal as Ernest Hemingway's macho posturing. His drinking increased, his health deteriorated. Dubliners were shocked by his demise on 20 March 1964 at the age of 41 in the Meath Hospital, where James Clarence Mangan had earlier died. 'Dublin is empty tonight,' a former neighbour mourned.

John Coll's Drumcondra canal sculpture captures Brendan in full conversational flow. He is also commemorated in St. Patrick's Park. Beatrice Behan wrote a moving autobiography, *My Life with Brendan*. She died in 1993 and was buried beside him in Glasnevin Cemetery.

Beatrice frequently recalled one of their happiest occasions, the 1959 French premiere of *The Hostage* in the Sarah Bernhardt Theatre, Paris. In contrast to earlier custodial escorts, Brendan was welcomed by a guard of honour in black-and-white uniforms with gold epaulettes. The audience gave him a three-minute ovation and the cast no fewer than ten curtain calls. Beatrice recollected: 'The cries of "Auteur!" at the final curtain had an exciting ring. Brendan spoke to the audience in French, telling them how proud he was to have his play presented in the most civilised city in the world. His triumphal return to Paris was probably the highlight of his literary life.'

Brendan Behan with his wife Beatrice

1 Pembroke Road

MAEVE BINCHY
(1940-2012)

1 Pembroke Road

*I tell a story and I want to share
it with my readers.*

James Joyce and Samuel Beckett revelled in riddles, a windfall for generations of academics. Maeve Binchy never used a difficult word where a simple one would suffice. A former teacher at 1 Pembroke Road, her sales totalled more than the pair of them together. Before she died in 2012 at the age of 72, the Dubliner had sold forty million copies of her novels, which had been translated into thirty seven languages. She finished ahead of Jane Austen, Charles Dickens and Stephen King in a poll for World Book Day, 2000. Her work reflected the warmth and positivity which distinguished her life. Unpretentious and related with a natural conversational fluency, her books were page-turners. Maeve preached no message and offered no incredible solutions. She told *The Chicago Tribune*: 'There are no makeovers in my books. The ugly duckling does not become a beautiful swan. She becomes a confident duck able to take charge of her own life and problems.'

The eldest of four children, Maeve was born on 28 May 1940 in Knocknacree Road, Dalkey, ten miles from Dublin. Her barrister father and her mother, a nurse, encouraged their children to read and tell stories: 'Because I saw my parents relaxing in armchairs and reading and liking it, I thought it was a peaceful grown-up thing to do, and I still think that.' Maeve described her youth as being full of enthusiasms and fantasies, and urges to be famous or to become a saint. She attended a local convent school until the age of sixteen. Her six foot stature made her instantly recognisable at University College Dublin, where she studied history and French. She graduated in 1960 with a B.A. in education.

Maeve taught history, Latin and French in the private school which Miss Kathleen Meredith opened in 1929 at 1 Pembroke Road. Its students included pioneering journalist and broadcaster, Mary Raftery. In the heart of Dublin's Bohemia close to Parsons Bookshop, poet Patrick Kavanagh regularly chatted to pupils and teachers through its railings. One of Maeve's students was Caroline Walsh, daughter of novelist, Mary Lavin. Maeve was a regular guest at Mary's parties, where she met writers Frank O'Connor, Tom Kilroy, Desmond Hogan and John McGahern. Visitors drank something stronger than tea. Maeve recalled: 'Mary Lavin had her children so well trained that not a word of this ever leaked out to the pupils. No tales were ever told that Miss Clarke and Miss Binchy might have been boisterous in civilian life.'

Summer holidays allowed Maeve to travel. Her writing career commenced without her knowledge. Her father sent her chatty travel letters to the *Irish Independent* which promptly published them. After seven years, Maeve abandoned teaching and became a journalist with the *Irish Times*. The security of her home life was shattered by her mother's death from cancer. Her father died three years later. It was a low period in Maeve's life. She moved to a small flat in Dublin, where she sought solace in drink and a rash friendship with a married man.

Maeve was appointed women's editor of the *Irish Times* in 1968, at the age of 28. She became a London correspondent after falling in love with BBC producer and children's writer, Gordon Snell, whom she married in 1977. Samuel Beckett was among Maeve's London interviewees, before she started to write short stories. Thirty rejection slips later, she published her first books, *Central Line* in 1978 and *Victoria Line* in 1980: 'Every day, millions of people travel on London's Underground, yet everyday life is not nearly as mundane as we think. At Notting Hill, the secretary, harbouring her secrets travels to work; at Highbury and Islington, Adam has a sudden change of heart...'

The Irishwoman was over 40 when she attempted her first long novel. Accepted by the sixth publisher she approached, *Light a Penny Candle* was published in 1982, shortly after she and Gordon had bought a cottage in Dalkey. It was the story of a girl growing up in Ireland and Elizabeth, a conservative English war-evacuee. The relationship between opposites led to a life-long friendship. Maeve followed her debut novel with *Echoes*, a story of ambition and betrayal which commenced with two children shouting their wishes into the echo cave: 'if you shouted your question loud enough in the right direction, you got an answer instead of an echo.'

In 1987, Maeve published *Firefly Summer*. An American millionaire returns to a small Irish town in the 1960s, to realise his dream of restoring a long-neglected hotel on ancestral land. His arrival causes discontent and jealousy and disturbs the equilibrium of the locals. The book's success enhanced Maeve's reputation. She wrote from seven each morning until early afternoon on her novels, all of which were set in Ireland. She liked James Joyce's work, but she quipped:

'If you're going on a plane journey, you're more likely to take one of my stories than *Finnegans Wake!*'

The Dalkey writer published sixteen novels and four short-story collections. 'Maeve's Week' *Irish Times* column delighted readers for three decades. Her 1978 play, *Deeply Regretted By*, won an award at the Prague Film Festival. Several of her books were televised and encouraged social change in Ireland. Two were made into successful films, *Circle of Friends* and *Tara Road*, which sold over one million hardback copies. *Tara Road* featured two women, one from Ireland, the other from America, who swop houses, despite being strangers. The Irishwoman is trying to cope with her husband's infidelity, the American lady has lost a son. The pair discover much about themselves, female friendship becomes a source of strength.

Maeve's fans were dismayed when she announced in 2000 that *Scarlet Feather* would be her last book. But she soon returned to the keyboard. Five more books followed, including her celebration of life in old age, *A Time to Dance*. Maeve's philosophy was: 'I tell a story and I want to share it with my readers.' The appeal of her writing lay in strong characterisation and entertaining storytelling. Good invariably triumphed, community spirit prevailed. Criticised for her laxity with punctuation, one critic found Maeve's work 'so nice, that my own reserves of warmth and understanding were failing fast by the final page'.

Readers thought otherwise and, as well as heading bestseller lists, Maeve was feted on chat-shows around the world. She explained the appeal of Irish writing on the US *Oprah Winfrey Show*: 'I think the Irish are lucky in that we never had the Victorian concept of waiting until you have something to say before you say it! We value good talkers much more than good listeners, and we love telling stories. This fluent delight in telling what happened is easily translated into writing down our thoughts.'

Like Brendan Behan, Maeve was a larger-than-life figure, whose presence, natural warmth and sense of fun endeared her to everyone who knew her. She took fame and wealth lightly and never lost her childhood friendships. She continued to live in her Dalkey cottage with her husband until she died on 30 July 2012, aged 72. Hundreds lined the streets of the village for her funeral, the applause echoed off the walls of the houses she had known since childhood. Maeve's last years were clouded by arthritis and heart problems. But she insisted: 'If you woke up each morning, and immediately dwelt on your ills, what sort of a day could you look forward to?'

Maeve Binchy's beloved Dalkey

47 Lower Gardiner Street

DION BOUCICAULT
(1820-1890)

47 Lower Gardiner Street

Oh my land! My own land! Bless every blade of grass upon your green cheeks! The clouds that hang over ye are the sighs of your exiled children, and your face is always wet with their tears
— Arrah-na-Pogue.

Irish playwrights made a unique contribution to English theatre from Oliver Goldsmith and Oscar Wilde to George Bernard Shaw and Sean O'Casey. But few matched the influence on both the English and American theatre of Dion Boucicault, who lived at 47 Lower Gardiner Street, following his birth on 27 December 1820. An outstanding actor, playwright and director, the Dubliner was also an innovative theatre manager. He revolutionised the status of playwrights by instituting the royalty system of payment. In the USA, where he died, he was acclaimed equally as a playwright, theatre manager and the person responsible for the passing of the country's first dramatic copyright law in 1856. He was famous in Ireland as the author of *The Wearing of the Green*.

Writing was in the family blood. Dion's mother, Anne Boursiquot, was sister of the Romantic poet, George Darley. The circumstances of the playwright's parentage were appropriately theatrical. Dion's original name was Dionysius Lardner Boursiquot. It is likely that he was the son of scientific writer Dr Dionysius Lardner, rather than of his mother's older husband, Samuel Boursiqot. Lardner later became involved in another romantic scandal. Dion followed in his footsteps, eloping once and marrying three times.

In 1828, Lardner was appointed Professor of Philosophy and Astronomy at University College London. Anne Boursiquot followed, with Dion. After a succession of institutions, Dion was enrolled at the university's grammar school. Writing for the school magazine proved more congenial than studying, his wit and ability to mimic his teachers marked him out from fellow-pupils. Mother and son returned to Dublin in 1836. Dion completed his education at the Geoghegan Academy on Stephen's Green, with future war correspondent, William Howard Russell.

Dion was soon in the wars himself. He moved back to London, where Lardner employed him as an apprentice civil engineer. To his father's discomfiture, it was a short-lived partnership. The London-Harrow line could not match the lure of West End theatre, to which Dion had been introduced by former classmate Charles Lamb Kenney, son of dramatist, James Kenney. Like Bram Stoker, the world of the imagination provided him with a romantic escape from mundane reality and a convoluted home life.

To his credit, Lardner maintained his allowance when Dion set off in 1838 at the age of seventeen to become an actor. He haunted the stage door of Cheltenham's Theatre Royal, until its manager finally gave him a part. Using the stage-name Lee Moreton, Dion made his debut in *Richard III*. Despite his brogue, he was praised for his performance as the Duke of Norfolk. The Dubliner's ability was matched by unrestrained confidence and enthusiasm. He was hired as a fulltime actor and put his accent to good use in Samuel Lover's *Rory O'More*, playing the title role only weeks after his stage debut.

From then on, the theatre was Dion's world. But, like compatriot, Charles Maturin, his rapid success proved a mixed blessing. He squandered money on expensive clothes, imported fruits and Havana cigars. Biographer Richard Fawkes revealed: 'He was as arrogant and assured off stage as he was on. Although he was only seventeen, he was already showing signs of the dandy personality he would effect once he made his name in London.'

Refining his acting, Dion built on his school magazine experience by writing plays. He enjoyed a unique eighteenth birthday present in December 1838, when Bristol's Theatre Royal staged his third effort, a one-act farce, *Lodgings to Let*. Exactly a year later, his first full-length play, *Jack Sheppard*, was performed in Hull's Theatre Royal. London's West End seemed light years from Hull. But, in 1841, Dion scored a major hit at Covent Garden with his comedy, *London Assurance*. He became the talk of the capital and a welcome guest at literary salons. His success encouraged him to drop his Lee Moreton stage alias. Henceforth, he was known as Dion Boucicault.

Dion did not let his socialising deflect him from writing. In 1842, he published a new play, *The Bastile*, which, with four subsequent dramas, was performed at Her Majesty's Theatre. Despite some less popular plays, he was hailed as a master of melodrama and dramatic construction. He knew what audiences wanted. With fresh and racy dialogue and a weave of unlikely incidents, he entertained them with fast-moving and action-packed plots. In the 1850s, he adapted French plays for London consumption, including *The Corsican Brothers*, which Queen Victoria enjoyed five times. He was acclaimed for his acting in his plays, *The Vampire* and *Andy Blake*.

Women were attracted to Dion, despite his slight stature and premature baldness. In 1853, the 33-year-old playwright eloped to the USA with 20-year old actress, Agnes Robertson. He took over a theatre which he renamed the Winter Garden Theatre. He wrote many successful plays including *The Octoroon*, which criticised the slave trade. In 1860, he published the *Colleen Bawn*, which played in all the major British and US cities. Dion returned to England in 1869 and achieved further success with *The Shaughran*, about a man who has returned to Ireland after escaping from transportation in Australia. Dion was lauded for his portrayal of the play's rogue, Con.

> *Oh Paddy dear, and did you hear*
> *The news that's going round?*

Despite his international success, Dion did not neglect his native country. He supported Charles Stuart Parnell and the Land League, and composed the patriotic anthem, *The Wearing of the Green*. In a pamphlet published in 1881, he complained that Ireland's 'elder sisters of the British family seemed to regard her with indifference and contempt, as one fitted for a sordid life of servitude'. The hero of *Arrah-na-Pogue* was Beamish Mac Coul, returned from America to free his countrymen: 'Oh my land! My own land! Bless every blade of grass upon your green cheeks! The clouds that hang over ye are the sighs of your exiled children, and your face is always wet with their tears.'

Dion himself was greeted as a returning hero when he staged *Arrah-na-Pogue* at Dublin's Theatre Royal. He was cheered in the streets, both for the play and for his portrayal of the character, Shaun the Post. Another fan was Oscar Wilde, whom Dion defended when he was ostracised by the English establishment after his arrest. Wilde insisted that 'beneath the fantastic envelope in which his managers are circulating him, there is a noble, earnest, kind and lovable man'. Dion was responsible for the 1874 statue of his friend, Michael William Balfe, which now stands in London's Theatre Royal.

In 1885, Dion once again fell for a younger actress, Louise Thorndike. They moved to New York and married. He died there on 18 September 1890, aged 69. No Ibsen or Shaw, Dion insisted that his duty was to please the public, which he did with unparalleled success for half a century. He wrote or adapted over 130 plays, many of which are still staged around the world. Donald Sinden, who starred in *London Assurance*, reiterated that the Dubliner was 'clearly one of the major figures, not just of British theatre but of world theatre'.

Dion's financial management did not match his writing skills. He died a poor man. His own dramatic life is overdue a play.

The Custom House beside Boucicault's brthplace

15 Herbert Place

Elizabeth Bowen
(1899-1973)

15 Herbert Place

I think the main thing, don't you, is to keep
the show on the road.

Samuel Beckett, Patrick Kavanagh and Brian O'Nolan are each associated with Europe's most literary waterway, Dublin's Grand Canal. Novelist Katherine Tynan was born close to Portobello Bridge. But Elizabeth Bowen was the only writer to boast the distinction of a canalside birthplace. She was born at 15 Herbert Place on 7 June 1899. An only child of Anglo-Irish parents, Elizabeth enjoyed a privileged upbringing unknown to Joyce and company. The canal's reflections played on the Sheraton chairs and tapestries of her first-floor drawing-room. Her early memories were of piano recitals, Victorian song and full-dress Sunday morning services at her nearby baptismal church, St. Stephen's.

As soon as Elizabeth could negotiate the nine steps from her front door, the canal became her favourite recreational area. She recalled in her autobiography, *Seven Winters*: 'The house was filled by the singing hum of the saw-mill across the water, and the smell of the newly-planed wood travelled across. Stacks of logs awaiting the saw over-topped the low tarred fence that ran along the bank of the opposite side. The woodyard was served from some of the barges that moved slowly up or down the canal, sinking into, then rising from the locks.'

The future author spent happy holidays at her ancestral family home, Bowen's Court, Kildorrery, County Cork, close to where James Joyce's forebears once lived. Family wealth, however, could not insulate the Bowens from domestic tragedy. Elizabeth's childhood idyll ended at the age of six, when her father, Henry, suffered a mental breakdown. Her mother, Florence, removed her at night to her maternal grandparents' Clontarf home, before taking her to live in England in 1906.

While Henry slowly recovered, Florence herself became ill. She died six years later of cancer. Elizabeth's relatives did not allow her to attend the funeral. Elizabeth was brought up by aunts in Hythe, before being sent in 1914 to a boarding school. Her disrupted childhood left her with a lifelong stammer. The sense of being orphaned informed such subsequent work as *The Death of the Heart*.

The Dubliner's interest in writing commenced when she joined her school's literary group. She abandoned studies in 1917 to work in a hospital for shell-shocked war victims. Two terms at the London Council School of Art convinced her that her future lay in writing. But she maintained her artist's eye, later noting: 'often when I write, I am trying to make words do the work of line and colour. I have the painter's sensitivity to light. Much (and perhaps the best) of my writing is verbal painting.'

After a brief course in journalism, Elizabeth made her print debut in the *Saturday Westminster* in 1921. Encouraged by novelist Rose Macauley, her first story collection, *Encounters*, was published two years later, when she was 24. More angular than flowing, her writing reflected her personal qualities, courage, discipline, lack of cant and an urge to do the decent thing: 'The best that an individual can do is to concentrate on what he or she can do, in the course of a burning effort to do it better.'

Elizabeth's second book, *The Hotel*, featured a heroine who attempts to cope with a life for which she is unprepared. Tall with a long distinguished face, well-spoken and mannered, Elizabeth married Alan Cameron in 1923. Recovering from First World War gas poisoning, he became an educational administrator in Oxford. Here, Elizabeth wrote her first novels and met authors Maurice Bowra and John Buchan. She dissected the secrets that lay beneath respectability, 'life with the lid on and what happens when the lid comes off'.

She also explored the ambivalences of Anglo-Irish identity. The newly-independent Ireland was the beginning of the end of the Anglo-Irish class, many were shot dead in the Cork area of Bowen's Court. Elizabeth's 1929 novel, *The Last September*, is based on the tragedies of landed neighbours during the political anarchy of 1920. Author Stacey D'Erasmo insisted that she 'had a genius for conveying the reader straight into the most powerful and complex regions of the heart. On that terrain, she was bold, empathic and merciless. She wrote about the aftermath of wars, about affairs and about childhood with equally piercing insight and a thorough comprehension of the consequences of politics and desire.'

Elizabeth moved to London and continued her writing with *The House in Paris*, which the *Times Literary Supplement* hailed as 'A compelling story, inspired with a deep insight into human nature'. Published in 1938, *The Death of the Heart* reflected Bowen's feeling of being orphaned. It is the story of a sixteen-year-old orphan, Portia, who moves to London to live with her half-brother. She falls in love with a family acquaintance, Eddie, who almost destroys her. She endeavours to recover: 'After inside upheavals, it is important to fix on imperturbable things...'

During the Second World War, Elizabeth became an air warden. She also worked for the Ministry of Information and returned to Dublin to report on Irish attitudes to the war. The London Blitz reinforced her conviction of the immediacy of life. Like fellow-Irish writer Leland Bardwell, Elizabeth was lucky to escape from the bombing of her Regent's Park home. Wartime London featured in her short story collection, *The Demon Lover*. It also provided the backdrop to one of her most significant books, *The Heat of the Day*: 'Apathetic, the injured and dying in the hospitals watched light change on walls which might fall tonight.'

Regarded by a friend as being Irish in England and English in Ireland, Elizabeth acknowledged: 'At an early though conscious age, I was transplanted. I arrived young, into a different mythology – in fact, into one totally alien to that of my forefathers... From now on there was to be (as for any immigrant) a cleft between my heredity and my environment – the former remaining in my case the more powerful.' The war strengthened Elizabeth's loyalty to England. But while she spent most of her life there, she always regarded herself as an Irish novelist: 'As long as I can remember I've been extremely conscious of being Irish – even when I was writing about very unIrish things such as suburban life in Paris or the English seaside.'

Elizabeth's marriage to Alan Cameron was companionable rather than sexual. She had affairs with Canadian diplomat Charles Ritchie, Irish writer Sean O'Faolain and the American poet May Sarton. When Cameron retired, the couple spent more time in Bowen's Court. Death intruded again, when he died in 1952. Between journalism and American lecture tours, Elizabeth kept Bowen's Court afloat until 1959. She was finally forced to sell it and return to England. 'I think the main thing, don't you, is to keep the show on the road,' she told BBC interviewer, James Mossman.

The Irishwoman spent her last years in Hythe, where she had lived after her father's hospitalisation. Her final novel *Eva Trout, or Changing Scenes* won the James Tait Black Memorial Prize in 1969. She was awarded the CBE and Honorary Doctorates in Literature from Oxford University and Trinity College, Dublin. An ardent smoker, Elizabeth died from lung cancer aged 73 on 22 February 1973. She was buried beside her husband in Farahy, close to Bowen's Court. Recognised as one of the most important women writers of the twentieth century, her discipline and dedication resulted in a legacy of over thirty books. Commemorative plaques mark both her London and canalside Dublin homes.

Elizabeth Bowen's childhood recreational area

54 Stannaway Road, Kimmage

CHRISTY BROWN
(1932-1981)

54 Stannaway Road, Kimmage

Until the age of seventeen I could not talk except by my eyes and foot and a queer sort of grunting language understood only by my family.

The lives of many writers have been marathons of struggle. Rejection, poverty, the challenge of a blank page each morning. Born into a working-class family at 54 Stannaway Road, Christy Brown faced more prohibitive odds. Oxygen deprivation at birth resulted in severe cerebral palsy. He was left unable to speak or walk. Yet, by the time of his death at the age of forty nine, he had written eight novels and poetry collections. His autobiography, *My Left Foot*, was made into an Academy Award-winning film.

Christy Brown was born on 5 June 1932, the twelfth of a family of twenty two, of whom nine died in infancy. Doctors advised his mother, Bridget, that he should be put into a home. Mrs Brown decided to bring him up just like the rest of her children. The Browns were a close family. Love was never spoken of but it permeated their home. Christy's bricklayer father, Patrick, brought him to the toilet each morning before he went to work. His taller brothers and sisters played with him and pulled him around the neighbourhood in a succession of box-carts. His mother read to him each night and taught him the alphabet.

One December evening, while his sister, Mona, was writing on a slate, five year old Christy seized her yellow chalk with his left foot. Holding the stick between his first and second toes, he drew a small line. His mother then wrote the letter 'A' on the slate and asked him to copy it. He made several attempts but failed. Biographer Georgina Louise Hambleton recorded his ultimate success: 'He wrote another line and the chalk broke. He sank his teeth into his lips, pressed his fingernails into his palms and connected the lines. The lines formed the letter "A".'

Christy's mother tolerated his tantrums of frustration until he finally inscribed complete words on their stone floor. His left foot had enabled him to escape his imprisoned body. Writing and reading became his passions until the age of ten, when he was given a box of paints. Encouraged by social worker Katriona Delahunt and Dr Robert Collis, he won a newspaper painting competition. An orthopedist and playwright, Robert Collis improved his speech and physical coordination and encouraged his writing. Christy also became addicted to classical music. It encouraged 'an undercurrent of emotion that made me calm and hopeful, that brought with it a vague promise or message of something to come'.

As his growing siblings developed outside interests, Christy had more time to himself. At the age of eighteen, he started to laboriously record the story of his life that would become *My Left Foot*. Influenced by whichever author he was currently reading, his early drafts mirrored the prose of Charles Dickens. Robert Collis provided helpful criticism and lent him books by modern authors. With film director John Huston, singer Burl Ives and Bridget Brown in attendance, Collis read out an excerpt from her son's work at a Dublin benefit event. The crowd cheered Christy's writing: 'My tension left me. I forgot my queer hands twisting and twining in my lap. I forgot my crooked mouth and shaking head...'

Christy returned renewed to his self-appointed mission. Detailing his childhood and struggle to be heard, *My Left Foot* became an immediate success when it was published in 1954. He celebrated: 'I have made myself articulate and understood to people in many parts of the world, and this is something we all wish to do whether we are crippled or not...' The book was serialised in the UK and the USA and translated into several languages. Equally importantly, it resulted in the gift of a typewriter from a Dublin company. Now, Christy could write further and faster – once he had trained his toes to use the keyboard.

His success changed his life, he travelled to town by taxi and indulged his growing interest in drinking. The mixed blessing of alcohol relaxed his muscles, improved his speech and introduced a hitherto unknown camaraderie. Christy embarked on his first love affair with American teacher, Beth Moore, one of many who had written to congratulate him. He flew to Connecticut in 1960 to meet her. She showed him New England, they enjoyed Broadway shows. Christy learned to drink with a straw. He missed Moore on his return. Describing Dublin as a cul-de-sac, he embarked on drinking sprees.

Christy's ambition to write still burned brightly. Despite the rejection of two plays, he persisted on his second book. He flew to the US, where Beth Moore prescribed a strict working regime. In 1970, after ten years' work, he produced the fictional autobiography, *Down All the Days. He* dedicated it: 'For Beth, who with such gentle ferocity, finally whipped me into finishing this book.' Christy was now 38, a more introspective and more articulate man. His new book was emotional and humorous, packed with observation of local life and characters. It was translated into fifteen languages.

Sadly, Christy's mother died before the publication of *Down All Those Days*. His younger sister, Ann, took on Bridget Brown's role in caring for him. The proceeds of his book enabled Christy to move into a specially constructed house beside Ann and her husband in Rathcoole, outside Dublin. He was now a celebrity, regularly interviewed and appearing on television. He did not allow the publicity to interfere with his work. In 1971, he published the first of three collections of poems, *Come Softly to My Wake*.

Christy had rowed with Beth Moore on his last American visit. He met 23-year-old nurse, Mary Carr, at a London party. Mary was a heavy drinker and had been previously married. The Brown family felt she would be unable for the responsibility of looking after Christy. But he fell in love with her and they married in Dublin in October 1972. Soon, however, Mary was spending weekends in London without her husband.

Praised by Brendan Kennelly for its emotional honesty, Christy's *Background Music* poetry collection was published in 1973. It was followed a year later by the novel, *A Shadow on Summer*, a thinly disguised account of Christy's affair with Beth Moore. By this time, Christy and Mary had moved to a cottage in Kerry. Their lives became increasingly chaotic, both were hospitalised for alcoholism. Nevertheless, Christy worked on another novel, *Wild Grow the Lilies*. Published in 1976, it was criticised for overwriting and over-long descriptions. His final poetry collection, *Of Snails and Skylarks*, was published in 1977.

At Mary's behest, she and Christy moved to Parbrook, Somerset in 1980. Anchorless without his family, friends and familiar places, he wrote to poet Paul Bura: 'I've more or less imposed upon myself a sort of Trappist-Monk seclusion from the rude outer world.' Before he had reached maturity as a writer, the 49-year old Dubliner choked to death while eating his dinner on 6 September 1981. He was buried in Glasnevin Cemetery, across the road from his former friend, Brendan Behan.

Christy's final novel, *A Promising Career*, was published posthumously. The 1989 film of *My Left Foot* won two Academy Awards. The *London Times* wrote: 'The extraordinary thing about this remarkable human being was the first impression he made on people was of a particularly cheerful and gregarious man. Few can have met him without finding the experience life-enhancing...'

Bridget Brown taught her son Christy how to write

Francis Street

WILLIAM CARLETON
(1794-1869)

Francis Street

*It is in his pages, and his alone, that future
generations must look for the truest and fullest
pictures of those who will ere long have passed away
from that troubled land – from the records of history,
and from the memory of man forever.*
– The Edinburgh Review

Lauded for his realistic portrayal of rural life, William Carleton played a pivotal role in Irish literature. A precursor of the Celtic Revival and his country's first great short story writer, he was the link between the old oral tradition and the modern printed word. W.B. Yeats wrote: 'He was but half articulate, half emerged from Mother earth, like one of Milton's lions, but his wild

Celtic melancholy gives to whole pages of *Fardorougha* and of *The Black Prophet* an almost spiritual grandeur.'

William walked from Tyrone to Dublin in 1818 in search of work. He stumbled on both accommodation and rare reading material for two shillings a week in Francis Street. He recalled: 'I was now, at least in my own opinion, a very comfortable young fellow. I had a good cheap bed in a snug back room off the parlour, with the whole circulating library for my amusement. It would be useless to attempt anything like a description of my enjoyment. I think I could not have read less than from twelve to sixteen hours a day.'

The Tyrone man was born on 20 February 1794 in Prillisk, the youngest of fourteen children, six of whom died young. His father, James, was a tenant farmer. His mother, Mary Kelly, an accomplished singer. Fluent in Irish and English, and a noted storyteller, James passed on his store of local lore to his son. Tall and athletic, William acquired a reputation as a sportsman and daredevil. Badly injured by a man-trap while raiding an orchard, he narrowly escaped drowning in a flooded river.

William witnessed scenes of poverty, evictions and political violence. As his family moved from one small farm to another, he received a basic education at various hedge schools. But, by the age of nine, he could recite by heart the play, *The Battle of Aughrim*. He learnt Latin and read Virgil, but his hunger for literature was not appeased until he found an odd volume of *Tom Jones* in a friend's house. He recalled: 'Such was the delight with which I read, and such my disappointment that there was no more of it, that I actually shed tears.'

After progressing to *Gil Blas*, 25-year-old William set out to seek books and work in Dublin. He exchanged his shirt for accommodation in Drogheda and arrived in the capital early in 1819 with two shillings and ninepence in his pocket. The newcomer shared a cellar in Bridgefoot Street with beggars and down-and-outs, before finding the room with the library on the lefthand side of Francis Street. He spent every spare hour studying and writing in nearby Marsh's Library. Tutoring enabled his theatre-going. He married Jane Anderson in 1822, adopted her Protestant faith and became a clerk with a Sunday School.

William had been writing essays for many years on the characters and events of his youth, in the manner of the *Spectator's* Joseph Addison. Marsh's acting librarian William Sisson showed some to literary friends. After initial features for the *Westmeath Guardian*, the aspiring writer contributed a series of essays to Caesar Otway's evangelical *Christian Examiner*. The first in 1828 was 'A Pilgrimage to Patrick's Purgatory'. It was based on a youthful journey to Lough Derg, where a fellow 'pilgrim' had relieved him of his clothes and money while he slept.

The magazine published thirty sketches over the next two years. William's reputation was sealed with their 1830 publication in book form as *Traits and Stories of the Irish Peasantry*. Based on his first-hand experiences, the stories offered a vivid insight into the minds of the people he had known, farmers, labourers and craftsmen. A further selection, *Tales of Ireland*, followed three years later. The Tyrone writer's work was imbued by his appreciation of landscape: 'As I took a solitary road across the mountains, the loneliness of the walk, the deep gloom of the valleys, the towering height of the dark hills, and the pale silvery light of a sleeping lake, shining dimly in the distance below, gave me such a distinct notion of the sublime and beautiful as I have seldom since experienced.'

William met Samuel Ferguson and Robert Maturin and was invited to contribute to the influential *Dublin University Magazine*. Despite his growing popularity, he did not escape criticism. Some remarked that his work lacked the humour of Charles Lever and Samuel Lover. Catholics were displeased that his work appeared in a Protestant journal. Professional patriots were offended by his perceived criticism of the Irish character. William reiterated that he was equally the 'historian of their habits and manners, their feelings, their prejudices, their superstitions and their crimes'.

William's first novel, *Fardorougha, the Miser*, was serialised by the *Dublin University Magazine* in 1837-8. Dealing with the Irish hunger for land, it was praised by Walt Whitman and adapted for the stage. William published seven further novels over the next decade, including three which dealt with the Famine. Some revealed a didactic strain. *Parra Sastha* encouraged hard work and thrift, *Rody the Rover* condemned agrarian violence. *Art Maguire* warned of the dangers of alcohol, a substance not unknown to its author. One of his most popular books was *Willy Reilly and His Dear Cooleen Bawn*, which was serialised in the *London Independent* and reached over 40 editions.

A tall grey-bearded Tolstoyan figure, William was one of Dublin's most recognisable figures. In addition to his stories, he contributed to *The National Magazine*, *The Irish Penny Journal*, *The Dublin University Review and Quarterly*. And to *The Nation*, whose columnist, Lady Wilde, told him: 'You give a meaning to the Irish character no other writer has done.' Reading was hazardous in those pre-electric days but a boon for opticians. Artist Alexander Williams revealed that Mr. Chancellor of Sackville Street presented William 'with a beautiful pair of gold rimmed spectacles, telling him that so many people had damaged their sight reading his tales and stories that his business had benefitted'.

Despite his literary earnings, William's drinking ensured that he was rarely above the poverty line. He was awarded an annual government pension of £200 in 1848. He lived briefly at 2 Marino Crescent and died in Sandford, in a house now demolished, on 30 January 1869 aged 78. He was buried in Mount Jerome Cemetery. *The Dublin University Magazine* wrote: 'There is none, we repeat, with whom he can be compared: he stands alone as the portrayer of the manners and customs of our people – as the man who has unlocked the secrets of the Irish heart, and described the Irish character, without caricature or exaggeration, by that mighty power of genius which portrays reality while it frames its own creations – and produces those wonderful conceptions, which are at once truth and fiction.'

Carleton featured in Seamus Heaney's 'Station Island' and became the subject of an annual summer school. Shaded by chestnut trees, his Mount Jerome obelisk was restored by the William Carleton Memorial Committee and unveiled in August 1989. Critic Thomas Flanagan, novelists Ben Kiely and David Hanly and former *Envoy* editor John Ryan were among the attendance. Recollecting Carleton's stories, the party dallied too long in the summer sunshine and were locked in, ironically, by an impatient fellow-Northern gatekeeper.

St Nicholas of Myra Church in Francis Street

15 Mountjoy Street

Austin Clarke
(1896-1974)

15 Mountjoy Street

Burn Ovid with the rest. Lovers will find
A hedge-school for themselves and learn by heart
All that the clergy banish from the mind...

Austin Clarke resided from the age of three until fourteen at 15 Mountjoy Street, close to Parnell Square. His family moved there after his birth at 83 Manor Street on 9 May 1896. Austin's father was a Superintendent of Waste Water for Dublin Corporation. Austin's mother ensured that he and his three sisters were regular churchgoers. They lived in the shadow of the island Black Church, around which the children frequently ran with playmates. But only twice, local legend had it that the devil would appear to anyone who circled the church three times.

Austin grew up to the morning clatter of milkcarts, which he observed through the parlour window aspidistras. And to the smell of paraffin, with which neighbours primed their fires. The day was further enlivened by the clip-clop of the cabs and sidecars which hastened to the Galway trains at Broadstone station. Austin first observed the city from the crossbar of his father's bicycle. At the age of seven, his father showed him the Gordon Bennett racecars heading to the Phoenix Park Speed Trials.

Austin soon experienced the local streets on foot, from Dominick Street to Parnell Square. In Capel Street, he discovered Dublin's first free municipal library, which James Joyce had also frequented. At the age of thirteen, he was one of the earliest visitors to Dublin's first cinema, the Volta, which Joyce opened in Mary Street in 1909. Years later on a visit to Joyce in Paris, the latter revealed that Capel Street was his favourite Dublin thoroughfare. A regular theatregoer from the age of seventeen, Austin shared his compatriot's musical interests and studied the violin and piano in the Rathmines School of Music. He also acquired Joyce's religious scepticism. Like Joyce, his elder by fourteen years, he progressed from nearby Belvedere College to University College Dublin, where he became lecturer in English in 1917.

George Russell encouraged Austin's interest in poetry. Maunsell & Company published his first narrative poem in 1917. Widely acclaimed, *The Vengeance of Fionn* was a retelling of an Ossianic legend. In 1920, Austin embarked on a short-lived marriage which caused a nervous breakdown. As the ceremony had taken place in a registry office, the university did not renew his lectureship. He fled to London.

Compatriot Robert Lynd found Austin work as a literary critic. The 25-year-old Dubliner contributed to the *Observer* and the *Times Literary Supplement*. He progressed his poetry and endeavoured to escape his Catholic baggage and the giant shadow of W. B. Yeats.

Religious zealots cast a darker mantle. The Irish Censorship Board banned his first two novels. *The Bright Temptation*, a romance published in 1932, and the 1936 *The Singing Men at Cashel*. Austin's *Collected Poems* were also published in 1936. But he suffered another setback when *The Oxford Book of Modern Verse* editor, W. B. Yeats ignored his work, while according twelve pages to his friend, Oliver St John Gogarty.

Undaunted, Austin returned to Ireland in 1937 and published the collection, *Night and Morning*. A devotee of the Palace Bar, he featured in Alan Reeves' cartoon with fellow-poets Patrick Kavanagh and Ewart Milne, and Robert Smyllie, who provided *Irish Times* reviewing commissions. Though a mild-mannered man, Austin was the unwitting cause of 'The Battle of the Palace Bar'. He allegedly insulted Louis MacNeice, who was immediately defended by his friend, Fred Higgins. Poetic punches were exchanged. Patrick Kavanagh recorded the resultant shenanigans:

> *They fought like barbarians, these highbrow*
> > *grammarians,*
> *As I have recorded for the future to hear.*
> *And in no other land could a battle so grand*
> *Have been fought over poetry, but in Ireland so dear.*

'The sound of poetry is part of its meaning.' In 1941, Austin co-founded the Dublin Verse-Speaking Society with Roibeard Ó Faracháin: 'to save from neglect the tradition of verse drama left to us by Yeats'. It later metamorphosed into the Lyric Theatre Company, for which Austin wrote several verse plays. He launched a weekly poetry programme on 2RN, the national radio station, which was to last for a quarter of a century. The censor struck again in 1952, banning Austin's new novel, *The Sun Dances at Easter*. Three years later, the Dubliner wrote a new collection of poems, *Ancient Lights*. He followed this with the memoirs, *Twice Round the Black Church* and *A Penny in the Clouds*.

Mirroring Sean O'Casey's incandescent prose, Austin's poems satirised church and state, while also celebrating sexuality. Tall, grave and distinguished in appearance, courage and honesty were Austin's hallmark. More concerned with social issues than his contemporary, Patrick Kavanagh, he spoke out against clericalism, unemployment and injustice, as in 'Unmarried Mothers':

> *In the Convent of the Sacred Heart,*
> *The Long Room has been decorated*
> *Where a Bishop can dine off golden plate:*
> *As Oriental Potentate.*
> *Girls, who will never wheel a go-cart,*
> *Cook, sew, wash, dig, milk cows, clean stables*
> *And, twice a day, giving their babes*
> *The teat, herdlike, yield milk that cost*
> *Them dearly...*

Austin's university studies had introduced him to the folk and bardic strands of Irish poetry. He applied the technical means of classical Irish language poetry to writing in English. Regard for the techniques of Gaelic verse did not preclude an interest in avant-garde poets, he also wrote on Ezra Pound. Austin and Patrick Kavanagh were the only writers Pound asked to see, when he visited Ireland in 1965. Kavanagh frequently denigrated his more erudite compatriot. Critic Sean Lucy countered: 'Clarke showed a new generation of Irish poets how a true modern voice could emerge from their own tradition, a voice capable of profound ironies and satire, as well as a new relaxation and a gentle pleasure of the sensual.'

Liam Millar's Dolmen Press published the Dubliner's work. Austin liked being independent and launched his own Bridge Press.

Altogether, he wrote twenty volumes of poetry and numerous plays. Unfairly caricatured in Samuel Beckett's *Murphy* as 'a distinguished indigent drunken Irish bard', Austin's dedication gained him several honours. He was elected president of Irish PEN, Honorary member of the United Arts Club and awarded the Gregory medal by the Irish Academy of Letters. He survived two heart attacks to read with Brendan Kennelly and Eavan Boland at the 1967 dedication of the W.B. Yeats Memorial in St. Stephen's Green. His *Collected Poems* was published in 1974.

Austin died on 19 March 1974 at the age of 77. His final address was Bridge House, Templeogue, beside the river Dodder. In 1984, he became the first Dublin writer to have a bridge named called after him, when the new Templeogue span was named Austin Clarke Bridge.

Capel Street – favourite street of Austin Clarke and James Joyce

Eden Road, Glasthule

Padraic Colum
(1881–1972)

Railway Cottage, Eden Road, Glasthule

My eyelids red and heavy are
With bending o'er the smould'ring peat...

Glasthule is a long remove from Longford, where Padraic Collumb was born on 8 December 1881. He was the first of eight children of Susan and Patrick Collumb, master of the local workhouse. Padraic later changed his name to Colum. Walking to fairs with his uncle, he met the wanderers and ballad singers who would feature in his poems. He recalled: 'I was born where waifs, strays and tramps congregated. I heard stories before I could read them, and songs and scraps of poetry before I could learn at any school.'

Padraic's father lost his position in 1889 and left to seek his fortune in the Colorado Gold Rush. He returned empty-handed in 1892 and was appointed assistant stationmaster at Sandycove. The family settled at Railway Cottage in Glasthule, where Padraic spent his formative years. Studying at Glasthule national school, he delivered railway parcels in his spare time. Nearby Dun Laoghaire provided bookshops and sea walks. And the stimulation of a port, to which ships arrived daily from England and further shores.

The security of Padraic's home life was shattered by his mother's death in 1897. The family split up and 16-year old Padraic went to live in various south Dublin boarding-houses: 18 Longwood Avenue, 26 Rugby Road and 30 Chelmsford Road. In 1898, he became a clerk in the Irish Railway Clearing House in Dawson Street. Close to the National Library, where he could study and write. His first poems were published in the *Irish Independent* and *The United Irishman* in 1902. They included 'An Old Woman of the Roads' and 'The Drover':

> *To Meath of the pastures,*
> *From wet hills by the sea,*
> *Through Leitrim and Longford*
> *Go my cattle and me.*
> *I hear in the darkness*
> *Their slipping and breathing.*
> *I name them the bye-ways*
> *They're to pass without heeding.*

Later that year, Padraic won a competition with the anti-army recruitment play, *The Saxon Shilling*. He acted in dramas by George Russell and W.B. Yeats, before deciding to concentrate on his writing. Russell informed artist Sarah Purser: 'He is a rough jewel at present, but a real one.' In 1903, the Irish National Theatre Society staged Padraic's second play, *Broken Soil*. He met James Joyce, who shared his affection for Oliver Goldsmith. The following year was a momentous one for the pair. Joyce abandoned Dublin for the Continent. Padraic relinquished his job to study and write full-time, thanks to a scholarship from wealthy American, Thomas Kelly. Hailed by Tom Kettle and other critics, Padraic's 1905 play, *The Land*, was an early Abbey Theatre success.

This was an exciting period in Dublin's history, with a heady blend of nationalism and an emerging literary movement. Padraic worked closely with the Literary Revival's leading figures. *Wild Earth*, his first major poetry collection was published in 1907. Far removed from Yeats's mythic and symbolic work, it was a reiteration of Padraic's commitment to poetry that was 'close to the ground'. It featured 'An Old Woman of the Roads' and the much-quoted 'A Poor Scholar of the 'Forties':

> *My eyelids red and heavy are*
> *With bending o'er the smold'ring peat.*
> *I know the Aeneid now by heart,*
> *My Virgil read in cold and heat,*
> *In loneliness and hunger smart.*
> *And I know Homer, too, I ween,*
> *As Munster poets know Ossian.*

The Abbey Theatre staged two more of Padraic's plays, *The Fiddlers' House* and *Thomas Muskerry*. Their directness of style established him as a master of peasant realist drama. Described by Micheal MacLiammoir as one of the finest Abbey plays, *Thomas Muskerry* was also shown in New York. Padraic did not neglect his politics. His short, stocky figure belied his fearlessness, he was one of the Irish Volunteers who were fired on by British soldiers at Bachelor's Walk in 1913.

Padraic married teacher Mary Gunning Maguire in 1912. They lived at 2 Belmont Avenue, Donnybrook for two years before sailing to New York, where Padraic lectured on Irish literature. The outbreak of war turned the Colums' holiday into an eight-year sojourn. Padraic wrote a further volume of poetry and a book of Irish folk stories. *The Adventure of Odysseus* and *The Children of Odin* introduced many children to classical literature. Published in 1923, his first novel, *Castle Conquer*, dealt with the Irish land war. It was followed by two books of essays on Ireland and three volumes of Hawaiian folklore.

In 1931, following their return from America, the Colums made the first of two long visits to France. Padraic, now 50, renewed his friendship with James Joyce. His former Dublin boon companion celebrated in *Finnegans Wake*: 'The S. S. Paudraic's in the harbour'. Padraic wrote the Foreword to the American edition of *Anna Livia Plurabelle*. The Colum and Joyce families holidayed together in Nice. In Paris, Joyce introduced Padraic and Mary to Sylvia Beach and Ernest Hemingway. Padraic typed and regularly read for his near-blind compatriot, who plumbed his historical and topographical expertise when finalising *Finnegans Wake*. With war on the horizon in 1938, Joyce saw the Colums off to the Le Havre boat train: 'We don't want you to go but, anyhow, you'll be safe in America.'

Both Padraic and Mary lectured at Columbia University. Apart from brief visits home, they spent the rest of their lives in America. As well as *The Show-Booth*, produced in 1948, Padraic wrote five other plays based on the tradition of Japanese Noh drama. He retold Irish legends in *A Treasury of Irish Folklore*. His semi-autobiographical novel, *The Flying Swans*, followed in 1957, the year his wife died.

Mary Colum bequeathed her own record of the period and their relationship, *Life and the Dream*. Three years later, Padraic published *Our Friend James Joyce*, which Mary and he had co-written. One of his last and most important works was *The Poet's Circuits: Collected Poems of Ireland*. It detailed the growth of a versifier's mind and the relationship between the Irish poet and the land and its traditions.

Padraic died in Connecticut aged 90 on 11 January 1972. He was buried beside his wife in Saint Fintan's Cemetery, Sutton in the shadow of Sheilmartin Hill, an area appropriately rich in legend. A poet, novelist, playwright, children's author and collector of folklore, Padraic was one of his country's most versatile writers. His love of Irish traditions and his fresh style endeared him to readers of several generations. Author Patricia Boylan described him as possessing many graces but no airs: 'There was a kind of incandescent innocence about him.'

Grave of Mary and Padraic Colum in Sutton

House 38, Trinity College Dublin

James Patrick (J.P.) Donleavy
(1926–)

House 38, Trinity College Dublin

The Ginger Man is the picaresque novel to stop them all, lusty, violent, wildly funny... – Dorothy Parker

Dublin was no exception to the explosion of artistic vitality which energised the early 1950s. Nikos Kazantzakis catapulted Zorba the Greek into existence. The Angry Young Men revolution spawned playwright John Osborne, Jack Kerouac hit the American trail. But Ireland produced the most widely-sold classic of the period, J.P. Donleavy's *The Ginger Man*, which Dorothy Parker described as 'one of those books which reveals its quality from the first line'.

Trinity College became Donleavy's first Irish home when he enrolled there at the end of 1946 as an American GI Bill of Rights student. The college represented the start of a career he could never have anticipated. He combined light study with pursuing his painting ambitions and vain efforts to match the drinking exploits of Brendan Behan and fellow-student Gainor Crist, the original Ginger Man. Donleavy's fondly-remembered quarters at House Number 38 featured a sitting room, bedroom and scullery: 'the quarterly rent of eighteen pounds, eight shillings and elevenpence also included gas and electricity, a daily bottle of milk and an evening meal!'

James Patrick Donleavy was born on 23 April 1926 in New York, the son of a Galway mother and a Longford father, who grew orchids for one of the city's biggest hotels. The family lived in Brooklyn Heights before moving to sedate Woodlawn. Beside Herman Melville's cemetery, which would later feature in his work. Donleavy studied at Fordham Preparatory School but was expelled in 1942 for entertaining members of his fraternity in a saloon. An enthusiastic boxer with the New York Athletic Club, he enlisted in the US navy in 1944. He discovered James Joyce's work in a naval academy library and commenced his own creative career by ghost-writing essays for fellow-pupils. Discharged at the age of twenty, he decided to study in Joyce's Dublin.

Shoeless children selling newspapers was a shock. And the cold which permeated Donleavy's Trinity quarters. Dimly-lit pubs provided a cosier alternative. He soon encountered Brendan Behan, art student John Ryan, aspiring sculptor Des MacNamara and fellow-American, Gainor Crist. Though of compact build, Donleavy's neat attire and beard ensured he stood out in the crowd. Being 'different' in 1940s Dublin was a risky business. But his boxing expertise stood him in good stead. Brendan Behan desisted from a rash Davy Byrne's challenge when he saw the visitor's rapid warm-up.

John Ryan encouraged Donleavy to take up painting. The newcomer's quarters were transformed into a studio. In 1948, he staged the first of four exhibitions and married English student, Valerie Heron. Though Ernest Gebler and other friends bought pictures, Donleavy's catalogue introduction and equally lurid nudes garnered more publicity than financial reward. His love of art was matched by his continued interest in writing. He concentrated on poetry and short stories. John Ryan published his fist story in the April 1950 issue of *Envoy*. Writing soon superseded art.

In 1951, Donleavy commenced the book which within a few years propelled him to world fame. He described its genesis to *Paris Review* interviewers, Molly McKaughan and Fayette Hickox: 'I realized that the only way you could ever tackle the world was to write something that no one could hold off, a book that would go everywhere, into everyone's hands. And I decided then to write a novel that would shake the world. I shook my fist and said I would do it.'

'Today a rare sun of spring. And horse carts clanging to the quays down Tara Street and the shoeless white faced kids screaming.' *The Ginger Man* was published by Olympia Press in Paris in 1955, when Donleavy was 29. It was based on the antics of his red-haired former Trinity mate, Gainor Crist, a native of Dayton, Ohio. Like Gainor, the Ginger Man dreamt of wealth and peace. Allergic to work, he spent more time in pubs than with his wife. Admired by women, addicted to good company, he was dogged by unpaid landlords and distrustful in-laws. But his poetic vision and natural charm never deserted him, as he navigated his riotous way through Bohemian Dublin. After an uninvited reading of the manuscript, Brendan Behan proclaimed: 'This book is going to go around the world and beat the Bejasus out of the Bible!'

Brendan proved a perceptive critic. Within a short time, Donleavy's debut novel had become a twentieth century classic. It was published in twenty five languages, including Japanese and Russian, and sold several million copies. Banned in Ireland for its sex content, it was included in the Modern Library's Best 100 English-Language Novels of the Twentieth century. It was also turned into a successful stage play in London, with Richard Harris in the title role. The play enjoyed a shorter run in Dublin, a church prelate had it removed after three performances.

Anything after *The Ginger Man* was certain to be anti-climactic. But Donleavy went on to write twenty-four other books and plays. These included the hilarious, bitter-sweet *The Beastly Beatitudes of Balthazar B*, about a rich boy born in Paris who seeks love: 'The world has an instinct. Waits to deliver blows at the moment when it knows it will hurt most. Not nice.' The Darcy Dancer trilogy, a comic treatise on more positive thinking, added to Donleavy's reputation. *Leila: Further in the Destinies of Darcy Dancer*, captured the decline of the Anglo-Irish class in the 1950s and 1960s. Mouldering big houses with leaking roofs, bills yellowing on sagging floors. One reviewer noted: 'It takes about ten seconds to become hopelessly addicted to Donleavy's style and about five seconds to fall in love with Darcy Dancer and his adventures.'

Donleavy set some of his books in the US. Displaying his trademark humour and melancholy, these included *A Fairy Tale of New York* and *A Singular Man*, which he described as his personal favourite. The singular George Smith was rich but lonely, and being pursued by his former wife and their children for a share of his fortune. *Time* magazine insisted: 'Once the reader overcomes the resentful suspicion that the fractured-telegram style of interior monologue must take less time to write than to read, he will find Smith the most lushly loony character of the year. Donleavy simply cannot help being comic even when the symbols and portents crowd thickest.'

Following two divorces, Donleavy currently lives with one of his two children, Philip, in a Westmeath country house which features a sauna and a gym. An appropriate address for a Joycean, it was visited in 1900 by the author of *Ulysses*. Joyce recorded in *Stephen Hero*: 'It was reached by an untended drive and the ground behind it thick with clumps of faded rhododendrons sloped down to the shore of Lough Owel.' The lake found its way into *Ulysses*.

Donleavy looks younger than his age, thanks to a lifelong keep-fit regime. In 2012, he celebrated his 86th birthday with an exhibition of his paintings at Dublin's Matthews Gallery. Generous with advice, the man who recorded Bohemian Dublin like no other joked that his lack of an education was an advantage when he commenced writing. He counselled aspiring authors to write as if corresponding with a friend: 'Being a good novelist really comes down to being a good newspaper reporter: you're trying to get what you've written on your page into a reader's mind as quickly as possible, and to keep them seeing it. That is why I use the short, truncated, telegraphic sentences.'

The Ginger Man's Trinity College alma mater

Camden Street's De Luxe Hotel

Ernest Gebler
(1914-1998)

Camden Street Cinema (now hotel)

*Gebler was, for all his sometimes dour qualities,
one of that rare breed, a consummate gentleman.*
— J.P. Donleavy

C amden Street's Theatre De Luxe cinema acquired a reputation for unreliability during the 1940s. While rain swept the exterior street and a cowboy chase neared a bloody climax in sun-baked Arizona, the screen would suddenly go blank. It was a regular occurrence at the Art Deco cinema which opened in 1912. 'Change the bloody reel,' aficionados would shout up to the projection room. Minutes later, the cowboys would reappear and the dust would fly again, to ironic cheers.

The culprit was aspiring writer Ernest 'Ernie' Gebler. Notebooks danced in every perforated pocket as he pedalled, habitually late, from a shack in Ashtown. Ernest was not only a projectionist, he was also the cinema rat-catcher. His writing activities in the De Luxe eventually paid off. He became the most affluent and widely-read Irish author of the period. The jacket was replaced by tweeds, the bike by a sportscar, and his Ashtown room by a country mansion. One of his books became an Oscar-winning film, a play won an American Academy Award.

The arts were in the Gebler blood. Born in Dublin on 31 December 1914, Ernie was the son of Czechoslovak-born Adolphe Gebler, who also had cinema associations. Once a silent film accompanist in Waterford, he became First Clarinettist with the Radio Éireann Symphony Orchestra. According to sculptor Des MacNamara, Adolphe disliked the conductor and sought every opportunity to annoy him. When resting during a critical symphonic moment, he would spread a handkerchief over his knees and clean his clarinet. The audience looked at nothing else.

Largely self-educated, Ernie Gebler worked backstage at the Gate Theatre in the 1930s before deciding to concentrate on writing. He read voraciously and acquired an encyclopaedic knowledge of literature, astronomy, chemistry and physiology. Like Jack London and many self-educated, he would later tend to err on the didactic side. No one showed him how to write. He commenced an arduous apprenticeship, with a discipline which reflected his granite features. While working in Camden Street, he wrote stories for the religious *Rosary* and *Messenger* magazines. Replicating Sean O'Casey's contributions to a card manufacturer, his first book was a compilation of In Memoriam verses, for which he was paid seven shillings and sixpence each.

But Ernie persisted, like fellow-Northsider Brendan Behan, who shared his passion for swimming and politics. Through Brendan, he met Des MacNamara, who became one of Ernie's closest friends. Des recalled: 'Some people have described Ernie as an obsessive, as if that were an entirely negative quality. But without that focus against all the odds, he would have remained backstage at either the Gate or the Camden cinema. He simply wrote and wrote and though publication came comparatively late, at the age of 30, it was achieved through singularly hard graft and not by ingratiation.'

In 1946, Ernie published his first novel about a Dublin childhood, *He Had My Heart Scalded*. His hopes of fame and solvency were unrealized when, like Behan's debut work, the book was banned in Ireland. Its publication, however, enhanced Ernie's self-belief as a writer. No more would he swop film reels or chase rodents. Packing his dictionary and few possessions, he sailed to London. He embarked on a four-year marathon at the British Museum, researching and writing the hitherto unchronicled story of the Mayflower voyage. Encouraged by actress Sally Travers, he subsisted by selling stories to magazines such as *Envoy*, and filching milk from morning porches.

The Dubliner's dedication was rewarded: *The Plymouth Adventure* was published in 1950. Superbly characterised, the fictionalised account of the pilgrims' seventeenth century Atlantic endurance sold five million copies in the USA alone. It was filmed, with Spencer Tracy in the lead role. Ernie's social and financial status changed overnight. The 36-year-old, tall, high-domed Dubliner embraced the good life on a 200-acre estate and big house under the Wicklow hills near Roundwood. While not neglecting his writing, he fished and bathed in Lough Dan, which lapped the edge of the pine-shaded grounds.

Ernie's life was further enriched by a new wife, nine years his junior. The glamorous Leatrice Gilbert, Trinity College student and daughter of American silent movie star, John Gilbert. The couple married in New York in 1950. Sadly, Ernie's remote manor and the malevolent Wicklow gales proved no match for Californian sunshine. Lea disappeared two years later, together with their baby son,

Karl. Once home, she divorced Ernie. He gradually resumed the only security he had ever known, his writing. Like fellow-Dubliner Sheridan le Fanu, he worked through the night in the Gothic silence of his mist-shrouded mansion. His loneliness alleviated by classical music and Irish whiskey.

Ernie's next romance was with a much younger lady who, ominously, had writing ambitions of her own. It proved equally disastrous. The relationship between their daughter and a divorced older man anguished Edna O'Brien's parents and friends. In 1950s Catholic Ireland, it was easy to raise a posse and intimidate a pagan with a foreign-sounding name. Ernie was badly beaten by a gang which included a priest who brandished a cross. Ernie and Edna married in 1954 but another divorce ensued. Ernie's old friends proved more durable. Des and Skylla MacNamara and Alan and Carolyn Simpson of the Pike Theatre regularly visited. Also, budding novelist, J.P. Donleavy.

Donleavy remembered the Dubliner advising him on the mistakes made by authors who fall into unexpected riches: 'Mike, they buy binoculars, shotguns, sports cars and fishing rods, and a big estate to use them on. And then outfitted in their new life, along with new bathrooms, wallpaper and brands of soap, they make a fatal mistake and change their women. To schemingly get toasted and roasted on glowing hot emotional coals, and subjected to a whole new set of tricks and treacheries.'

Despite his problems, Ernie never neglected his writing. Working with what Donleavy described as 'implacable application', he published several more novels including *A Week in the Country* and *The Love Investigator*. The *Times* described his 1969 book, *Shall I Eat You Now?*, as 'immensely entertaining and poignant.' The story of a lecherous employer who lusts after his secretary was filmed as *Hoffman*, starring Peter Sellers and Sinead Cusack. Ernie's many plays included *She Sits Smiling*, *The Spaniard in Galway* and *A Cry for Help*. He also wrote screenplays and television dramas such as

Why Aren't you Famous and *A Little Milk of Human Kindness*. Though he never repeated the blockbuster success of the Oscar-winning *The Plymouth Adventure*, he won an American Academy Award for his television drama, *Call Me Daddy*.

Ernie's writing proved more successful than his relationships. Jane, his companion for over a decade, collapsed in 1989 with a heart attack while mowing their lawn in Dalkey. Ernie went into decline. His lingering death from Alzheimer's disease was ironic for a man who had trained his mind to accomplish miracles. He died in the Grove Nursing Home, Killiney on 26 January 1998, aged 83. He left three sons. Sasha, Karl, who was renamed John by his American mother, and Carlo, who carries on the family writing tradition.

J.P. Donleavy was among those who mourned his demise. When Donleavy was missing Ireland in McCarthyite America, Ernie invited him to return and offered to support him while awaiting a publisher for *The Ginger Man*. Forever appreciative of Ernie's encouragement, Donleavy insisted: 'Gebler was, for all his sometimes dour qualities, one of that rare breed, a consummate gentleman.'

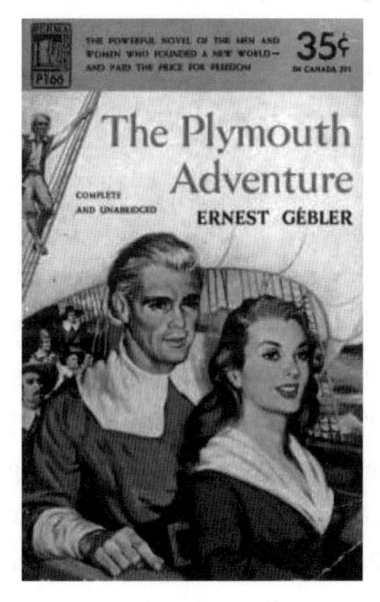

Sold 5 million copies in USA alone

5 Parnell Square East

OLIVER ST. JOHN GOGARTY
(1878–1957)

5 Parnell Square East

Gogarty, the arch-mocker, the author of all the jokes that enable us to live in Dublin. – George Moore

Italian philosopher Mario Rossi, a friend of W.B. Yeats, described Oliver St John Gogarty as: 'A man who recalls the great Italians of the Quattrocento... to know Gogarty was to realise the enthusiasm of the man who lives with full consciousness for that admirable phenomenon which is called life.'

Few people packed as much into one existence as the Dubliner, who was born at 5 Rutland Square East, now Parnell Square, on 17 August, 1878. He achieved fame as a poet, writer, surgeon, aviator and racing cyclist. Five feet nine, stockily built and an accomplished swimmer, he was awarded a Royal Humane Society bronze medal for three times rescuing drowning men from the Liffey. His familiarity with the river enabled him to escape would-be executioners during the Civil War. He became a senator and was the inspiration for Buck Mulligan in James Joyce's *Ulysses*.

Unlike Joyce, Gogarty grew up in affluent circumstances. His father, Henry, was a successful physician with a second imposing residence in Glasnevin. Its gardens and nearby Tolka river inspired Gogarty's lifelong love of nature. Margaret Gogarty was an energetic woman who passed on her vivacity and sense of humour to her son. Railing against gloom, he advised: 'Life is plastic: it will assume any shape you choose to put on it.' Gogarty suffered three colleges, before commencing medical studies in 1898 at Trinity College. Known for his bawdy rhymes, less disreputable verse won him three Vice-Chancellor's prizes for poetry between 1901 and 1903.

In 1904 and 1905, Gogarty published poems in *The Venture* and *Dana*. He became friends with W.B. Yeats and James Joyce. He accommodated Joyce in the Sandycove Martello Tower, in which the fellow-Dubliner later set the opening scene of *Ulysses*. Tower visitor, William Bulfin, noted their contrasting characters. While Joyce listened in silence, Gogarty 'was a wayward kind of genius who talked in a captivating manner, with a keen, grim humour, which cut and pierced through a topic in bright, strong flashes worthy of the rapier of Swift'. Gogarty applauded Joyce's poetry but was repelled by *Ulysses* – 'a triumph of ugliness, chaos and ineffectuality'.

Gogarty married Martha Duane in 1906. After graduating from Trinity College, he commenced his career as a surgeon at the Richmond Hospital. He bought the balconied former home of National Library architect, Sir Thomas Deane at 15 Ely Place, where he also treated private patients. He later opened consulting room at 27 St. Stephen's Green. His regular Friday evening guests included Yeats, George Russell, Horace Plunkett, James Stephens and Tom Kettle, who assisted his campaign for better housing and the abolition of Dublin's slums. And, occasionally, neighbour George Moore, who marvelled at his photographic memory and remembered him fondly in *Salve* as: 'Gogarty, the arch-mocker, the author of all the jokes that enable us to live in Dublin – Gogarty, the author of the *Limericks of the Golden Age*, the youngest of my friends, full in the face, with a smile in his eyes and always a witticism on his lips, overflowing with quotations.'

Courage as well as wit distinguished Gogarty. He supported Arthur Griffith's campaign for an independent Ireland and sheltered rebel leader Michael Collins in Ely Place. Later, he had the unenviable responsibility of performing postmortems on both men, when they died during the Civil War. Created a senator by the new Free State government in 1922, 44-year old Gogarty himself was kidnapped by anti-government gunmen. 'Should I tip the driver?' he enquired as he was bundled into a house opposite Islandbridge weir. He feigned a stomach upset, flung his coat at his captors and escaped the waiting firing squad by diving into the freezing Liffey. The republicans avenged his escape by burning his Renvyle, Connemara home.

Gogarty wrote plays for the Abbey Theatre, including *Blight: The Tragedy of Dublin: An Exposition*. Its criticism of unhealthy tenements mirrored his frequent Senate outrage on the subject and influenced Sean O'Casey's later work. In the 1920s and 1930s, his collections of poetry included the award-winnng *An Offering of Swans* and *Wild Apples*. Appropriately for an athlete, his 'Tailteann Ode' won a bronze medal at the 1924 Olympic Games in Paris. Gogarty was unsurprised that his poetry had its detractors: 'Possibly because I set my face against the revival of folk poetry and Padraic Columism: and insisted that there were better things to hear and still finer things to see in Ireland than turf smoke and cottage songs.' Close to Joyce, the Colums never warmed to Gogarty. Mary Colum described his lack of reserve as 'an incontinence of speech', which prevented him from being a companionable man.

In 1936, Gogarty published the autobiographical *As I Was Going Down Sackville Street*. A nostalgic voyage, it recalled Dublin's literati and characters such as Endymion: 'Quaintly he came raiking out of Molesworth Street into Kildare Street, an odd figure mouldered by memories, and driven mad by dreams which had overflowed into life, making him turn himself into a merry mockery of all he had once held dear.' *Tumbling in the Hay*, a comic novel about medical students in turn-of-the-century Dublin, followed in 1939.

A familiar figure in his yellow Rolls-Royce, Gogarty the aviator showed his city from the air to Yeats, George Russell and artist, Sarah Purser. After failing to enlist in the RAF at the outbreak of war, he departed in September 1939 for a lecture tour in the United States. Delayed there by the conflict, he published further poetry, novels and memoirs. These included *Rolling Down the Lea* and *It Isn't This Time Of Year At All!*, further snapshots of intellectual Dublin in the early 1900s. He subsequently took out US citizenship and, apart from holidays in Ireland, lived there for the rest of his life.

Like Joyce, George Moore and George Russell, Gogarty died far from the land whose literature he had enhanced. Shortly after enquiring about purchasing the Sandycove tower, the 79-year-old writer suffered a fatal heart attack in New York on 22 September 1957. He retained his sometimes caustic wit to the end. When a bar conversation with friends was interrupted by the jukebox, Gogarty exclaimed: 'Oh dear God in Heaven, that I should find myself thousands of miles from home, an old man at the mercy of every retarded son of a bitch who has a nickel to drop in that bloody illuminated coal scuttle.'

Gogarty was buried in Ballinakill Cemetery, close to his former Renvyle house. His epitaph is from one of his own poems, 'Non Dolet':

Our friends go with us as we go
Down the long path where beauty wends
Where all we love forgathers, so
Why should we fear to join our friends?

Despite Gogarty's generosity, Joyce repaid his former boon companion badly. *The Bell* editor, Sean O'Faolain wrote: 'Joyce did him an immense and cruel injustice in *Ulysses* in presenting him to posterity as something approaching the nature of an inquisitive lout whose only function in life was to offset the exquisite sensitivity and delicacy of Stephen Dedalus. Gogarty was a kind and sensitive man, full of verve and zest. His essential nature, which nobody could ever possibly gather from *Ulysses*, was his nature as a poet – he was a fine poet.'

James Joyce did Gogarty an injustice

73 Upper Leeson Street

Patrick Lafcadio Hearn (Koizumi Yakumo)
(1850–1904)

73 Upper Leeson Street

We are all compounds of innumerable lives, each a sum in an infinite addition – the dead are not dead, they live in all of us, and move us, stirring faintly in every heart beat.

'Oh! the dawnless glory of tropic morning! – the single sudden leap of the giant light over the purpling of a hundred peaks – over the surging of the mornes!' Patrick Lafcadio Hearn was Ireland's Paul Gauguin. Like the Frenchman – whom he may have met in Martinique – he forsook the increasingly commercial West for the more exotic and traditional East. He settled in Japan in 1890 and became one of its best-loved writers.

He died there in 1904, a long way from his Dublin home at 73 Upper Leeson Street.

Few writers matched Patrick's Homeric voyaging. He was born on 27 June 1850 on the Ionian island of Lefkada, from which his second name is derived. His mother, Rosa Kassimati, was Greek. His Offaly father, military surgeon Charles Hearn, transferred to the West Indies, leaving two-year old Patrick and his mother at 48 Lower Gardiner Street, Dublin. When Charles returned, Rosa departed for Greece. Re-posted to India, Charles entrusted Patrick to a great-aunt. Charles died of a fever and was buried at sea. Patrick never saw either of his parents again. He later wrote of his mother: 'I would rather have her portrait than a fortune.'

Patrick's guardian was Sarah Brenane, a prosperous widow, with whom he lived at 73 Upper Leeson Street, 21 Leinster Square and 3 Prince Arthur Terrace. The childless Sarah lavished attention on her black-haired charge. They enjoyed holidays at Bel Air house in seaside Tramore and with relatives in Redhill, Surrey. In Wales, a Bangor sea captain entertained Patrick with stories of the Far East. Patrick's favourite holidays were at Lough Corrib with his aunt, Mrs Elwood, who sang Moore's melodies to him.

When Patrick was thirteen, Mrs Brenane sent him to a Catholic boarding school at Ushaw near Durham. His myopia was compounded when a fellow-student accidentally blinded him in one eye with a knotted rope. Patrick startled his teachers by announcing that his love of nature had changed him from Catholicism to Pantheism. The school head recalled: 'As a student he shone only in English writing: he was first in his class the first time he composed in English, and kept first, or nearly first, all the time he was here.'

After leaving Ushaw in 1867, Mrs Brenane sent Patrick to the Petits Précepteurs at Yvetot. Near Rouen, this was the alma mater of Guy de Maupassant, whose works he would later translate. Patrick was unhappy there. He stole a gate key and fled to Paris. He probably lodged with his uncle, Richard Hearn, a Barbizon School pupil of artist Jean Francois Millet. Biographer Nina H. Kennard suggested that it was his Paris experiences which sowed the seed of Patrick's ambition to succeed as an artist. After a year in London, an uncle paid his way to a distant relative in Cincinnati.

The 19-year-old immigrant worked at odd jobs and learned to set type and proofread. He contributed stories to local newspapers and in 1872 became a crime reporter for the *Cincinnati Daily Enquirer*. He and artist Henry Farny also launched a weekly literary and satirical journal. Referring to Patrick's scant five feet three inches, a contemporary noted, 'He suggested a small, shy, studious, shipwrecked sailor.'

In 1877, Patrick moved to New Orleans, where he spent nine years. He contributed features, illustrated with his own woodcuts, to local and national publications including *Harper's Weekly* and *Scribner's*. Enthusiastic about French literature since his Paris days, he translated stories by de Maupassant, Anatole France and Pierre Loti, precursors of subsequent full-volume works. He preferred Parnassianism to George Moore's naturalism, and praised Leconte de Lisle's *Poèmes antiques* as 'exquisitely classics finished and polished like an antique marble, full of music, light and the old Greek spirit of the Beautiful'.

Patrick wrote his first book in 1884, *Stray Leaves from Strange Literature*, an anthology of tales from various lands. In 1885, he published two books on Creole culture and cuisine. These were followed by a novella, *Chita*, and *One of Cleopatra's Nights and Other Fantastic Romances*. Impressed with Patrick's impressionistic descriptions, *Harper's* magazine sent him to the West Indies in 1887. He wrote *Two Years in the French West Indies* and possibly met artist Paul Gauguin, who was in Martinique at the same time. Equally repelled by Western materialism, both men were captivated by the pace of life in Martinique, where people had not lost touch with nature.

Forty-year-old Patrick's life took a fateful turn when he was redirected to Japan in 1890, a year before Gauguin sailed to French Polynesia. Patrick immediately felt at home in the country whose culture seemed to unite the material and spiritual. He was captivated by the pace of life, the sounds of old temple bells, the silent fall of cherry blossoms: 'Elfish everything seems, for everything as well as everybody is small, and queer, and mysterious: the little houses under their blue roofs, the little shop-fronts hung with blue, and the smiling little people in their blue costumes.'

Patrick taught at a school in western Matsue and married 22-year old Koizumi Setsu, the daughter of a local samurai family. He became a naturalized Japanese and assumed the name Koizumi Yakumo. In 1896, he began teaching English literature at Tokyo Imperial University. Patrick's understanding of the country's culture and traditions endeared him to his hosts. His awareness of nature and the world around him made him one of the first Westerners to read and appreciate haiku. A contemporary noted: 'Of all modern writers in English, his prose was possibly the most polished, beautiful, lyrical.'

The Irishman once worked for eight months to perfect seventy-three lines. He wrote in *A Japanese Miscellany* of several dragonfly haiku he had translated: 'They help us to understand something of the soul of the elder Japan. The people who could find delight, century after century, in watching the ways of insects, and in making such verses about them, must have comprehended, better than we, the simple pleasure of existence.'

As interest grew in Japan and its art, Patrick's books informed millions of readers in Europe and the USA, for whom the country was a mystery. In fourteen years, he wrote twelve books including *Japan: An Attempt at Interpretation*, *Japanese Fairy Tales*, *Gleanings in Buddha Fields* and *Out of the East: Japanese Lyrics*. His work remains a unique record of pre-industrial Japan:

Wafted into my room, the scent of the flowers of the plum tree
Changes my broken window into a source of delight.

Patrick was only 54 when he died from a heart attack on 26 September, 1904, a year after Gauguin died in the Marquesas. When his wife went into his study that morning, Patrick exclaimed: 'I dreamed an extraordinary dream last night, I made a long travel, but here I am now smoking in the library of our house at Nishi Okubo. Life and the world are strange.'

Survived by his widow, three sons and one daughter, Patrick was buried in Zoshigaya cemetery, Toshima, Tokyo after a Buddhist funeral. His former New Orleans residence has been preserved as a historic building, as has his Matsue home and the garden and pond which feature in his writings. Matsue also boasts the Lafcadio Hearn Memorial Museum. Streets are named after Patrick in Lefkada and Fort-de-France, Martinique. His Dublin addresses are marked by plaques.

Lafcadio Hearn Museum in Matsue, Japan

41 Brighton Square, Rathgar

JAMES JOYCE
(1882-1941)

41 Brighton Square, Rathgar

To live, to err, to fall, to triumph, to recreate life out of life! – A Portrait of the Artist as a Young Man

'Once upon a time and a very good time it was there was a moocow coming down along the road...' *A Portrait of the Artist as a Young Man* opens to James Joyce's memory of the story of a fairy cow who spirited little boys away. The tale was one of many told to him by his father on the grassy space opposite red-brick 41 Brighton Square, where the future writer was born on 2 February 1882. The upmarket square was an appropriate address for Mary Jane and civil servant, John Stanislaus Joyce. Mary, an accomplished pianist, passed on her love of music to James, who would later sing at the age of six in a Bray concert with both his parents. Singer and raconteur John Stanislaus recalled the period of his son's youth as providing 'all the happiest moments of my life'.

James Joyce was the eldest of ten children. The year of his birth was momentous in Irish politics. His father celebrated Parnell's prison release and attended the unveiling of the monument to Catholic Emancipation hero, Daniel O'Connell. He also frequented a surfeit of pubs. By the time James left Ireland in 1904, he had endured an accommodation odyssey worthy of *Ulysses*. Brighton Square was followed by 23 Castlewood Avenue and, in 1887, 1 Martello Terrace, Bray. Five years later, 23 Carysfort Avenue, Blackrock, 34 Fitzgibbon Street, 2 Millbourne Avenue and, in 1895, 17 North Richmond Street. The downward spiral continued to 29 Windsor Terrace, 13 Richmond Avenue, 8 Inverness Road, 32 Glengariff Parade and in, 1902, 5 St. Peter's Road, Phibsborough.

Joyce excelled at Clongowes and Belvedere schools. But, like George Moore, he resented the dead hand of the powerful Catholic church. His brother, Stanislaus, insisted: 'Some inner purpose transfigured him.' Joyce proclaimed in *A Portrait of the Artist*: 'I will not serve that in which I no longer believe whether it call itself my home, my fatherland or my church: and I will try to express myself in some mode of life or art as freely as I can and as wholly as I can, using for my defence the only arms I allow myself to use, silence, exile, and cunning.'

He enrolled in 1898 at University College Dublin, where he studied English, French, and Italian. His debut 1900 *Fortnightly Review* article on Henrik Ibsen's *New Drama* stimulated a note of thanks from the playwright. Joyce graduated in 1902 and left for Paris to study medicine. He lived precariously for a few months, before returning to St. Peter's Road, where his mother was dying of cancer. She did not survive to hear him sing in 1904 with John McCormack at the Antient Concert Rooms. According to boon companion Oliver St John Gogarty, he did not confine his singing to the concert hall:

James Joyce

There is a young fellow named Joyce,
Possessed of a sweet tenor voice.
He goes down to the kips
With a song on his lips
And biddeth the harlots rejoice.

In March 1904, 22-year-old Joyce rented a flat at 60 Shelbourne Road. He met 20-year old chambermaid Nora Barnacle, with whom he walked out on June 16, the day he immortalised in *Ulysses*. Three months later, he stayed for six nights at the Sandycove Martello Tower where *Ulysses* commences. In October 1904, he and Nora left for Trieste, where he taught English and their children Giorgio and Lucia were born. Despite illness and poverty, Joyce progressed his writing in the port city which had earlier welcomed compatriot Charles Lever and Dante. He returned briefly to 44 Fontenoy Street in 1909 and 1910, and saw Dublin for the last time in 1912.

Joyce's first book, the poetry collection *Chamber Music*, was published in 1907. After years of argument with publishers, 1914 saw the launch of *Dubliners*, stories which reflected the stagnation of Dublin society. *A Portrait of the Artist as a Young Man* followed in 1916. It depicted his childhood, adolescence and coming of age as an artist. Ezra Pound championed Joyce's work. He invited him to Paris, which became the Dubliner's home from 1920 until 1939. Pound introduced him to Harriet Shaw Weaver, whose patronage enabled Joyce to concentrate on writing. He completed *Ulysses*, which Sylvia Beach published on his fortieth birthday in 1922.

'Stately, plump Buck Mulligan came from the stairhead...' *Ulysses* occupied Joyce for seven years. The eighteen chapters, each covering roughly one hour, are a study of Dublin and the peregrinations of several citizens on June 16, 1904. The book's experimental use of language, interior monologue and stream of consciousness technique established Joyce as Europe's leading Modernist writer.

Ulysses celebrated human values and the ordinary man. Author Anthony Burgess advised: 'Before we start reading we ought to put off the mask of solemnity and prepare to be entertained.'

Many compatriots visited Joyce in Paris, including James Stephens, Austin Clarke and Padraic Colum, who described the writer: 'Slender, well-made, he holds himself very upright: he is tastefully dressed, and wears a ring in which there is a large stone. The pupils of his eyes are enlarged because of successive operations, but his gaze is attentive and steady. There is a small tuft of beard on his chin. The flesh of his face has softness and colour – the glow that a child's face has.'

Joyce endured innumerable eye operations and long periods of partial blindness during the sixteen years on his final work, *Finnegans Wake*. His life was further clouded by the worry of imminent war and the mental instability of 'my blueveined child', his daughter, Lucia. Biographer Gordon Bowker revealed that, despite his problems, Joyce used his influence to enable up to sixteen Jewish acquaintances escape the Nazi net.

The Dubliner left most of his possessions behind when he fled occupied France in 1940. He died only months later in Zurich on 13 January 1941 aged 58. No Irish government representative attended his funeral. Swiss admirers fashioned an Irish harp-shaped wreath which stood out against the snow-mantled ground. A local tenor sang a Monteverdi aria. Joyce had lived most of his life outside Ireland. British minister to Berne, Lord Derwent, said it was appropriate that he had died in Zurich, because he had chosen to be a European.

Patrick Kavanagh suggested that Joyce did more for Ireland than Yeats and Irish Literary Revivalists: 'The most important thing that was happening in Dublin at this time was not the activity of Yeats and his followers but the fact that wandering in the city, unknown and ignored, was a young man whose observant eye and ear was capturing the epic city that is to be found in *Ulysses*.'

Derided in Ireland in his lifetime, one newspaper described Joyce as a yahoo who had 'reviled the religion in which he had been brought up and fouled the nest which had been his native city'. This attitude mellowed to the music of cash tills, as increasing numbers of visitors arrived to follow Dublin's *Ulysses* trail. The Joyce industry mushroomed, with commemorations, museums and plaques galore. The writer who had long endured poverty was commemorated from 1993 on the Irish ten pound note.

62 Pembroke Road

PATRICK KAVANAGH
(1904-1967)

62 Pembroke Road

On Pembroke Road look out for my ghost,
Dishevelled with shoes untied...

Patrick Kavanagh penned his most enduring work, including his canal poems, in the first-floor flat which he occupied at 62 Pembroke Road from 1943 to 1958. Poverty and cold were constant companions, his first bed was a mattress stretched over bricks and milk crates. His brother, Peter, recalled: 'The rooms were very large and each had a fireplace with marble mantle. The ceilings were ten feet. In each room were two six-foot windows that leaked cold air. Wooden shutters were on each of the windows but even when closed tight failed to stop a strong breeze which blew through the rooms.'

The poet became the area's most notable character. Tall and ungainly, he loped along in a belted gaberdine, down-brimmed hat and horn-rimmed glasses, muttering to himself and kicking at imaginary obstacles. He chatted to the local beauties, children behind the railings of Miss Meredith's private school and houseproud wives, who vainly remonstrated with him for his rural spitting. His first call each morning was to Parsons Bookshop on Baggot Street Bridge.

Patrick was born on 21 October 1904 near the village of Iniskeen, County Monaghan, the fourth of the ten children of Bridget Quinn and shoemaker, James Kavanagh. Patrick left school at the age of thirteen to work their small farm and play goalie for the local football team. Frugality and gossip marked his youth. Recalling the deprivation of his family and neighbours, he later commented: 'The real poverty was lack of enlightenment'.

A schoolmate's recitation of James Clarence Mangan sparked Patrick's interest in poetry. A neighbour allowed him access to the works of Byron, Shelley, and Goldsmith. Poems from Palgrave's *Golden Treasury* fueled Patrick's day-dreaming. Biographer Antoinette Quinn discovered a poignant signpost to his future in the Cobbler's Account Book: 'I'm sitting on a bag of oats on the loft: the sun is shining most beautiful on me: 8th May 1923.'

The Monaghan man first appeared in print at the age of 24, with two poems in the *Irish Weekly Independent*. A new world opened when he came across the *Irish Statesman* at a Dundalk market. Editor George Russell accepted three poems in 1929, including 'Ploughman':

> *I turn the lea-green down*
> *Gaily now,*
> *And paint the meadow brown*
> *With my plough.*

Patrick wrote by candlelight after a day's farming. *The Dublin Magazine*, *John O'London* and *The Spectator* published further poems. Jonathan Cape included 'Ploughman' in its anthology, *Best Poems of 1930*. Mirroring hero William Carleton, Patrick walked for three days in 1931 to meet his Dublin mentor, George Russell. The editor gifted him books by Emerson, Dostoevsky, James Stephens and George Moore. Their weight concerned the muddied traveller, but not their contents, as he settled down for the night in Dublin's Iveagh Hostel, where Liam O'Flaherty had earlier lodged.

Back home, Patrick savoured his treasure trove while working the fields, just as Doctor Johnson had studied Ovid in Lichfield's equally remote meadows. His confidence was boosted when the *Irish Times* accepted four poems in 1935. Macmillan printed his first collection, *Ploughman and other Poems*, in its 1936 Contemporary Poets series. After a short period in London, during which he published the autobiographical *Green Fool*, 35-year old Patrick moved to Dublin in 1939. In the hope of commissions, he drank in Fleet Street's Palace Bar, where *Irish Times* editor Bertie Smyllie held sway. Patrick's use of colloquial speech and his studies of the lives of real people did not endear him to Dublin's literati. For them, he was a figure of derision, with his uncouth manner and seven-league boots.

Schoolteacher brother Peter Kavanagh subsidised Patrick's early years in Dublin. Columns in the *Irish Press* and the *Standard* newspapers introduced him to a wider public. The poet stayed in 51 Upper Drumcondra Road and 35 Haddington Road, before moving to Pembroke Road in 1943. The 1942 publication of the emotionally powerful *The Great Hunger* established Patrick as a major poet. A howl of sexual repression, the poem described the privations and hardship of rural existence. Patrick's social realism mirrored Joyce and drew a line under the Literary Revival's romantic peasant. Macmillan published the well-reviewed collection, *A Soul for Sale* in 1947. *Tarry Flynn*, a more lyrical account of farming life, followed.

Like Dr. Johnson, Patrick became synonymous with his adopted city. A target of visiting journalists, Larry Morrow dined with him: 'Patrick Kavanagh, without warning, suddenly crosses his legs, jerks the table a good two feet in the air, cups and dishes a-jingle-jangling, and continues his conversation as if no earthquake had occurred. Or he as suddenly hunches the enormous, mountainous shoulders, and chairs, table, walls even, seem to shiver with him. Nuclear fission (one reflects) is a ripple in a teacup compared to Mr Kavanagh in a tea-shop.'

Envoy provided Patrick with a valuable mouthpiece. *The Bell* published the watershed *Intimate Parnassus* and nurtured his progress to a more humorous and confessional mode. When *Envoy* closed, Peter Kavanagh poured his savings into a weekly magazine which the brothers jointly wrote. One of the most extreme periodicals ever seen in Dublin, *Kavanagh's Weekly, A Journal of Literature and Politics* attacked almost every Irish institution from April, 1952 until its demise thirteen weeks later.

Ironically, Patrick then sued a journal which he felt had ridiculed him. He was hospitalised with cancer shortly after meeting Louis MacNeice's friend, Patrick Leigh Fermor, who impressed him with his recitation of *The Dead* at Clonmacnoise. The warm summer of 1955 marked Patrick's rebirth at the age of 51. He convalesced close to Parsons Bookshop in what he called his Parnassus. Reunited with the beauty of nature and the magic of light, he scooped up baptismal canal water from under Baggot Street Bridge:

> *Leafy-with-love banks and the green waters of the canal*
> *Pouring redemption for me, that I do*
> *The will of God, wallow in the habitual, the banal,*
> *Grow with nature again as before I grew.*

After fifteen years, the poet left Pembroke Road at the end of 1958: 'I will confess that I walked into every room in turn and prostrated myself on the floor, concentrating the while that this would be my last look out the window. I gazed out the window and concentrated and tried to fix in my imagination all those images. And if the truth must be told, I wept.'

Patrick achieved overdue national recognition, when RTE broadcast a televised profile in 1962. He married his longtime friend, Katherine Moloney, in April 1967. Seven months later, on 30 November, the 63-year old poet succumbed to pneumonia in the Merrion Nursing Home, 21 Herbert Street, where Samuel Beckett's mother had also died.

Patrick's giant presence still pervades his beloved Baggotonia. A nocturnal dog-walker claims to see him regularly on the crest of the canal bridge, gazing in the window of what was once Parsons Bookshop. The adjacent Grand Canal features a memorial bench erected in 1958 and, opposite, John Coll's 1991 sculpture seat.

119 Morehampton Road

BENEDICT KIELY
(1919-2007)

119 Morehampton Road, Donnybrook

*Every man at the end should return to the place
he started in.*

Benedict Kiely was a proud native of County Tyrone. The birthplace of his hero, William Carleton, playwright Brian Friel, and distant cousin, Flann O'Brien. Like Carleton a century earlier, Ben also migrated to the big city for work. And in time, he became a well-know figure on the Dublin literary and broadcasting scene – though, as he once explained, never a Dublin man. The definition of a Dublin man was one who didn't go home for Christmas, he was *at* home. Nevertheless, the city was Ben's home for over sixty years. After living in Dollymount and Rathgar, he spent his last productive forty years with his wife, Frances, at 119 Morehampton Road, Donnybrook.

The youngest of the six children of Thomas and Sara Alice Kiely, Ben was born on 15 August 1919 in Dromore, close to William Carleton's birthplace. A Boer War veteran and a chainman for the Ordnance Survey, Thomas became a bank porter when the family moved to Omagh. Despite the Catholic-Protestant divide, people mixed easily in Omagh. The only discrimination Ben experienced was from his own side. A soccer player for Omagh Corinthians, he was suspended from the Gaelic Athletic Association for playing a 'foreign' game.

Thomas Kiely regaled his son on long walks with tales of his African travels and adventures. Like Carleton, Ben enjoyed the essays of Joseph Addison. And, between surreptitious perusals of *Dracula* and Zane Gray thrillers, the textbooks of Hilaire Belloc and G.K. Chesterton. He would read late by the fireside, when the family had gone to bed: 'The only night I ever let the fire go out, because I was afraid to go out into the dark and root for more fuel, was the night I finished reading *The Master of Ballantrae*: one of the only two books that ever gave me the creeps.'

Ben became involved with a local theatrical group. One of his favourite teachers, Brother Rice, 'made us realise that there was a world where books mattered'. Dreaming of being a writer, Ben progressed to George Bernard Shaw and Jonathan Swift. When he was seventeen, he started work as a sorting clerk in Omagh Post Office. He decided to study for the priesthood but, after hospitalisation with a spinal injury, he abandoned the Jesuits. Awaiting a place in University College Dublin in 1939, he worked as a part-time journalist with the local *Weekly Standard*. The experience confirmed his determination to earn his living by the pen. Ben subsidised his Dublin studies by writing for a periodical and a weekly newspaper. He also found time to help rescue victims of the 1941 German bombing of North Strand. He graduated in 1943 with a B.A. in History and Letters.

In 1944, Ben married and, the following year, he joined the *Irish Independent* as a critic and leader-writer. He progressed his serious writing and published his first book in 1945 at the age of 26. *Counties of Contention* was a non-fiction account of the Ireland's partition. This was followed by his first novel, *Land Without Stars*, a story of sectarian dissension set in Donegal and Tyrone. *And Poor Scholar*, a critical biography of William Carleton.

Ben's next book earned him the distinction of being added to the list of proscribed Irish writers. *In a Harbour Green* was the story of seduction in the west of Ireland, which failed to seduce the Censorship Board. Ben took the news lightly: 'A writer here felt out of it if he were not banned.' The event, however, soured his relationship with the *Independent*. In 1950, Ben left to become literary editor of the *Irish Press*, where he was to remain for fifteen years and meet his future second wife, Frances. He celebrated the move by publishing *Modern Irish Fiction: A Critique*, an acclaimed first survey of Irish authors published between 1919 and 1948.

Four more novels followed before Ben moved in 1964 to America. Adventuring in the footsteps of Padraic and Mary Colum, he became a visiting professor of creative writing at four institutions: Atlanta's Emory University, Hollins College in Virginia, the University of Oregon and, later, the University of Delaware. A natural and indefatigable raconteur, his affability and easy delivery ensured his popularity as a teacher. He remained in the US for four years and acquired a new audience with short stories and articles in the *New Yorker* and other journals. He contributed to the *New York Times Book Review* and wrote 'Letters from America' for *The Irish Times*. On his return to Ireland, he inaugurated the long-running 'Sunday Miscellany' radio programme.

Ben produced some of his best work in his new home at 119 Morehampton Road. Dwarfed by a voluminous desk in his front-room study, he wrote *Proxopera: A Tale of Modern Ireland*, which dealt with a terrorist kidnapping and was described by Anthony Burgess as 'nearly flawless as a piece of literature'. *Nothing Happens in Carmincross* also focused on violence and sectarianism: 'John O'Leary, the Fenian whose nobility had affected the poet Yeats, said that there were things a man might not do, not even to save his country: he meant telling lies, being dishonourable, not being a gentleman.'

Among Ben's Donnybrook visitors were Thomas Flanagan, Seamus Heaney, John Montague, James Plunkett and Val Mulkerns. Nearby were two pubs, where Ben dallied with legendary fellow-broadcasters, Ciarán MacMathuna and Seán MacRéamoinn. Like his friend, Patrick Kavanagh, Ben viewed Donnybrook as his village: 'To step out on the simplest errand may mean a lot of friendly talking with neighbours, young and old. A great time-waster, you may say. But also, it warms the heart.'

The adopted Dubliner drew on his Tyrone, Dublin and US experiences to write seven acclaimed short-story collections. These included *A Journey to the Seven Streams*, *A Ball of Malt and Madame Butterfly* and *A Letter to Peachtree*. He also edited *The Penguin Book of Irish Short Stories*. Gregarious by nature, Ben's work featured digressions, old sayings and poetry quotations. A colleague wrote: 'This is the filter through which we hear the stories themselves, and it gives them their characteristic weight. It's as if we are listening to the voice of a whole culture, the stories being mined in front of us out of a rich lode.'

Ben's stories were distinguished by benevolent humour, but he was equally adept at portraying grief and loss. His consciousness of Ireland's history and its natives' contradictions added an occasional sombre note. He only gave vent to indignation in his last novels, about the inhumanity of kidnappers and bombers. He was equally unafraid to ask questions of himself. Like many another writer, he wondered if all the invented characters were only pretexts: 'Does the novelist wander about like a blind man feeling faces, among his own people, searching for himself?'

The Tyrone man's broadcasts, journalism and literary work spanned six decades. A rare phenomenon in Dublin, he was equally popular among such diverse literati as Brendan Behan, Patrick Kavanagh, Father Senan Moynihan, Brian Friel and Thomas Kilroy. His honours included the 1996 Award for Literature from the Irish Academy of Letters. He was a household name before he died on 9 February 2007 at the age of 88. Ben never escaped his consciousness of William Carleton but, unlike him, he returned to be buried in Omagh in his native Tyrone. He had written in one of his first books: 'Every man at the end should return to the place he started in.'

11 *Upper Lad Lane, Baggot Street*

Mary Lavin
(1912-1996)

11 Upper Lad Lane, Baggot Street

Sorrow is an ingredient of happiness
– a necessary ingredient.

The late *Irish Times* literary editor Caroline Walsh had happy memories of the mews house at Upper Lad Lane, which her widowed mother, Mary Lavin, bought in the late 1950s. Though the nearby Pike Theatre was a converted mews, the little houses were still unfashionable and malodorous. Only a short time earlier they had stabled the horses of Fitzwilliam Street gentry. Scrap-metal dealers and welders enlivened the lane by day. Evenings were filled with birdsong from local gardens and canal bank trees. Wild flowers sprouted from high stone walls. Architect Sam Stephenson helped Mary transform the neglected coach house into a reflection of her own natural exuberance. It boasted two bedrooms, one for Mary, one for her three children. A dining and sitting area faced a small patio.

The mews remained the Lavin home for a quarter of a century. Mary served Italian food and wine to Maeve Binchy, Brian Friel, Desmond Hogan, Tom Kilroy, Frank O'Connor and Nuala O'Faolain. Caroline Walsh recalled: 'Our house was always full of writers, people like Patrick Kavanagh and Padraic Colum and younger writers such as John McGahern and Tom MacIntyre.' The camaraderie of Mary's favourite bookshop added to the charm of Lad Lane life. Frequented by fellow-writers and artists, Parsons Bookshop was only a stroll away along the canal. Here, Caroline the scholar regularly waited for her mother to collect her after a morning's writing in the National Library.

One of Ireland's most popular short story writers and novelists, Mary Lavin was born on 10 June 1912 in East Walpole, Massachusetts. The only child of Irish immigrants, Tom and Nora Lavin. When Mary was nine, the family returned to Athenry, where they spent a year before moving to Dublin. Athenry would resurface in her stories. Mary's accent led to her being teased by schoolmates. She attended Loreto College on St. Stephen's Green, and studied English and French at University College Dublin.

Mary received her M.A. in English in 1936 with a thesis on Jane Austen. Interested in literature from a young age, one of her favourite stories was James Joyce's 'The Dead'. Biographer Leah Levenson quoted Mary on her early tastes: 'I loved the Russian writers and later when I was at college I grew to love French literature, particularly Racine, not so much for the content as for the technique.'

Mary's writing career commenced in 1939. Composing a thesis on Virginia Woolf, she suddenly realised: '*She's not writing a thesis!*' Mary turned the pages over and commenced what would be her first published story. Accepted by the *Dublin Magazine* after numerous rejections, 'Miss Holland' dealt with an outsider in a boarding house: 'Supper was an ordeal that she dreaded. She was very nervous of walking into the public dining-room of a boarding house and facing a crowd of strangers. She went downstairs feeling the same way that she felt as a child on her first day at school.'

Frank O'Connor praised Mary's next contribution to the *Atlantic Monthly*, which introduced her to an American audience. With encouragement from novelist Lord Dunsany and editor, Seamus O'Sullivan, she bravely made her way in a male-dominated world. Her first collection of stories about life in rural Ireland was published in 1942. Widely acclaimed, *Tales from Bective Bridge* won the James Tait Black Memorial Prize.

Mary fell in love while at university with a fellow-student, Michael Scott. He, however, became a priest. In 1943, she married lawyer William Walsh. She continued her writing, while also rearing three children. After its *Atlantic Monthly* serialization, her first novel was published in 1945. *The House in Clewe Street* was the saga of a traditional provincial Catholic family, in which the main protagonist, Gabriel, attempts to escape the 'mind-forged manacles'.

The writer's marriage ended when William died suddenly in 1954. At the age of 42, Mary bade farewell to their farm beside Bective Abbey and moved with her children to Dublin. From writing on the kitchen table by the left bank of the river Boyne, she now composed on the left bank of the Grand Canal. Her subsequent stories on the emotional challenges of widowhood are considered to be among her finest. *Happiness and Other Stories* features a lady who also rears three children alone. While some of her work was criticised for intrusive narration, critic Maurice Harmon insisted: 'Quite clearly she has important things to tell us about ourselves and does so with sophistication, warmth and intelligence.'

A slightly distracted air complemented Mary's trademark smiling features, as she tried to balance her writing schedule with the demands of her growing children. Continental family trips in a Volkswagen Beetle provided the only light relief. Family responsibilities fulfilled and impervious to distraction, Mary wrote tediously in longhand in such diverse locations as St. Stephen's Green, the Clog cafe and the National Library. The late Maeve Binchy saw her running one day to the Library: 'She said she pretended she had to clock in, otherwise the day ran away with her.'

Though her three novels were well received, Mary's favourite form of expression was the short story, which she described as 'a flash of lightning lighting up the whole landscape all at once'. She maintained: 'I don't think a story has to have a beginning, middle and end. I think of it more as an arrow in flight.' Her deft use of monologue and her caring and sympathetic narrative earned praise on both sides of the Atlantic. Her early American upbringing enabled a fruitful objectivity. Richly nuanced, her tales and novels about the conflicts and frustrations within Irish hearts and homes had a universal appeal. She wrote on feminist concerns in a country which was largely controlled by zealots and political backwoodsmen.

Mary followed *Bective Bridge* with several further collections of stories. *The Long Ago, The Becker Wives, A Single Lady, The Patriot Son* and, in 1957, *A Likely Story*. Compared to those of Katherine Mansfield and Anton Chekhov, her stories were translated into several languages including Russian and Japanese. She gained many honours. The Katherine Mansfield Prize and Guggenheim Fellowships in 1959 and 1961, and an honorary doctorate from UCD in 1968. Equally popular in the US, she won the 1979 American Irish Literary Award, a windfall of seven thousand dollars.

In a twist which could have come from one of her stories, Mary's personal life took a turn for the better. She unexpectedly heard from her former university heartthrob, Michael Scott. He had obtained release from the priesthood in 1968 and returned to Ireland. Though

Mary unconvincingly protested 'I'd had a whale of a time as a widow', they married the following year in Bruges.

Mary's marriage did not deter her from participating in the sit-in at Wood Quay to protest the development of a key Viking site. Though her Bohemian spirit clashed with Michael's abstemious ways, they were a close couple. He accompanied her to the Baggot Bridge party which marked the closing of Parsons Bookshop in 1989.

Michael died two years later and Mary followed him on 25 March 1996, aged 83. She was buried in St. Mary's Cemetery, Navan. Her legacy included fifteen short story collections and three novels. Crediting Mary with extracting a universal truth from the depths of the unremarkable, William Trevor concluded his *Guardian* tribute: 'As a person, she was both humble and certain, complicated and simple – an apt reflection of her role as an artist. The short story of today owes her a very great debt.'

The House by the Churchyard, Chapelizod

Joseph Sheridan le Fanu
(1814-73)

70 Merrion Square

The clouds, column after column, came up sullenly over the Dublin mountains, rolling themselves from one horizon to the other in one black dome of vapour, their slow but steady motion contrasting with the awful stillness of the air. There was a weight in the atmosphere, and a sort of undefined menace brooding over the little town... – The House by the Churchyard

The Liffeyside village of Chapelizod features in many stories by Joseph Sheridan le Fanu. Born at 45 Lower Dominick Street on 28 August 1814, the tall handsome Dubliner was the father of the Victorian ghost story and one of the period's most popular writers. His works include *Uncle Silas* and the murder mystery, *The House by the Churchyard*. Backing on to the church and cemetery, the house of the latter's title still broods over Chapelizod, where le Fanu spent eleven of his first twelve years. His work influenced James Joyce, who made the village the home of *Finnegans Wake* protagonists, Humphrey Earwicker and Anna Livia Plurabelle. Le Fanu described Chapelizod as: 'about the gayest and prettiest of the outpost villages in which old Dublin took a complacent pride'.

Descended from a Huguenot family which had originated in Caen, literature was in le Fanu's blood. His grandmother Alicia and his great-uncle, Richard Brinsley Sheridan, were playwrights. His clergyman father, Thomas possessed a library which the future writer enjoyed from an early age and in which he composed his first poems. After eleven years as chaplain of the Royal Hibernian Military School (now St. Mary's Hospital) in Phoenix Park, Thomas was transferred to Abington in Limerick.

Though he missed Chapelizod and the Phoenix Park military reviews, Limerick also inspired le Fanu junior. An elderly tutor introduced him to local supernatural traditions. He witnessed faction fights. Agrarian murders alerted him for the first time to the gulf between privileged Protestants and the deprived Irish majority. Le Fanu was himself lucky to escape an ambush in which his horse was killed. Describing the neighbouring countryside, he later wrote: 'What a mournful beauty is thine: dressed in loveliness and laughter, there is moral decay at thy heart.'

Le Fanu indulged his love of the classics when he entered Dublin's Trinity College in 1833. His wit and debating skills led to his Presidency of the Historical Society. He wrote his first story, 'The Ghost and the Bonesetter', for the *Dublin University Magazine*. This was followed by twelve further features between 1838 and 1840, later collected as *The Purcell Papers*. The stories, many of whose ideas were subsequently developed into novels, featured supernatural visitations, gloomy castles and nostalgia for the original dispossessed Irish Catholic aristocracy. The undergraduate also composed ballads, the most popular of which were the cautiously nationalistic 'Shamus O'Brien' and 'Phaudrig Croohore':

> *Muse of Green Erin, break thine icy slumbers!*
>   *Strike once again thy wreathed lyre!*
> *Burst forth once more and wake thy tuneful numbers!*
>   *Kindle again thy long-extinguished fire!*

Twenty-three-year old le Fanu graduated with a degree in law in 1837. But, instead of practising, he became co-owner of newspapers which were later amalgamated as the *Dublin Evening Mail*. Like Oscar Wilde, he was distressed by the premature death of a favourite sister, Catherine, at the age of 28 in 1841. Her demise may have sparked a later novella, *Spalatro: From the Notes of Fra Giacomo*. Spalatro, its bandit hero of noble parentage, was consumed by a necrophiliac passion for an undead blood-drinking beauty, '"The time draws nigh," said she, while death-paleness overspread her cheeks. "I foresaw this. I dreaded it. The time draws nigh – my mission will be ended."'

While endeavouring to complete his first full-length novel, le Fanu married Susanna Bennett in 1844. After a short spell at 2 Nelson Street, the couple lived beside the canal at 1 and 15 Warrington Place. They moved in 1851 to what is now 70 Merrion Square. Here, their four children played with young neighbours, Oscar and Willie Wilde. Le Fanu combined writing with managing his newspapers. In 1845, he published the first of eighteen books, *The Cock and Anchor*, a chronicle of old Dublin. Though a Unionist, he was depressed by the course of Irish politics. He supported John Mitchel and Isaac Butt in their campaign against government indifference to the potato famine.

Le Fanu's debut book was followed six years later by his first collection of short stories, *Ghost Stories and Tales of Mystery*. Death, sadly, paid him another visit. Unlike her non-churchgoing husband,

Susanna became increasingly neurotic and obsessed by religion. She constantly visited nearby St. Stephen's Church. Upset by the demise of close relatives including her father, she suffered a breakdown and died in April, 1858.

Three years later, le Fanu's 'primary confidante', his mother died. He exorcised his grief with obsessive writing. Clad in a long black velvet coat, he worked by candlelight under family portraits in his favourite back room. Stopping only for cups of tea, he produced a stream of novels and short stories. Increasingly reclusive, he was known locally as 'The Invisible Prince'. Charles Lever was one of his few visitors. Alfred Perceval Graves recalled that, at odd hours of the evening: 'He might occasionally be seen stealing, like the ghost of his former self, between his newspaper office and his home in Merrion Square: sometimes, too, he was to be encountered in an old out-of-the-way bookshop poring over some rare black letter Astrology or Demonology.'

A meticulous craftsman, le Fanu was soon one of the most widely-read Victorian writers. Appreciated both for his historical novels and his innovative ghost stories. He serialised his books in the *Dublin University Magazine*, before revising them for the English market. In 1863, the 49-year-old author published *The House by the Churchyard* and, the following year, *Uncle Silas*: 'The wild eyes of this strange old man were fixed on me as he rose: an habitual contraction, which in certain lights took the character of a scowl, did not relax as he advanced towards me with a thin-lipped smile.'

Published in 1872, *In a Glass Darkly* was a collection of horror and mystery stories. One of them, 'Carmilla', foreshadowed Bram Stoker's *Dracula*. Combining vampirism and lesbianism, the book's main character had lived for hundreds of years, before a stake was driven through her heart. Two medical examiners inspected her body: 'There was a faint but appreciable respiration, and a corresponding action of the heart. The limbs were perfectly flexible, the flesh elastic: and the leaden coffin floated with blood, in which to a depth of seven inches, the body lay immersed. Here then, were all the admitted signs and proofs of vampirism.'

Though most of his works were set in England at the behest of his publisher, le Fanu's final stories were inspired by Irish folklore. He died unexpectedly of bronchitis at his Merrion Square home on 7 February 1873, aged 58. His peers paid tribute to his learning, wit and pleasant conversation. Remarking on his later years, *The Freeman's Journal* lamented: 'His handsome, even distinguished face was wholly missed from society: and he was only known on the title page of his books.' Leaving a legacy of over twenty books, le Fanu was buried in the appropriately Gothic Mount Jerome Cemetery, close to former Trinity College fellow-student, Sir William Wilde.

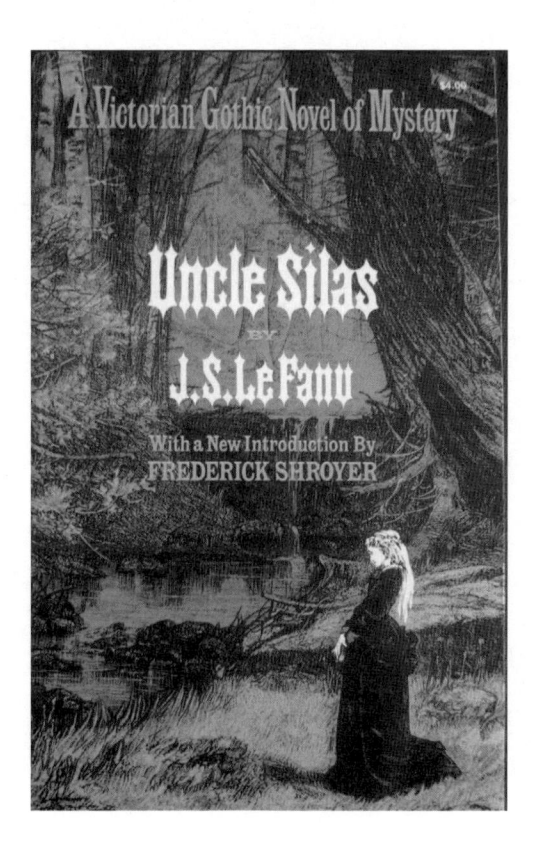

35 Amiens Street

CHARLES LEVER
(1806-72)

35 Amiens Street

Of all the men I have encountered, he was the surest fund of drollery – Anthony Trollope.

Famed for his unfailing wit and one of Ireland's most popular nineteenth century novelists, Charles Lever was born on 31 August 1806 at 35 Amiens Street. A railway bridge appropriately now spans the site of the much-travelled author's original home. Charles was the son of Julia Candler from Kilkenny and builder, James Lever, who was involved with the construction of Dublin's General Post Office. The Levers were liberal Protestants and one of Charles's first teachers was a Catholic. He enjoyed a happy childhood in a home where fires lit every winter room and where books and newspapers were read. He occasionally startled his parents by reading aloud an invented story from the morning paper. In his early teens, he scoured city book stalls. Later, he took to writing and performing dramas in an improvised theatre.

Charles Lever attended a succession of schools, where he was sometimes reprimanded for his practical jokes. Tall, fair-haired, confident and eloquent, he was popular with fellow-students. Residing at 2, Botany Bay Square, he established a reputation as a wit and raconteur at Trinity College, where he commenced medical studies in 1822. Briefly ensconced at 33 Molesworth Street, he followed in Oliver Goldsmith's footsteps and supplemented his allowance by composing ballads. Disguised, he sang these in the streets with fellow-student Robert Boyle. Lever's favourite author was Walter Scott: 'The glorious heroism of Scott's novels was a fine stream to turn into the turbid waters of our worldliness. It was of incalculable benefit to give men even a passing glance of noble devotion, of high-hearted courage, and unsullied purity.'

Lever regularly holidayed in Portumna, where his brother, John, was a curate. He became a favoured guest of the Countess of Clanricarde and observed the Connaught squires at play. He improvised romances based on the stories he heard of duelling, steeple-chasing and romance, which he related to fellow-students. A friend remembered that when he relayed these stories, he 'would so identify himself with the events as to impart to them all the vitality and interest of personal adventure'.

The storyteller graduated from Trinity College, Dublin in 1827, and obtained a position as a medical officer on an emigrant ship to Canada. He remained there for several months, some of which he spent with a tribe of Red Indians. On his return, he tramped across northern Europe and studied medicine in Gottingen in Germany. He visited Paris, Vienna and Weimer, where 'in rapt astonishment', he heard a talk by the ageing poet, Goethe.

Back in Dublin, Lever resumed his medical research at Steevens' and Sir Patrick Dun's Hospitals with fellow-student, William Wilde. Tired of dinners where professionals talked only shop, he and novelist Samuel Lover established a debating and dining club in Dame Street's Commercial Buildings. Lever qualified as a physician in 1831 and briefly practised at 74 Talbot Street, before taking up an appointment in Kilrush. His kindness and humour encouraged both patients and fellow-doctors during the 1832 cholera epidemic. He transferred to Portstewart, where he met William Hamilton Maxwell, famous for his adventurous *Stories of Waterloo* and *Wild Sports of the West* books, which influenced Lever's later writing.

Lever's literary career commenced in 1830, when *The Dublin Literary Gazette* serialised an account of his continental travels, *The Log-Book of a Rambler*. Three years later, he married Catherine Baker, with whom he had fallen in love as a teenager. Catherine encouraged his writing and, in 1837, the *Dublin University Magazine* commenced the serialisation of his first comic adventure novel, *The Confessions of Harry Lorrequer*. An Irish Tom Jones, it featured duels and elopements and became a bestseller when it was published in book form, with drawings by Charles Dickens' illustrator, 'Phiz'.

Lever continued his writing when he and Catherine moved to Brussels. In 1841, he published *Charles O'Malley*, a series of adventures involving student Frank Webber. The student was modelled on Lever's former fellow-balladeer, Robert Boyle, who, 'capable of anything, he spent his youth in follies and eccentricities: every one of which, however, gave indications of a mind inexhaustible in resources, and abounding in devices and contrivances that none other but himself would have thought of'.

Though George Moore would later deride his work as 'a sort of restaurant gravy that makes everything taste the same', the public was in the mood for light-hearted novels. Lever's popularity almost rivalled that of Charles Dickens. In 1842, the 36-year-old Dubliner forsook medicine to write fulltime. He returned to Ireland to edit the *Dublin University Magazine* and settled in Templeogue House, where he indulged his love of cards, horses, swimming and rowing. Among his guests were William Carleton and Sir William Wilde. And William Thackeray, then working on his *Irish Sketch Book*, which he later dedicated to his host.

Lever published three further novels in quick succession. Dublin, however, offered too many distractions and he returned to Brussels with his wife in 1845. Continuing his writing, he embarked on another tour of central Europe in the family coach. He met Charles Dickens in Germany and travelled to Como and Florence where, in 1850, he wrote one of the last of his entertaining novels, *Roland Cashel*.

The Dubliner studied the disadvantaged as well as the privileged: 'My notion is that the poor man that has neither fine houses nor fine clothes nor servants to amuse him, that Providence is kind to him in another way and fills his mind with all manner of droll thoughts and queer stories and bits of songs and the like.' His light-hearted work, however, peeved nationalists, who thought literature should be harnessed to highlight British misrule. Accused himself once of the same charge, William Carleton attacked Lever's alleged caricatures of Irish people. Lever also fell foul of Unionist extremists, for ridiculing the British administration and for detailing yeomanry violence in one of his books. His only probable crime was the literary one of loose construction.

Lever's humorous work gradually went out of fashion and his final books displayed a more serious style. Notably, *The Daltons*, influenced by Honore de Balzac. And *Davenport Dunn*, about a financier whose wizardy attracted the aristocratic types who had humiliated him in his charity-school youth. As well as hoping to finance a tunnel through the Italian Alps, Dunn planned to develop a quality tourist resort in the west of Ireland. Lever wondered: 'The old feudalism that had linked the fate of a starving people with the fortunes of a ruined gentry was to be extinguished at once, and a great experiment tried. Was Ireland to be more governable in prosperity than in adversity?'

In 1867, Lever was appointed British consul in Trieste, where James Joyce would later toil. Saddened by his son's premature death in 1863, his health gradually declined after his wife, Catherine died in 1870. His final novel, *Lord Kilgobbin: A Tale of Ireland in our Own Time*, featured a Fenian hero and was published in 1872. Lever made one final visit to Dublin, before dying of a heart attack in Trieste on 1 June 1872 at the age of 65. He is buried there, as is James Joyce's brother, Stanislaus. The anniversary of his birth was marked by a symposium in Italy in 2006.

Lever wrote thirty novels and five volumes of essays and short stories. He dedicated his final book to the childhood sweetheart who became his wife: 'To the memory of one whose companionship made the happiness of a long life, and whose loss has left me helpless...'

Charles Lever in middle age

60 Grafton Street

SAMUEL LOVER
(1797-1868)

60 Grafton Street

'Sam Lover' had no enemy, secretly or publicly
– The Athenaeum

Born on 24 February 1797 at 60 Grafton Street, Samuel Lover was a poet, painter, novelist, and grandfather of songwriter Victor Herbert. His parents were Abigail Maher and stockbroker, John Lover, whose other children all died in infancy. Abigail encouraged her son's aptitude for drawing and music, his father bought him a piano at an early age. The future writer studied at Whyte's Grafton Street Academy, whose roll-call included the Duke of Wellington and executed rebel, Robert Emmet. Lover was much affected by government repression and, unlike most fellow-Protestants, he sympathised with Irish nationalists. His happy childhood came to a premature end when his mother died while he was only thirteen. He immersed himself in art and music, to the discomfiture of his father, who insisted he join the family stockbroking business.

Lover endured four office years, before leaving to seek an uncertain living as an artist and book illustrator. He also studied music. Encouraged by leading portraitist, John Comerford, he concentrated on miniature painting. His delicate compositions stimulated many private commissions. He exhibited miniatures and landscapes at the Royal Hibernian Academy, which appointed him Secretary in 1828, a year after his marriage to architect's daughter, Lucy Berrel. The couple lived at 9 D'Olier Street.

Lover also contributed humorous stories to magazines. *The Dublin Literary Gazette* published his debut features, 'Ballads and Singers' and the 'Story of a Gridiron'. His interest in folklore led to his first book in 1831, *Legends and Stories of Ireland*, which he also illustrated. His commissions waned, however, with the production of *The Parson's Horn-Book*, whose criticism of the established church was enhanced by his apposite illustrations. Following widespread acclaim for his miniature of Nicolo Paganini at the Royal Academy, Lover moved to London in 1834.

Now 37, the Dubliner's songs and writing quickly gained him further popularity. Poet Thomas Moore praised his singing and introduced him to his literary acquaintances. Lightly built, with humorous eyes and an open, frank expression, Lover became a popular guest at London receptions. Including Lady Blessington's evenings, where he sang his own songs. He published *Songs and Ballads*, which included such favourites as 'Molly Bawn', 'The Low-Backed Car' and 'The Four-Leaved Shamrock'. And the lyric of the incurable optimist, Brian O Linn, a favourite of later writer, Oliver St John Gogarty:

> *The bridge it broke down and they all tumbled in,*
> *'We'll go home by water,' says Brian O Linn.*

Lady Morgan was also impressed by his talents. He composed 'Rory O'More' after she suggested he should write about genuine Irish characters rather than caricatures. The song led to his first novel of the same name, which was acclaimed on its 1837 publication. Combining romance with social commentary, the book centred on Rory and the patriotic Horace de Lacey, who had arrived home from France to organise a rebellion against English rule. The book launched the epigrams 'Better safe than sorry' and 'There's luck in odd numbers'. Starring Tyrone Power, a dramatised version of *Rory O'More* ran for one hundred nights at London's Adelphi Theatre.

In 1842, Lover published *Handy Andy, An Irish Tale*: 'Andy Rooney was a fellow who had the most singularly ingenious knack of doing everything the wrong way: disappointment waited on all affairs in which he bore a part, and destruction was at his fingers' ends.' *Handy Andy* became his best known work, which W.B. Yeats insisted: 'Like all he wrote, is full of truthful pages and poetic feeling.' The book featured one of his most popular songs, 'What will you do, love?':

> *What will you do, love, when I am going*
> *With white sails flowing, the seas beyond?*
> *What will you do, love, when waves divide us*
> *And friends may chide us for being fond?*

Briefly a librettist for fellow-Dublin composer, Michael William Balfe, Lover wrote operettas which were performed at Covent Garden. His plays, *The Hall Porter*, *The Happy Man* and *Olympic Picnic* were staged at London's leading theatres. He published almost twenty books and plays, which Justin McCarthy and other critics hailed for their pathos and humour. Lover did not neglect his painting and from 1851 to 1862, he exhibited landscape drawings at the Royal Academy. His last exhibited work in London was 'The Kerry Post on St. Valentine's Day', which later featured in the Royal Hibernian Academy.

The Dubliner found time to co-found the literary magazine, *Bentley's Miscellany*, with Charles Dickens. Lover had long been fascinated by the songs, stories and legends of rural Ireland. In addition to composing three hundred songs, he also collected folk songs from around the country. In 1858, he published a collection called *The Lyrics of Ireland*. His efforts ensured the preservation of many old lyrics which might otherwise have been lost. James Joyce's modest Trieste library featured a copy of his *Poems of Ireland*. Joyce featured his fellow-Dubliner's 'The Low-back'd Car' in *Ulysses*:

> *Oh, my heart would beat high*
> *At her glance and her sigh,*
> *Though it beat in a low-back'd car.*

Like Joyce, Lover's writing and painting sadly led to deteriorating eyesight. Photography also reduced the demand for miniature portraits. To compensate for his reduced income, Lover launched a series of public entertainments which he called 'Irish Evenings'. These recitations of songs and stories drew full houses. In 1846, he toured the US and Canada. His contribution to literature and art earned him a Civil List pension of £100. He remarried in 1852, four years after the death of his first wife. But, dogged by indifferent health, he was forced to retreat from London to Jersey, where he spent the last four years of his life.

The 71-year-old Dubliner died on 6 July 1868, in St. Helier. He was buried in London's Kensal Green cemetery, close to his friends Michael William Balfe and William Thackeray, and fellow-Dublin author, Anna Brownell Jameson. *The Athenaeum* wrote: 'Lover passed so softly and unassumingly along the various paths of life trodden by him that nobody was offended... "Sam Lover" had no enemy, secretly or publicly.'

London's National Portrait gallery features a marble bust of the author by Edward Arlington Foley. Lover is also commemorated by a tablet in Dublin's St. Patrick's Cathedral.

Directed by Sidney Olcott, one of the earliest movies made in Ireland was a 1911 film version of *Rory O'Moore*.

Lover's choice of art over stockbroking benefited American culture. His daughter, Fanny, married Edward Herbert and gave birth to a boy, Victor, in February, 1859. Edward died suddenly in Paris and Fanny and Victor went to live with Lover in Sevenoaks, Kent. Fanny regularly played the piano and sang Irish folk songs to her son. When Victor Herbert was seven, Lover encouraged Fanny to take him to study in Germany.

Having completed his studies, Victor played in France, Germany and Italy. Hailed as a cello virtuoso, he was appointed first cellist of the Vienna Strauss Orchestra in 1882. He emigrated to America and became the country's best-loved composer and songwriter, penning over forty operettas and operas. Sung around the world, his lyrics included 'Ah! Sweet Mystery of Life' and 'Gypsy Love Song'. Described as a grandfather of the modern musical theatre, he died in 1924. Philip Sousa, Jerome Kern and Irving Berlin attended his funeral, he was buried in Woodlawn cemetery close to writer Herman Melville. Victor's music-loving great grandmother, Abigail Lover, would have been as proud of him as she had been of her son, Samuel.

39 The Rise, Glasnevin

PATRICIA LYNCH
(1894-1972)

39 The Rise, Glasnevin

What I have tried to do in my books is to reveal the magic of ordinary life.

Dublin's reputation for literary talent is well matched by the southern county of Cork, whose roll-call includes Daniel Corkery, David Marcus, Lennox Robinson, Frank O'Connor, Sean O'Faolain and William Trevor. And one of Ireland's most prolific writers, the doyenne of children's storytelling, Patricia Lynch. Following a sojourn in England, Patricia lived for most of her life with her husband Richard Fox at 39 The Rise, in the northside Dublin suburb of Glasnevin. Becoming built-up in the 1930s, Glasnevin was still washed by green fields and the bubbling Tolka river. The travellers of Patricia's stories now camped further out of town but regularly announced their arrival to solder kettles and saucepans. The Rise provided Patricia with a much-loved garden and her first secure home. From here her books went out to delight children around the world, *The Turf-Cutter's Donkey*, *King of the Tinkers*, *The Bookshop on the Quay*.

Patricia Lynch was born in Cork city on 4 June 1894. Her father, Timothy, was a businessman in Egypt. When his activities contracted, his wife, Nora, moved Patricia and an older brother to the home of their grandfather, a scholarly man who taught Latin and Greek. An habitué of Cork's quayside bookshops, he passed on his fascination with the written word to Patricia. One of their regular visitors was Mrs Hennessy, a seanchai. All activity ceased when she began her storytelling. Patricia recalled in *A Storyteller's Childhood*: 'The people who lived in Ireland before the days of history were as well known to Mrs Hennessy as the neighbours in her village.'

When Patricia was five, her mother left to join her husband in Egypt. A contemporary photograph shows Patricia wide-eyed, pensive and anxious. Mrs Hennessy offered to mind her. They travelled by donkey and cart to Mrs Hennessy's home in West Cork. On the way, they met drovers and shepherds. Bantry Fair brought the additional excitement of ballad singers and travelling show people. A tribe of itinerants sparked a fascination for the nomadic way of life, which would permeate Patricia's work. The West Cork idyll was ended by the sudden death of Patricia's father in 1900. Her mother took her to London, where she hoped to sort out his affairs.

Like Elizabeth Bowen's displacement, this was the start of a lonely and peripatetic existence for the youngster, whose mother was frequently absent. Patricia soon lost her Cork accent. She lodged at many addresses, from the East End to a farm in Kent. Here, a cache of books included *The Magic City* by children's author, Edith Nesbit. Its escapism encouraged Patricia's hopes of also becoming a writer. When she was twelve, a junior magazine published her first article,

'Life Story of a Daffodil'. She bought a bicycle after a local newspaper printed some of her poems.

Soon, Patricia was on the road again. Her mother unexpectedly returned to take her to Egypt in search of her husband's legacy. Patricia fell ill en route and was left behind, with a family in Bruges. She had a fortuitous meeting with an English journalist: 'Miss Carmichael wrote travel articles and would pound them out on her typewriter. I brought her hot, creamy coffee in the mornings and we talked. I told her about my family and their quest for riches. "Perhaps writing will be your gold mine," she said. "You've had a few little nuggets already. You should learn shorthand and typewriting. With them and a good knowledge of English, a girl can go through the world."'

Patricia's mother finally reappeared, solvent. Patricia followed Miss Carmichael's advice and enrolled at a commercial school. At the age of 21, she finally embarked on her long-dreamed-of career in journalism. She supported the Suffragette Movement and joined the staff of the weekly *Workers' Dreadnought*. Editor Sylvia Pankhurst sent her to Dublin to report on the 1916 Rebellion.

After having learned her trade at the *Dreadnought*, Patricia progressed to the *Christian Commonwealth*. One of her interviewees was Edith Nesbit, whose advice she would always remember: 'I love children, but books for children cannot be written by those who merely like or study them. It is only possible for those who remember what one felt like as a child, and have never quite grown away from it.' Nesbit encouraged the Irishwoman's own story writing ambitions.

Patricia's life was disrupted once more, when her mother and brother died in quick succession. But, in October 1922, she commenced the happiest chapter of her life when she married the journalist and former imprisoned conscientious objector, Richard Michael Fox. She and her husband returned to Ireland and in 1923 moved into 39 The

Rise. George Russell found work for Richard, and Patricia finally commenced her own creative career.

She published her first book, *The Green Dragon*, in 1925. Six years later, she won the Tailteann Literary Award for *The Cobbler's Apprentice*, about an ill-treated boy who found companionship with a cat and a dog. *The Irish Press* serialised a number of stories, *The Turf-Cutter's Children*. These featured the adventures of two children, Seamus and Eileen, and 'Long Ears', the donkey they had rescued from cruel travellers. Published in 1934, *The Turf-Cutter's Donkey* and *King of the Tinkers* became bestsellers.

Patricia's books were illustrated by some of Ireland's leading artists, Sean Keating, Harry Kernoff, Elizabeth Rivers and Jack B. Yeats. Keating's work enlivened *The Grey Goose of Kilnevin*, which was acclaimed as one of the best adult or children's books published in the US in 1941. *The Grey Goose* describes a girl's quest for love and acceptance, as she and the goose experience many adventures, including meeting the Children of Lir. Reflecting on her earlier rootless life, Patricia explained why all her books were based in Ireland: 'I often felt very lonely and driven in on myself when I was left at a new, strange school. I would dream about Ireland and think of its people, its hills and valleys. These dreams would centre on Cork and I would try to recapture all the stories I had ever heard in Ireland. Perhaps that is one reason why all my books are rooted in Irish life and character.'

Patricia's work was regularly broadcast in Ireland and England and translated into many languages including French, German, Swedish and Japanese. Her slight build belied her discipline and energy. Summarising her work once, she explained: 'What I have tried to do in my books is to reveal the magic of ordinary life.' The *Brogeen* stories and the non-fantasy *The Bookshop on the Quay* consolidated her international reputation. The daughter of the proprietor of Ormond Quay's Four Masters' Bookshop saw a boy outside the window: 'He gazed at *Gulliver's Travels* displayed there as if he were meeting a friend. Craning her neck, Bridgie saw that his coat was muddy and wrinkled, and he carried an untidy bundle under his arm.

"'The poor boy!" she said to Mog. "He's lost!'"

Patricia was devastated when Richard Fox died suddenly in 1969. After forty-five happy years at The Rise, she moved into the Monkstown house of the puppeteers, Eugene and Mai Lambert. The Lambert children adopted her as their resident grandmother. Patricia died on 1 September 1972 aged 78 and was buried in Glasnevin Cemetery beside her husband. Like James Stephens, she had transmuted childhood deprivation and love of legend into a golden legacy. The fifty books she bequeathed provided a happy introduction to reading for generations of children.

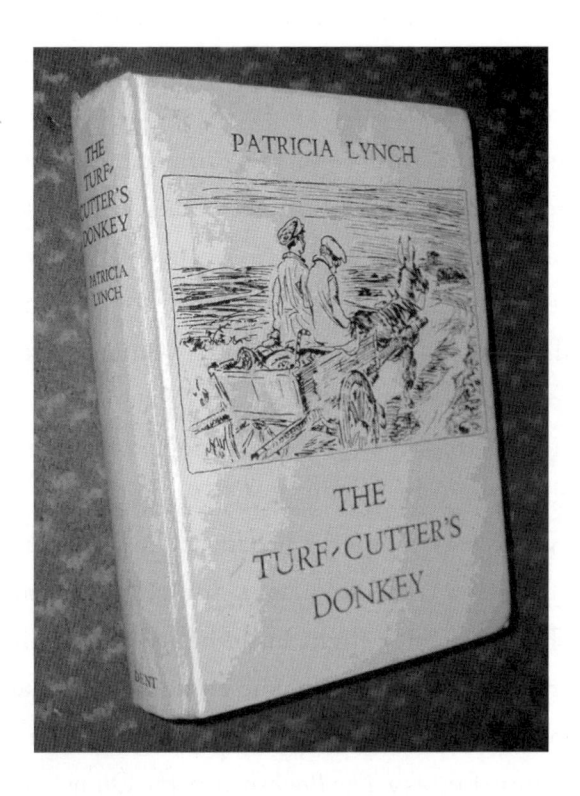

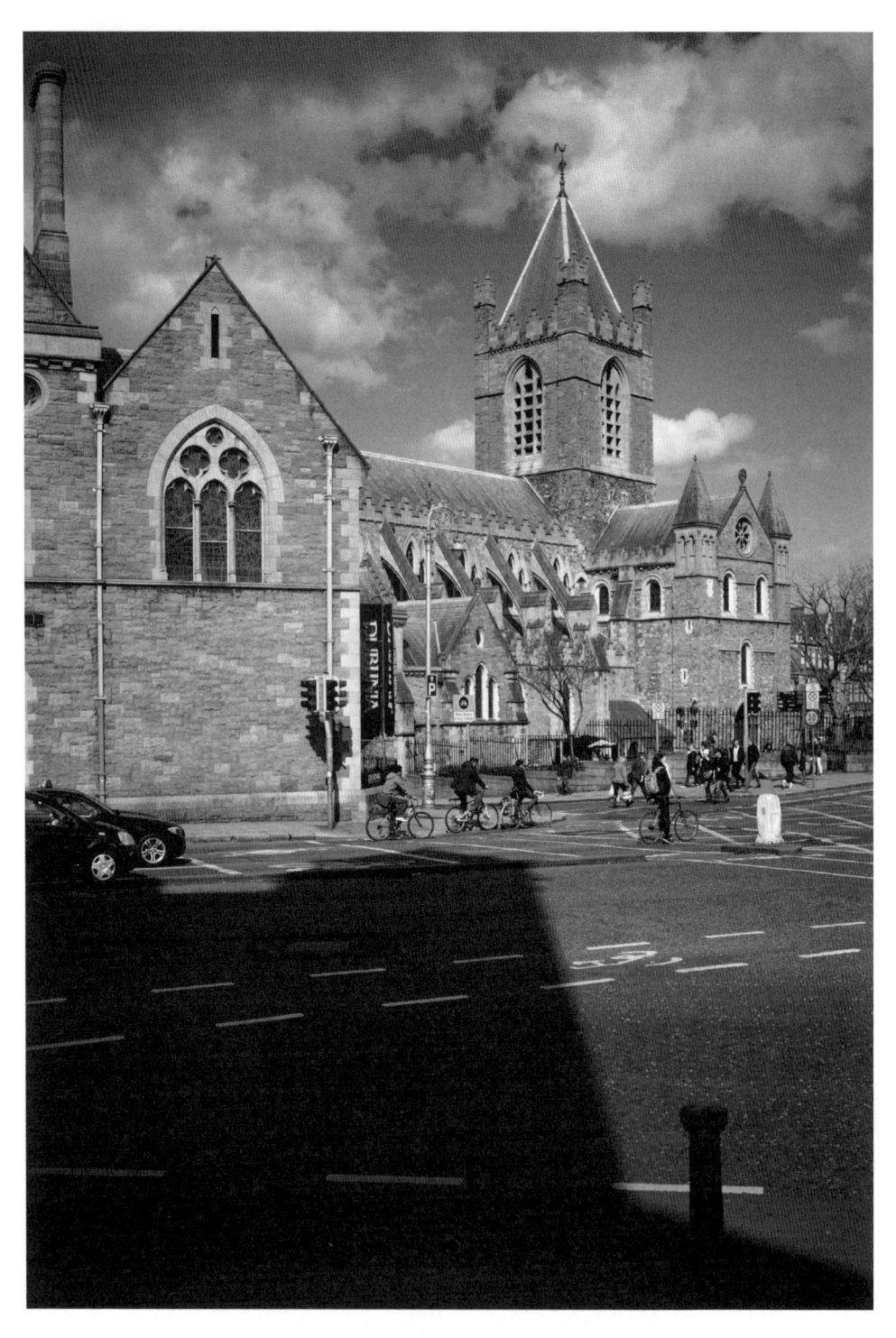

Mangan's birthplace faced Christ Church Cathedral

JAMES CLARENCE MANGAN
(1803-1849)

5 Lord Edward Street

He, too, had tears for all souls in trouble,
Here and in Hell – 'The Nameless One'

Named after the medieval fish market, Fishamble Street is one of Dublin's oldest thoroughfares. Henry Grattan lived here for his first eleven years. Also, Archbishop James Ussher, who claimed that the world had been created in October 4004 BC. Handel's *Messiah* had its debut in the local New Musick Hall in April, 1742. Seventy years later, the poet Shelley spoke alongside Daniel O'Connell at a pro-Catholic Emancipation meeting in the Fishamble Street Theatre.

But the street's best-loved resident was the short-lived poet, James Clarence Mangan, who was born at Number 3 on 1 May, 1803. He was the quintessential Dubliner. Unlike most writers, he lived all his life close to his birthplace opposite Christ Church Cathedral. He inspired many poets, including Patrick Kavanagh, whose interest in verse was first sparked by a recitation he heard of Mangan's 'A Vision of Connaught in the Thirteenth Century':

> *I walked entranced*
> *Through a land of Morn:*
> *The sun, with wondrous excess of light,*
> *Shone down and glanced*
> *Over fields of corn*
> *And lustrous gardens aleft and right...*

A pub marks the site of Mangan's birthplace, now 5 Lord Edward Street. Highly appropriate, some have noted. Mangan frequented hostelries and was allegedly partial to opium. But he was much more than a mere inebriate. W.B. Yeats and James Joyce acknowledged him as one of Ireland's finest, most innovative and most skilful poets. The latter maintained that, in his best work, he produced 'an exalted lyrical music and a burning idealism that revealed themselves in rhythms of extraordinary and unpremeditated beauty'. Joyce often recited his poem, 'The Nameless One'. Mangan's word-play predated *Finnegans Wake* by a century. A Modernist before his time, he was also the first Irish poet to deal with alienation in society.

Like Tom Moore, Mangan's parents were also country people. His mother, Catherine, came from Dunsany, County Meath. His father, James, was a former hedge school teacher from Shanagolden, Limerick. James ran a small grocery but lived extravagantly and lost his money in property speculation. His son was educated at three different institutions in Werburgh Street and Chancery Lane. A Jesuit priest taught him French, Italian, Spanish and the classics. An early interest in literature provided an escape from his dictatorial father.

When James Mangan's business foundered, the family moved to a tenement house in Chancery Lane. Young James toiled from the age of fifteen to support his parents and their family of four. His hands became permanently ink-stained from copying documents as a scrivener in a legal office at 6 York Street: 'dull drudgery ... my heart felt as if it were gradually growing into the inanimate material I wrote on'. Ireland's un-sung historian and illustrator, George Petrie, found him more congenial work in the Irish Ordnance Survey office. He later became a cataloguer in Trinity College Library.

Mangan's first contributions appeared in *Grant's Almanac* and the *New Ladies Almanac* in 1818. He progressed to the *Comet*, the newspaper of a political and satirical club whose members included Samuel Lover and Daniel O'Connell's son, Maurice. Mangan's reputation spread, he was invited to contribute to the newly-launched *Dublin Penny Journal* in 1832. His poems appeared over the pen-name Clarence, henceforth he was known as James Clarence Mangan. The original Clarence was a character in Shakespeare's *Richard III*, who had drowned in a barrel of wine. Mangan frequently repeated the line: 'Clarence is come – false, fleeting, perjured Clarence.'

The mysticism of the German poets appealed to Mangan's melancholy and introspective nature. In 1834, the *Dublin University Magazine* published the first of the 31-year-old's translations from German, a poem by Heinrich Heine. This and other translations were later published in two volumes. Mangan's poems were one of the main attractions of the *Irish Penny Journal*, which was inaugurated in 1840. His reputation was further enhanced by his translations of old Gaelic poems, particularly 'O'Hussey's Ode to the Maguire' and 'Roisin Dubh'.

A prolific writer and energetic craftsman, Mangan experimented with contrasting styles. Equally adept at prose, he published critical articles and a brief autobiography. He assisted John O'Donovan with the *Annals of the Four Masters*. Poverty and a fondness for the punch-bowl unfortunately resulted in missed deadlines and contributed to his general ill health. According to lecturer Sean Ryder: 'He appears to have written a great deal in public houses, where he was able to get ink and paper for free: we also know from his correspondence that he sometimes composed in libraries and that he wrote with great speed and with little revision.'

Like Oscar Wilde, Mangan was also tormented by the early death of a much-loved younger sister. As the poet's fame spread, so did his reputation for eccentricity. Poor eyesight forced him to wear enormous spectacles. A friend described him 'dressed in a blue cloak (mid-summer or mid-winter), and a hat of fantastic shape, under which golden hair as fine and as silky as a woman's hung in unkempt tangles, and deep blue eyes lighted a face as colourless as parchment'.

Regularly working in Marsh's Library, Mangan wrote some of his best work for the *Nation*, the paper which Charles Gavan Duffy and the Young Ireland party started in 1842. Duffy proved to be one of most consistent benefactors. He remembered the poet fondly: 'He was as truly born to sing deathless songs as Keats or Shelley'. Mangan witnessed the horror of the famine and there was no doubting his great love for his country. Ironically, he is most remembered for a handful of patriotic verse out of the one thousand he composed. Including one of his last, 'Consolation and Counsel':

> *Knowledge is Power, not Powder. That man strikes*
> *A blow for Ireland worth a hundred guns*
> *Who trains one reasoner...*

During the 1849 cholera epidemic, Board of Health officers found Mangan dying in a Bride Street hovel. He was taken to a public ward in the Meath Hospital, Physician William Stokes recognised him, provided him with proper clothes and transferred him to a private room. Mangan died a few days later on 20 June at the age of 46.

Three mourners attended his burial in Glasnevin Cemetery, where his uncle, Michael Smyth, later erected a headstone.

A much-admired bust of the poet by Oliver Shepherd now graces St Stephen's Green, close to the memorial to W.B. Yeats. Sean Ryder's *James Clarence Mangan: Selected Writings*, provides a stimulating introduction to Mangan's work and genius. In 'The Nameless One', published posthumously, Mangan wrote what might be a fitting epitaph:

> *Him grant a grave to, ye pitying noble,*
> *Deep in your bosoms: there let him dwell!*
> *He, too, had tears for all souls in trouble,*
> *Here and in hell*

Mangan regularly wrote in Marsh's Library

37 York Street

Charles Robert Maturin
(1782-1824)

37 York Street

He sank for a few moments into a fit of gloomy abstraction, till the sound of the clock striking twelve made him start. It was the only sound he had heard for some hours, and the sounds produced by inanimate things, while all living beings around are as dead, have at such an hour an effect indescribably awful...
– Melmoth the Wanderer

Emasculated by property developers, it is hard to believe that York Street was once lined with elegant Georgian residences. For almost half of his 42 years' life, it was home to Dublin's first Gothic novelist, Charles Maturin. His work influenced such writers as Honore de Balzac, Edgar Allan Poe and grandnephew, Oscar Wilde. A curate in nearby St. Peter's Church, Maturin moved to 37 York Street in 1804. Since demolished, the site of his home is now part of the Royal College of Surgeons, on the lefthand approach to Stephen's Green. Though he regularly wrote on a small desk in the seclusion of Marsh's library, Maturin completed most of his work here, including *Melmoth the Wanderer* and *The Wild Irish Boy*. In York Street, he also indulged his passion for dancing and staging the extravagant soirees which helped to bankrupt him.

Maturin's oratory matched his intense writing. His Sunday sermons attracted hundreds, entertained equally by his quick wit and colourful appearance. A tall man with a permanent aura of distraction, he was York Street's most eccentric figure. James Clarence Mangan, who had worked at Number 6 and was no mean nonconformist himself, described the writer as 'one of those three-cornered men whom society insists upon infixing into circular cavities'. When composing, Maturin pasted a wafer on his forehead to discourage interruption. Mangan once met him returning after officiating at a funeral: 'He stalked along York-street, with an abstracted, or rather distracted air: the white scarf and hat-band which he had received remaining still wreathed around his beautifully-shaped person, and exhibiting to the gaze of the amused and amazed pedestrians whom he almost literally encountered in his path, a boot upon one foot and a shoe on the other!'

The distracted clergyman was descended from Huguenot refugees who originated east of Bordeaux. Maturin's great great grandfather, Gabriel Maturin, arrived in Ireland in 1715. He was crippled after twenty-six years imprisonment on the Ile Saint Marguerite, where a fellow-prisoner was the legendary Man in the Iron Mask. Charles Maturin was born on 25 September 1782 to Fidelia and William Maturin, a civil servant. Brought up in Fitzwilliam Street, he entered Trinity College at the age of fifteen. A voracious reader, he won an award for written composition and graduated in 1800. He was ordained in the Church of Ireland three years later and appointed curate in Loughrea. He was transferred to St. Peter's in Aungier Street, where he ministered for the rest of his life. Since replaced by a hostel, St. Peter's was Dublin's largest Church of Ireland parish. Its worshippers included Robert Emmet's family. In 1804, Maturin married the singer Henrietta Kingsbury, the aunt of Jane Francesca Wilde, mother of Oscar Wilde.

Lack of money, as much as literary ambitions, drove Maturin to write. To support his parents, he also tutored pre-college students. Because of his clerical career, he published his first three books under a pseudonym, Dennis Jasper Murphy. He was influenced by the Gothic novelists, Matthew Lewis and Ann Radcliffe, and by such writers as Cervantes, Swift and Sterne. His first work in 1807 was *The Fatal Revenge: or, the Family of Montorio*. Set in the late seventeenth century and featuring banditti, murder and suicide, it was a lurid Gothic novel of usurpation and vengeance. Praised by Walter Scott, Samuel Taylor Coleridge described it as 'a novel of no small reputation in the bold and terrific line'.

Maturin's next book, *The Wild Irish Boy*, was set in Loughrea and intended to capitalise on the success of Lady Morgan's *Wild Irish Girl*. In 1812, he published *The Milesian Chief*. He followed this with the play, *Bertram*, which he sent to Walter Scott. The novelist described the verse-tragedy as 'grand and powerful, the language most animated and poetical, and the characters sketched with a masterly enthusiasm'. Scott forwarded the play to Alfred Lord Byron, who arranged its 1816 launch at Drury Lane Theatre. With Edmund Kean in the title role, it proved a huge success.

The 34-year-old Dubliner dissipated the resulting windfall on extravagant entertaining and bailing out his father and a bankrupt relative. He returned to his writing desk. His next two plays, *Manuel* and *Fredolfo*, did not repeat his Drury Lane triumph. To add to his problems, *Bertram's* irreverent sentiments displeased church authorities and aborted his hopes for advancement. In 1818, between writing the sermons which filled St. Peter's, he published *Women: or, Pour et Contre*, a suspenseful romance which also reflected his opposition to religious fanaticism: 'He was startled by the cries of a female voice, piercing, but suddenly stopped: – he rushed forward, – a carriage thundering over the bridge passed him rapidly, and in a few moments the rolling of the wheels at a distance, as it pursued the way to the country, was the only sound to be heard.'

Maturin published his most famous work, *Melmoth the Wanderer*, in 1820. Rated as one of the finest examples of Gothic fiction in the English language, it opened in a remote Wicklow country house. *Melmoth* told the Faust-like story of a seventeenth-century scholar who sold his soul to the devil in exchange for a prolonged life. An indictment of intolerance and man's inhumanity to man, the book's hero, Melmoth, was the archetypal outsider: 'I laugh at human passions and human cares, vice and virtue, religion and impiety: they are all the result of petty localities, and artificial situation. One physical want, one severe and abrupt lesson from the colourless and shrivelled lip of necessity, is worth all the logic of the empty wretches who have presumed to prate it, from Zeno down to Burgersdicius.'

Melmoth's freshness and its attention to the psychology of despair and the torments of religious doubt, distinguished it from rival Gothic works. Its complicated plot, however, and Maturin's pedantic style displeased some commentators, as did the graphic detail of torture and murder. But such violence was not unknown to the Maturins. Apart from Gabriel's prison experiences, another of the family replaced a rector in Donegal who had been beaten to death in 1797.

The writer returned to the theme of religious fanaticism in his final historical romance, *The Albigenses*. His industry, sadly, was matched by his impracticality and improvidence. He died at his home in York Street on 30 October 1824, aged 42, apparently from laudanum poisoning. James Clarence Mangan ascribed his death to an apothecary's blunder. Maturin was buried in St. Peter's churchyard, Aungier Street. This was the scene of a criticised 1980's exhumation, following which bodies were transferred to Mount Jerome Cemetery.

Maturin's work was neglected for many years until his reputation was revived with reprints in the 1890s. Highly regarded on the continent, his books were also translated into the language of his ancestors. Charles Baudelaire was an admirer, Balzac wrote a short sequel to *Melmoth*, entitled *Melmoth Reconciled*. Oscar Wilde related to the fictional outcast and used the pseudonym Sebastian Melmoth following his release from prison in 1897. Praising the York Street writer, the radical novelist William Godwin said: 'If there be any writer of the present day to whose burial-place I should wish to make a pilgrimage, that writer is Maturin.'

Oscar Wilde's visitng card – he used the pseudonym Sebastian Melmoth after his release from prison

4 Upper Ely Place

GEORGE MOORE
(1852-1933)

4 Upper Ely Place

I always feel better morally for being with him. I find most people humbugs, addicted to dishonest practices and thoughts. – John Butler Yeats

He almost became a jockey. But George Moore instead achieved fame as the first great modern Irish novelist. For half a century, he was a significant figure on the literary stages of Dublin, London and Paris. Informed by his knowledge of art and music, his work influenced James Joyce and W.B. Yeats. Indefatigable and dedicated, he was a pivotal figure in the Irish Literary Revival with Yeats, Edward Martyn and Lady Gregory. His ten years from 1901 at 4 Upper Ely Place were as eventful as his early career. When he exchanged Irish provincialism for Parisian sophistication and defied the English censor with *A Modern Lover* and *Esther Waters*.

In Ely Place, Moore wrote *The Lake*, *The Untilled Field* and the first volume of his controversial *Hail and Farewell* memoir. His arrival disturbed the quiet of the sedate and gated cul de sac. A Unionist neighbour threatened a lawsuit, when he painted his door a nationalist green. The next-door Drew sisters disliked *Esther Waters* so much, they tore it up and stuffed its pages through his letter box. Under his tilted bowler, Moore rattled his Malacca cane along their railings in retaliation. They hired an organ-grinder to interrupt his writing.

Son of Mary Blake and Catholic landowner and MP, George Henry Moore, the future novelist was born on 24 February 1852 in Moore Hall, Mayo, overlooking Lough Carra. His great grandfather, George, had made his fortune in the Spanish wine trade. His great-uncle, John, supported 1798 Irish rebels and was made President of Connaught before dying in British army custody. George Henry Moore had imported maize to feed famine victims. His parents' readings of Walter Scott stimulated young George's interest in literature. He was captivated at the age of eleven by Shelley: 'I read the dazzling stanzas by the shores of a pale-green Irish lake, comprehending little, and loving a great deal.'

Moore's playmates included Oscar and Willie Wilde, with whom he sailed on Lough Carra. Moore studied in an English college, from which 'I was expelled when I was sixteen, for idleness and general worthlessness'. Horsemanship was a family tradition. His uncle's death in the 1845 Grand National did not deter 17-year old Moore: 'To ride the winner at Liverpool seemed to me a final achievement and glory.' His riding came to a premature end when his father was reelected MP and the family moved to London.

Moore sidestepped his father's army ambitions, to study art in South Kensington. When his father died in 1830, Moore departed for Paris to continue his studies. His aptitude for painting matched that for rota learning. His failure depressed him: 'What a shock it is for a man to leave one self without knowing he can acquire another self.

I shed tears, and the bitterest.' Encouraged by playwright Bernard Lopez, he commenced to write.

Argument and controversy marked 1870s Paris, the world's cultural capital. Writers experimented with new forms, Impressionism developed in reaction to the academic establishment. Tall, blonde, moustached and somewhat ungainly, Moore became an habitué of the Cafe Nouvelle Athenes, the rue Pigalle's heart of artistic debate. He regularly met Edgar Degas, Claude Monet, Camille Pissarro and writers, Stephane Mallarme and Emile Zola. Edouard Manet and Auguste Renoir each painted him. Moore was an early champion of the derided Impressionists and a regular guest at Manet's studio. The Frenchman encouraged him to ignore critics, to write with candour and courage. In his *Confessions*, Moore quoted Manet: 'I am ashamed of nothing – I am a writer, 'tis my profession to be ashamed of nothing but to be ashamed.'

In 1877, 25-year-old Moore published his first book of poems, *Flowers of Passion*. Dealing with lesbianism and homosexuality, one critic declared it 'should be burnt by the common hangman'. Moore penned the equally provocative *Pagan Poems*:

> *Lifting a curtain suddenly, – what meets*
> *My gaze? – you, glittering like a precious stone*
> *Amid the splendours of black satin sheets.*

After seven years in Paris, Moore moved to London, where he finally found expression in writing novels. Published in 1883, *A Modern Lover* was a realistic portrayal of an artist's dalliances which was banned by the circulating libraries. As was *A Mummer's Wife*, whose frankness and Zolaesque style marked it as the first Naturalist novel written in English.

The books' proscriptions backfired. Interest grew in both Moore and the new style of writing, *A Mummer's Wife* was reprinted repeatedly. The 1894 novel, *Esther Waters*, about a seduced and abandoned servant, assailed Victorian hypocrisy and cemented Moore's literary reputation. He also impressed as an art critic. *Modern Painting* introduced Impressionism to an English audience, *Confessions of a Young Man* was a lively memoir of his Paris apprenticeship and his artist friends.

Opposed to the Boer War, Moore accepted cousin Edward Martyn's 1901 invitation to return to Dublin. Once settled in 4 Upper Ely Place, Moore, now 49, threw himself into the Irish Literary Revival and the founding of The Irish National Theatre. As well as W.B. Yeats and Lady Gregory, he became friends with artists Nathaniel Hone, John Hughes and Walter Osborne. Despite a reputation for boorishness, John B. Yeats, found the novelist's directness refreshing: 'I always feel better morally for being with him. I find most people humbugs, addicted to dishonest practices and thoughts.'

Ely Place boasted earlier literary associations. Oscar Wilde proposed to Constance Lloyd at number 1. Bram Stoker's surgeon-brother, Sir Thornley, lived at number 8 Ely House. During Moore's time, the street was a centre of artistic social life. Oliver St. John Gogarty entertained across the road, while Moore's Saturday Nights mirrored the excitement of his Café Nouvelle Athenes evenings. George Russell, Tom Kettle and Horace Plunkett passed through his door and artists Walter Sickert, Henry Tonks and John B. Yeats. They dined and debated under pictures by Moore's friends, Manet and Pissarro. Nationalist leader Douglas Hyde was taken aback when Moore suggested introducing Indian temple prostitutes – 'Divine Decanters' – to relieve sex-starved Irish prelates.

Moore's *The Untilled Field* and his stream-of-consciousness novel, *The Lake*, influenced James Joyce, thirty years his junior. Like him, Moore finally became disenchanted with his country and exiled himself to London in 1911. After Moore Hall was burnt down during the 1923 Irish Civil War, he lamented: 'I don't think I shall ever be able to set a foot in Ireland again.'

George Bernard Shaw and W.B. Yeats were among his London visitors. James Joyce pilgrimaged from Paris in 1929. Moore recorded: 'He was distinguished, courteous, respectful, and I was the same: he seemed anxious to accord me the first place. I demurred, and declared him the first in Europe. We agreed that our careers were not altogether dissimilar, and he added: "Paris has played an equal part in our lives."'

The Mayo writer never married but had affairs with Lady Cunard and Oscar Wilde's befriender, Ada Leverson. He enjoyed a cantankerous old age at 121 Ebury Street, where he died aged 80 on 21 January 1933. His ashes were buried on Castle Island, Lough Carra, within sight of the ruins of his Moore Hall birthplace. Among the attendance was his former Ely Place neighbour, Oliver St. John Gogarty. James Joyce sent a wreath from Paris.

Ruins of George Moore's birthplace

12 Aungier Street

THOMAS MOORE
(1779-1852)

12 Aungier Street

Dear Harp of my Country! in darkness I found thee,
The cold chain of Silence had hung o'er thee long.
When proudly, my own Island Harp, I unbound thee,
And gave all thy chords to light, freedom, and song.

Praised by Shelley and Lord Byron, the poet, songwriter and biographer Thomas Moore is popularly known as 'The Bard of Ireland'. He was a friend of such diverse figures as the revolutionary, Robert Emmet and British Prime Minister, Lord John Russell. In August, 1841, Moore visited his native Ireland for the last time. He requested the coachman to drive to his Aungier Street birthplace, where he had lived until the age of twenty. His companion, Dr. George Petrie recalled: 'Upon arriving opposite No. 12, he desired the car to be stopped and gazing at the well-remembered domicile, his eyes became suffused with tears. "I am looking, Petrie," he explained, "for the little gable window by which I penned my earliest verses, the *Melodies*".'

The poet retained happy memories of the family home, where his Kerryborn father, John Moore, opened a grocery store in the year of Tom's birth on 28 May 1779. Tom owed a particular debt to Anastasia Moore. He frequently recalled the musical parties organised 'by my joyous and social mother. Our small front and back drawing-rooms, as well as a little closet attached to the latter, were on such occasions distended to their utmost capacity, and the supper table in the small closet, where people had least room, was accordingly always the most merry'.

Anastasia encouraged her son's recitation and singing. He performed for assemblies of neighbours, artists and actors, and also appeared in amateur plays staged by his teacher, author Samuel Whyte of Whyte's Academy. Tom's subsequent success as a performer owed much to Whyte, who blunted his broad accent and taught him the value of pronunciation and expression. That effect 'does not so much depend upon the words we speak, as to our manner of speaking them'. Tom's reputation was in inverse proportion to his slight stature. Reporting on Whyte's July 1790 examinations, the *Dublin Chronicle* noted: 'A Master Moore, a boy not more than ten years old, distinguished himself in a remarkable manner, and was deservedly the admiration of every auditor.'

Tom made the headlines again at the age of fifteen, when the *Anthologia Hibernica* published two of his poems. He entered Trinity College in 1795 and joined the College Historical Society with his friend, Robert Emmet. Four years later, Tom moved to London and studied law at the Middle Temple. In 1800, the patronage of Lord Moira enabled his translation of the sixth century BC poet Anacreon, *The Odes of Anacreon*. This was followed by a collection of amorous poems, *The Poetical Works of Thomas Little, Esq.*

The Dubliner's singing and recitations gained him entree to the homes of the aristocracy, in 1803 he was appointed admiralty registrar in Bermuda. He travelled extensively in North America, where he criticised slavery and met President Thomas Jefferson. Back in England, Tom encouraged fellow-Dublin poet Mary Tighe and in 1806 published *Epistles, Odes, and other Poems*. This resulted in an aborted duel with a Scottish critic who had earlier bludgeoned John Keats and William Wordsworth. Lord Byron's comments on the duellists' allegedly 'leadless pistols' induced Tom to issue another duelling invitation. Luckily, Byron had left England before Tom's letter arrived. The poet shared Byron's passion for Greek Independence and the pair subsequently became close friends.

Tom regretted: 'During the prevalence of the Penal code, the music of Ireland was made to share in the fate of its people'. This prompted his *Irish Melodies*, which established his reputation in England, Ireland and on the Continent. Marrying verse to established airs, the first collection of Romantic lyrics was published in 1808. It included 'The Minstrel Boy', 'The Last Rose of Summer' and 'Erin! The Tear and the Smile in Thine Eyes'. Another favourite was 'She Is Far From the Land', about Sarah Curran, the fiancée of his executed friend, Robert Emmet.

Critic Norman Jeffares described the *Melodies* as 'the first successful manifestation of cultural nationalism: the turbulent present shimmers obliquely through the glorious past, which lights up a putative future'. Tom's success and natural charm ensured his continuing popularity in London. Lord Byron wrote: 'In society he is gentlemanly, gentle, and altogether more pleasing than any individual with whom I am acquainted.' The Dubliner's London popularity irked Irish nationalists. Ignoring the patriotic ardour of his lyrics, Thomas Davis criticised him as being elitist.

The 32-year-old poet married sixteen-year old actress, Bessy Dyke in 1811. It was to be a long and happy relationship. He wrote *M.P.*, a comic opera, and *National Airs and Sacred Songs*, which included the much-sung 'Oft in the Stilly Night':

> *Oft, in the stilly night,*
> *Ere slumber's chain has bound me,*
> *Fond memory brings the light*
> *Of other days around me:*

Tom published the epic *Lalla Rookh* in 1817. Repeatedly reprinted and translated, its success rivalled that of Lord Byron's works. Ostensibly an oriental drama on the struggle between Persians and their Moslem rulers, biographer Howard Mumford Jones noted: 'The overtones are unmistakably those of Irish rebellion, particularly the Robert Emmet episode.'

An agent in Bermuda left Tom liable for debts and he moved to Paris in 1819. He embarked on a Grand Tour with Lord John Russell. In Venice he met Lord Byron, who appointed him literary executor and instructed him to publish his memoirs should he die. Tom was later criticised for yielding to the Byron family's exhortations to destroy the frank reminiscences. After the poet's 1824 death, he published *Letters and Journals of Lord Byron, with Notices of his Life*. Tom's *Memoirs of the Life of Richard Brinsley Sheridan* further enhanced his literary reputation.

Tom journeyed to Ireland after his return from Paris. His observations of imperial rule led to *The Memoirs of Captain Rock*, which suggested that political violence was the result of misrule. Published in 1824, the book informed English readers of injustices in Ireland. Its popularity ensured a hero's welcome, when Tom revisited Dublin. An advocate of Catholic Emancipation, his patriotic credentials were further enhanced with the 1831 publication of the *Life and Death of Lord Edward Fitzgerald*.

The Dubliner became increasingly depressed after his five children succumbed to illness. He died aged 72 on 25 February 1852 at Sloperton Cottage in Bromham, Wiltshire. After a sparsely-attended service, he was buried in the nearby churchyard beside his daughter, Anastasia. Lord Byron wrote: 'He will live in his *Irish Melodies*: they will go down to posterity with the music: both will last as long as Ireland, or as music and poetry.'

Tom's poems have been set to music by composers Hector Berlioz and Benjamin Britten. He is commemorated by a statue in Dublin's College Green, and by bronze busts in New York's Central Park and at the Meeting of the Waters in Avoca, Wicklow. The poet's harp and books are held by the Royal Irish Academy in Dublin's Dawson Street. His parents' grave can be seen in St. Kevin's Churchyard, Camden Row, close to the family's former Aungier Street home.

Bromham graveyard where Tom Moore is buried

The National Library faced Lady Morgan's home

SYDNEY LADY MORGAN
(1776-1859)

39 Kildare Street

Born and dwelling in Ireland, amidst my countrymen and their sufferings, I saw and described, I felt and I pleaded: and if a political bias was ultimately taken, it originated in the natural condition of things.

As traffic drowns conversation in Kildare Street, it is hard to imagine that it once boasted Dublin's first noteworthy literary salon, where conversation were at a premium. The street's most famous house was Number 39, where best-selling writer, Sydney Owenson, better known as Lady Morgan, lived from 1813 to 1837. Censured by the Pope and the Austrian Emperor and the most discussed Irish writer of her generation, her forthrightness and personality were in inverse proportion to her height of a scant four feet. The Establishment derided her liberal opinions and support for

Catholic Emancipation. But Dubliners cheered her on the street and at the theatre. And her intelligence, wit and authorship of such bestsellers as *The Wild Irish Girl* and *Florence Macarthy* ensured her social success and overflowing soirees.

The circumstances of the writer's birth matched her most dramatic plots. Her parents had eloped, she was born on board the mail boat which crossed to Ireland from England on Christmas Day, 1776. Coy about her age, she once asked: 'What has a woman to do with dates?' Christened Sydney, she inherited her exuberance and performing skills from her Mayo-born actor father, Robert Owenson, a relative of Oliver Goldsmith. And her work ethic from her English mother, Jane Hill, who had married against her parents' wishes.

The family settled at 60 Dame Street. Jane died in 1789 and Sydney was sent to a Huguenot school in Clontarf. She started work as a governess in 1798, after her father's theatrical business failed. Her time with families in Tipperary and Westmeath provided an insight into the lives of both the landed gentry and landless locals. She blossomed as a conversationalist, harpist, singer and dancer. Her interest in literature sparked her own writing. In 1801, she published a volume of poems, which was followed by her first novel, *St. Clair: or, the Heiress of Desmond*. In 1805, she published *Twelve Original Hibernian Melodies*, a collection of translated Gaelic songs. Her next book was set in sixteenth-century France. The precursor of many historical novels, *The Novice of St. Dominick*, was praised for its imaginative and descriptive qualities.

The 1806 publication of *The Wild Irish Girl* ensured 30-year-old Sydney national fame. It focused on the relationship between young English landlord, Horatio, and harpist Glorvina, who sang and played old Irish melodies. The book denounced English policy in Ireland and celebrated the country's beauty, history and culture. Contrasting Irish imagination with English pragmatism, one of its characters insisted: 'The ancient Irish, like the modern, had more soul, more genius, than worldly prudence, or cautious calculating forethought. The feats of the hero engrossed them more than the exertions of the mechanist: works of imagination seduced them from pursuing works of utility.'

The subsequent *The Lay of an Irish Harp* cemented Sydney's patriotic credentials:

> *Why sleeps the harp of Erin's pride?*
> *Why with'ring droops its Shamrock wreathe?*
> *Why has that song of sweetness died*
> *Which Erin's harp alone can breathe?*

Sydney walked for two hours each morning before work, irrespective of the weather. Though a prolific scribe, her indecipherable writing was described by one acquaintance as 'a happy insolence of scrawl I never yet saw equalled'. She published *Patriotic Sketches and Metrical Fragments* in 1807. This was followed by *The Missionary: An Indian Tale*. Praised by Percy Bysshe Shelley, it was the story of a Christian missionary who fell in love with an Indian princess.

Writing briefly took a back seat in 1812, when Sydney married English surgeon, Sir Thomas Charles Morgan, seven years her junior. They set up house in Kildare Street, where the new Lady Morgan established the city's first literary salon. The home resounded to music, poetry and debate by Dublin's leading writers and personalities. Guests included Richard Brinsley Sheridan, Samuel Lover, Sheridan le Fanu, Charles Maturin, Felicia Hemans and Italian virtuoso, Nicolo Paganini. Thomas Moore visited: 'He sang some of his most beautiful songs then in his most delightful manner without stopping, some of them twice over.'

In 1814, Lady Morgan published the satirical *O'Donnel, a National Tale*. Praised by Sir Walter Scott, it was the first book in English literature to feature a governess as a romantic heroine. The book became another best-seller, but its sympathy with the dispossessed lost Lady Morgan some of her upper-class friends. In 1815, her publisher sent her to write a book on post-Napoleonic France. This, and a later Italian commission, resulted in many months of travelling by carriage on indifferent highways. Well known on the Continent, she was feted in Paris, where she met many celebrities and the revolutionaries, Lafayette and the Abbe Gregoire.

Published in 1817, *France* proved more political than topographical and was attacked by one critic as a compendium of licentiousness and impiety. It was followed by *Italy*, which was praised as 'fearless and excellent' by Lord Byron, but censured by the Pope and the Emperor of Austria, who barred its author from his territories. One of Lady Morgan's most venomous critics was the anti-feminist John Wilson Croker, who had also castigated John Keats and Alfred Tennyson. She had the last laugh when she caricatured Croker in the subsequent *Florence Macarthy*.

The Irishwoman's ideas influenced major Romantic authors, including her friends, Charles Maturin, Walter Scott and Percy Shelley. She also brought a Byronic association to Kildare Street. Byron's *Childe Harold* owed much to her book, *Woman: or Ida of Athens*. After attending Byron's funeral in 1824, Lady Caroline Lamb gave Lady Morgan a miniature of the poet. His last lover, Contessa Guiccioli, presented the Irishwoman with a locket containing a lock of Byron's hair. Sadly, the locket escaped its chain when Lady Morgan was pacing the street after a cold morning carriage ride. 'I have met with a loss which breaks my heart', she lamented.

In 1837, the Morgans left Kildare Street for London's Lowndes Square. Despite her criticism of English mismanagement in Ireland, Lady Morgan became the first woman to be awarded a civil-list pension for services to literature. Three years later, her eyesight failed and she reluctantly parked the gold pen which matched her habitually elegant attire. Compatriot author Anna Maria Hall was among her final visitors: 'Her head looked as noble as ever: the lines of her face had deepened, but her large, luminous eyes were bright and glistening, her voice was clear and firm... After some kind remarks, she gave voice to one or two little sarcasms, that showed her acuteness was undimmed.'

Having written thirty books, Lady Morgan died aged 82 on 16 April 1859. Death did not appeal to the happy agnostic: 'I shall be sorry to leave all the friends who have been so kind to me. The world has been a good world to me.' Her final unfinished book, *Woman and Her Master*, demonstrated her concern for the status of women. She was buried in Brompton Cemetery, Earl's Court, where suffragette Emmeline Pankhurst would later lie. David D'Angers' marble bust of Lady Morgan can be seen in London's Victoria and Albert Museum. Her portrait is displayed by the Royal Irish Academy in Dublin's Dawson Street.

ADVERTISEMENT.

THE PUBLISHER feels himself called upon to state, that the delay which has taken place in the appearance of this work, has arisen, in the first place through the very illegible state in which the manuscript was transmitted to him, and which, therefore, required twice the usual time to print: Secondly, in consequence of the author undertaking (without success) to procure a French translator for the Paris edition, the advantages of which it was incumbent on the publisher to secure, in order to reimburse himself for the very large sum paid for copyright: and thirdly, by the author's wish to have the French translation published without any of the political passages being suppressed, a proceeding which the reader will immediately perceive would have caused the confiscation of the work by the French government.

Conduit Street, Hanover Square,
June the 7th, 1817.

Lady Morgan's handwriting did not impress publisher of France *in 1817*

422 North Circular Road

Seán O'Casey
(1880-1964)

422 North Circular Road

I draw the line when I hear the gunmen blowin' about dyin' for the people, when it's the people who are dying for the gunmen! – The Shadow of a Gunman

The unprepossessing three-storey house at 422 North Circular Road witnessed the birth of the most memorable Irish dramas of the 1920s. They were written by Sean O'Casey, whose first-hand experience of the deprivation and exploitation of workers had led him into nationalism and trade unionism. A poor Protestant in a mainly Catholic city, O'Casey was equally frustrated by the blood-letting of 1916-1922 and the subsequent Civil War. He vented his rage with pen and ink in his first three plays between 1923 and 1926, before he fled to London. They were *The Shadow of a Gunman*, *Juno and the Paycock* and *The Plough and the Stars*.

O'Casey had much in common with fellow-Dubliner, James Joyce. Each suffered poverty, poor eyesight and a peripatetic life. But, while Joyce was faithful only to his art, O'Casey's art was harnessed to social reform. A lifelong socialist, he was the first playwright to write about Dublin's working class. He did so with unqualified passion. Northsider Aelish Gaynor's family knew the playwright: 'My aunt said it was amazing his manuscripts didn't burn up in the post! But while his plays were about tragic times, there was never anything as funny seen in Dublin. And they were also the first to show how it was the women who picked up the pieces and got on with life.'

Born on 30 March 1880 at 85 Upper Dorset Street, O'Casey was the youngest child of Michael and Susan Casey. Nine of their family of thirteen died in infancy. When O'Casey was two, the family moved to 9 Innisfallen Parade. Four years later, his father succumbed to a spinal injury, leaving Susan to feed her children on slender means. The future playwright spent the next two decades in the East Wall area, at 25 Hawthorne Terrace and 18 Abercorn Road. He was largely self-taught, apart from a spell at St Mary's National School, 20 Lower Dominick Street. Despite poor eyesight, he became a voracious reader. In the early 1890s, he and an older brother delivered recitations at parties. They joined a dramatic group and staged plays by Dion Boucicault and William Shakespeare in the family home. When he was fifteen, O'Casey acted in *The Shaughraun* at the Mechanics' Theatre, the site of the future Abbey which would one day stage his own plays.

Tall, fine-boned and with a determined set to his mouth, O'Casey experienced a variety of jobs from the age of fourteen. He was a labourer with the Great Northern Railway for nine years. His anger at the poverty of tenement dwellers converted him to socialism. He became an active trade unionist and also joined the Gaelic League. He wrote poems and political articles for the *Irish Worker* and participated in the 1913 Dublin Lock-Out. Appointed General Secretary of Larkin's Irish Citizen Army, he resigned over what he perceived as its takeover by middle-class Catholics. Recoiling from extremist rhetoric, he resented the fact that many more civilians than combatants had been killed in the 1916 uprising. Thereafter, he expressed himself though his plays.

Jim Larkin was O'Casey's hero. Asked once why he rejected religion, O'Casey replied: 'I never lost my faith, I found it. I found it when Jim Larkin came to Dublin and organized the unskilled workers. I found it in Jim's great socialist motto: "An injury to one is the concern of all". He was the saviour of Dublin. He put his faith in the people and their need to live a better and fuller life. And that's where I put my faith.'

Like George Bernard Shaw, success came comparatively late to O'Casey. He was 43 when the Abbey Theatre staged his first play, *The Shadow of a Gunman*. Set in 35 Mountjoy Square, where he had stayed before moving to North Circular Road, the 1923 play recorded the impact of revolutionary politics on Dublin's slum dwellers. Its comic-ironic pedlar, Seamus Shields, insisted: 'It's the civilians who suffer: when there's an ambush they don't know where to run. Shot in the back to save the British Empire, an' shot in the breast to save the soul of Ireland... I draw the line when I hear the gunmen blowin' about dyin' for the people, when it's the people who are dying for the gunmen!'

The Shadow played to capacity audiences and was quickly followed by *Juno and the Paycock*. Having already lost an arm fighting against the British, the 'Paycock's' son, Johnny Boyle, is taken away to be shot by republicans for allegedly helping the Free State cause. O'Casey's third play, *The Plough and the Stars*, which featured the comic character, Fluther Good, provoked riots at the Abbey in 1926. Outraged at the debunking of gunmen and the representation of an Irish girl as a prostitute, nationalists threw chairs and vegetables at the cast.

Juno and the Paycock won O'Casey the Hawthornden Prize. After supervising the play's West End production, he joined the long list of Irish writers who had found permanent refuge in London. He became friends with George Bernard Shaw, Augustus John painted his portrait. In 1927, the 47-year-old playwright married Eileen Carey Reynolds, a beautiful actress half his age. His fame spanned the Atlantic. Playwright, Eugene O'Neill was among those who welcomed him to America, where he lectured at Harvard University.

O'Casey later forsook the realism of his Irish plays for more experimental theatre. He explained in *The Flying Wasp* that the art of the theatre was to suggest, not to tell openly: 'Van Gogh, and particularly Cezanne, took from the extravagance of Cubism its possibilities and, uniting these with the greater possibilities of Realism and Impressionism, burst into a new art of painting. Now that is what I want to do in Drama!'

The Expressionist tragedy, *The Silver Tassie*, an attack on imperialist wars, received mixed reviews when it opened in London in 1929. But the playwright persisted and the 1942 *Red Roses for Me* about the Dublin Lock-Out attracted sell-out audiences. Seven years later, the tragicomedy *Cock-a-Doodle Dandy* was acclaimed at the Royal Court Theatre. Though Samuel Beckett praised his work, O'Casey was less smitten with his compatriot's plays: 'That Beckett is a clever writer... but his philosophy isn't my philosophy, for within him there is no hazard of hope: no desire for it: nothing in it but a lust for despair.'

In typical unrestrained style, the Dubliner wrote *I Knock on the Door* and five other volumes of autobiography between 1939 and 1954. Mirroring Joyce, he expressed his disenchantment with Kathleen Ni Houlihan: 'She had hounded Parnell to death: she had yelled and torn at Yeats, at Synge, and now she was doing the same to him.'

Sean O'Casey died in Totnes, Devon on 18 September 1964, aged 84. His ashes were scattered in the Garden of Remembrance at Golder's Green Crematorium. Commemorated by a new bridge in Dublin, his birthplace at 85 Upper Dorset Street is now a Mater Hospital outpost. In his last book, *Under a Coloured Cap*, he wrote what could be a fitting epitaph: 'Here, with whitened hair, desires failing, strength ebbing out of him, with the sun gone down, and with only the serenity and calm warning of the evening star left to him, he drank to Life, to all it had been, to what it was, to what it would be. Hurrah!'

Sean O'Casey Bridge

Court Apartments, Wilton Place

Frank O'Connor
(1903-1966)

Court Apartments, Wilton Place

I knew that nothing but the sight of the grave would convince him that we had to do it...
– Guests of the Nation

Novelist and short story master, Frank O'Connor, enjoyed the final five years of his life in a third-floor flat at canalside Court Apartments, Wilton Place. The Cork-born author retired here after suffering a stroke while completing the autobiographical *An Only Child in America*. It was an active retirement. He wrote, broadcast and lectured at Trinity College. Of medium build, Frank's moustache, mellifluous accent and brisk pace made him one of the Grand Canal's most striking habitues. Mary King of Parsons Bookshop recalled: 'He was also a very humane and understanding man which shows in those lovely stories. With his couture, white hair and warm manner, he breathed music into our tired bones whenever he called.'

Born on 17 September 1903 at 84 Douglas Street, Cork, Frank was the only child of Minnie O'Connor and former Munster Fuselier, Michael O'Donovan. Michael's drinking ensured a deprived upbringing, Minnie worked to feed the household. Like James Joyce's family, they moved to a less grand address. Before he left school at 14, Frank was taught by novelist Daniel Corkery, who inculcated a love of literature and the Irish language. Frank educated himself in the local library and learned to type at technical school. In 1918, he became involved in nationalist politics. He was interned during the subsequent Civil War. After a year's imprisonment, he noted: 'I was tired of war and I wanted to go home.'

On his release, Frank worked in libraries in Sligo and Wicklow. The latter's principal encouraged his writing and introduced him to George Russell, James Joyce's first publisher. Frank's literary career commenced with reviews and stories in Russell's *Irish Statesman*. After a period in Cork, he became librarian of Dublin's Pembroke Library in Anglesea Road in 1928. Working at night in his lodgings at 34 Chelmsford Road, his first book was a volume of short stories, *Guests of the Nation*. Published in 1931, it inspired Brendan Behan's *The Hostage* and Neil Jordan's film, *The Crying Game*. The title story was about the nationalist murder of two British army hostages: 'Donovan asked if there were any messages he wanted sent. "'No, chum," he said. "Not for me. If any of you would like to write to Hawkins's mother, you'll find a letter from her in his pocket. He and his mother were great chums. But my missus left me eight years ago."'

In 1932, Frank published his debut novel, *The Saint and Mary Kate*. His fluency in Gaelic led to the first of many translations into English. In 1935, he became a member of the Board of Directors of the Abbey Theatre, which produced two of his plays in 1937 and 1938.

Though few matched his short story talent, Frank revealed in a *Paris Review* that, after winning a painting scholarship, he almost became an artist. He told Andrew Whittier: 'From the time I was nine or ten, it was a toss-up whether I was going to be a writer or a painter, and I discovered by the time I was sixteen or seventeen that paints cost too much money, so I became a writer because you could be a writer with a pencil and a penny notebook.'

The 35-year-old Corkman abandoned librarianship for full-time authorship in 1938. The following year, he married Evelyn Bowen and became poetry editor of *The Bell*. He achieved unwanted fame in 1942, for defending the book, *The Tailor and Ansty*, which the Irish Censorship Board banned for its earthy language. He was soon on the proscribed list himself. In 1945, the Board banned his English translation of Brian Merriman's *Cúirt An Mheán Óiche*. Regarded by many as the finest poem written in the Irish language, its frank treatment of sexuality appalled the censors, who were unaware that its Gaelic original was freely available in government shops.

Frank protested the fate of young girls imprisoned or sentenced to death for infanticide, whose fate was ignored by the 'Christian' establishment which had banned his book. A 1949 *Irish Press* editorial denounced him as an 'anti-Irish Irishman' for an article on social conditions in Ireland. Larry Morrow captured Frank's demeanour in a profile in *The Bell*: 'His head, flung back fiercely proud, flashes a startling suggestion of the Yeats of thirty years ago . . . And in the darkness under the ostrich-egg brows chestnut eyes glow, burn, brazier-bright.'

The writer lived at 57 Strand Road, Sandymount from 1941 until 1949. His work was now well known in America and regularly published in *The New Yorker*. He agreed to lecture at Harvard in 1951. The following year, he published *The Stories of Frank O'Connor*, which included the popular 'My Oedipus Complex'. After the failure of his first marriage, he married Harriet Rich, whom he met while lecturing at Northwestern University. The couple lived in Brooklyn, where Frank worked at a table overlooking New York harbour and the Irish-bound liners.

Frank explained his love of writing to Andrew Whittier: 'To me, the novel is so human, the only thing I'm interested in - I can't imagine anything better in the world than people. A novel is about people, it's written for people, and the moment it starts getting so intellectual that it gets beyond the range of people and reduces them to academic formulae, I'm not interested in it any longer.'

The Corkman's writing was distinguished by sharp wit and straightforward prose. A perfectionist like favourites Chekhov and Hemingway, he constantly revised his stories which were published internationally. Unlike 'the outsider' Sean O'Faolain, the narrator in Frank's stories is also usually a participant. Frank published two volumes of autobiography and *The Big Fellow* biography of Michael Collins. An essayist and travel writer, his miscellaneous work included *Towards an Appreciation of Literature* and *The Art of the Theatre*. His literary criticism ranged from *Shakespeare: The Road to Stratford* to *The Backward Look: A Survey of Irish Literature*.

Frank visited Ireland frequently with his wife and daughter. While teaching at Stanford University, he suffered a mild stroke and returned home permanently in 1961 with his family. 'They think I'm on the way out,' he joked about the journalists who greeted his return. He was appointed Special Lecturer in Irish Literature at Trinity College, where students included future Joycean, David Norris. Exhibiting what V.S. Pritchett described as the savage indignant faith of Swift, Frank continued to campaign against censorship. He joined the Pike Theatre protestors who demonstrated against Alan Simpson's prosecution for staging Tennessee Williams' *The Rose Tattoo*.

Passionate about everything Irish, Frank also campaigned for the preservation of archeological remains and continued to translate old

Irish poems. One of the most beautiful Dolmen Press books was his *Little Monasteries* translation of lyrics from the seventh to the twelfth centuries. Frank's Wilton Place visitors included Irish-American critic, Thomas Flanagan. He lodged there while working on *The Year of the French*, which they discussed while walking the adjacent Grand Canal. Others to savour Frank's pungent pipe smoke were John Betjeman, Brendan Kennelly, Ben Kiely, Mary Lavin, Niall Montgomery and James Plunkett.

Trinity College awarded Frank an Honorary Doctorate of Literature in 1962. Ironically for an agnostic, his last lecture was given in the Catholic bastion of Maynooth College in February 1966. A fortnight later, he died of a heart attack on 10 March, aged 62. He was buried in Deansgrange Cemetery, close to another former canalside resident, Brian O'Nolan.

Frank O'Connor regularly walked this stretch of the canal

43 Parkgate Street

SEAN O'FAOLAIN
(1900-1991)

43 Parkgate Street

The truth is that the people have fallen into the hands of flatterers and cunning men who trifle with their intelligence and would chloroform their old dreams and hopes...

In 1940, unremarkable 43 Parkgate Street became one of Dublin's most significant literary addresses. Oblivious to the clattering of *Ulyssian* trams and Kingsbridge trains, Sean O'Faolain launched *The Bell* here, in his office in Cahill's Printers. The monthly journal represented a rare and vital outlet for Irish writers for the next fourteen years. Its first issue featured Elizabeth Bowen, Flann O'Brien and Jack B. Yeats. Subsequent numbers introduced newcomers Brendan Behan, John Montague and James Plunkett.

Reflecting its miniscule budget, *The Bell* was described as the only magazine in the world which was printed on lavatory paper with ink made from soot. What it lacked in paper quality, it made up for with courage. It became an outspoken liberal voice at a time of political and intellectual stagnation. Fearlessness was editor O'Faolain's second name. He risked his life fighting British rule in the 1920s and in the subsequent and equally bloody Civil War. He spent his middle age combating censorship and the insularity of the newly independent country he had helped to establish.

Sean O'Faolain's original name was John Francis Whelan. Born on 22 February 1900 at 16 Half Moon Street, Cork, he was the son of policeman Denis Whelan, whose erect bearing he inherited. His pious mother, Bridget, took in lodgers to supplement the family income. From early teens, the future writer immersed himself in the local library's dramas by Charles Dickens, Walter Scott and Alexandre Dumas. At the age of 17, he acted in a play by Daniel Corkery and met Frank O'Connor, who would remain a lifelong friend. Living opposite Cork Opera House, he became a regular playgoer. He was moved by Lennox Robinson's *The Patriot*, which dealt with the lives of ordinary recognisable folk: 'It brought me strange and wonderful news - that writers could also write books and plays about the common everyday reality of Irish life.'

O'Faolain won a scholarship to University College Cork, and graduated in English Language and Literature in 1921. His education was furthered by the fireside storytelling he heard on rural holidays. Reflecting the period's nationalism, he learned to speak Irish and became an independence fighter. In the ensuing Civil War, he heard the whine of bullets in lonely valleys where he had once enjoyed birdsong. He edited a newssheet, while his girlfriend, Eileen Gould, was imprisoned. Both tired of the bloodshed and fanaticism, he returned to university 'a more than disillusioned and embittered young man'.

The Corkman commenced teaching in Ennis and contributed his first short story to the *Irish Statesman* in 1926. 'I think you have a great talent', editor George Russell encouraged. He won a Fellowship to Harvard University and published a second story in *Hound and Horn* in 1928. He and Eileen married and moved to London, before returning to Dublin in 1933. Based on his fighting experiences, O'Faolain's first story collection was *Midsummer Night Madness*. Critic Eric Linklater described it as 'a wild and lovely book', but former fellow-rebels were annoyed by their unflattering portrayal. The depiction of a seduction led to the book being banned as indecent, as was the subsequent *Bird Alone*, which dealt with disillusionment and the taboo subject of sexuality

Further controversy followed 38-year-old O'Faolain's 1938 *King of the Beggars* biography of Daniel O'Connell. He suggested that the unsentimental constitutionalist was: 'a far more appropriate model for twentieth century Ireland, than any figure drawn from the sagas or the mists of Celtic antiquity'. The scene was set for a life-long battle between the writer and the triumphalists who had taken over his country. He concluded: 'The truth is that the people have fallen into the hands of flatterers and cunning men who trifle with their intelligence and would chloroform their old dreams and hopes, so that it is only the writers and artists of Ireland who can now hope to call them back to the days when these dreams blazed into a searing honesty.'

O'Faolain's wide-ranging work reflected his engagement with all aspects of Irish life and history. In addition to four novels which portrayed individual rebellion, he wrote biographies of Eamon de Valera, Cardinal Newman, Wolfe Tone and the Elizabethan chieftain, Hugh O'Neill. Published in 1942, *The Great O'Neill* was hailed as a startling fusion of O'Faolain's erudition and writing ability. *The Sunday Times* described it as: 'A series of pictures of wild grandeur and outlandish brilliance set against a background of Renaissance colour and turmoil.'

The Corkman also wrote meditative travelogues, *A Summer in Italy* and *South to Sicily*, and an autobiography, *Vive Moi*. A painstaking craftsman, his forte was the short story. Likened to Chekhov, he treated his subjects sympathetically and with humour. He commented: 'A short story, if it is a good story, is like a child's kite – a small wonder, a brief, bright moment.' He was less humorous about the erosion of social justice in mid-twentieth century Ireland. He was founder member and President of the Irish Association of Civil Liberty.

Though less confrontational than Frank O'Connor, novelist Honor Tracy described him as standing out like a rock in a foaming sea: 'In appearance he is like some respectable English burgher, tall and spare, rosy and blue- eyed: he pulls on a pipe in a calm English way and speaks in a manner imperturbable as it is urbane.' Tracy left her own record of *The Bell* era in her novel, *Mind You I've Said Nothing*. Her affair with the writer greatly anguished Eileen O'Faolain, who now had established herself as a writer of children's stories.

The Bell editor encouraged all his contributors. Without him, Michael Farrell's epic *Thy Tears May Cease* might never have been published. The journal provided a platform to promote both literature and the cause of literary freedom. It declared itself to be all-inclusive, belonging to 'Gentile or Jew, Protestant or Catholic, priest or layman'. The fear of academics to become involved ensured that it never matched the intellectual range of magazines such as *The Criterion*. But it broke ground with short stories and poems by new writers including James Plunkett and Michael McLaverty.

The Bell, which moved to 2 Lower O'Connell Street in 1945, also featured the first appearance of Patrick Kavanagh's *Tarry Flynn*. It published word-portraits of writers, including Elizabeth Bowen and Maurice Walsh, and documentary features on topics as diverse as prisons, hospitals and women in politics. It also highlighted such absurdities as the Gaelic Athletic Association's demand for the Defence Minister's sacking, because army members played golf and soccer which were not national games.

Sean O'Faolain enjoyed a long working life as a biographer, critic, playwright and novelist. Passionate to the end, he insisted: 'Youth should idealize and dammit, so should old age.' After three decades at 'Knockderry', Killiney, Eileen O'Faolain, 86, died in 1988. Sean spent his final years at 17 Rosmeen Park, Dun Laoghaire and died on 20 April 1991, aged 91. Like playwright Edward Martyn, he willed his body to medical science.

As for Joyce in distant Zurich, no politician or government member attended his memorial service. Conor Cruise O'Brien spoke of his 'Burkean magnanimity and generosity'. *The Irish Times* obituary concluded: 'If as a nation we have made any progress towards freeing ourselves spiritually, it was O'Faoláin and a few like him who urged us on our way.'

The O'Faolains' distinguished daughter, Julia, continues the family writing tradition.

Sean O'Faolain in his office in Boston College where he lectured in the 1960s

The Grand Canal beside Liam O'Flaherty's final home

LIAM O'FLAHERTY
(1896-1984)

Canalside Court Apartments, Wilton Place

One of the first of the modern revolutionary novelists, men like Hemingway and Malraux, who wrote about their experiences of rebellion and their own development as artists through it. – John Broderick

Liam O'Flaherty wandered the world as a deckhand, lumberjack, miner and soldier before achieving fame as a short story writer, novelist and author of *The Informer*, which John Ford filmed. He returned to Ireland in 1952 and moored for the final three decades of his life in the tranquil backwater of Dublin's Wilton Place. Tall, striking and always impeccably attired, Liam was an unmissable Baggotonian figure. Sean O'Faolain described him as bursting with energy and 'the most handsome man I had ever seen'. Heads turned when Liam walked to St. Stephen's Green or to revisit the Rotunda, where he had attempted to launch Dublin's first Soviet in 1922.

Canalside Court Apartments were a long remove from the Red Flagged-Rotunda and the trenches of World War One. But Liam knew the Grand Canal well and had written about it in his story, 'Wolf Lanigan's Death': 'A large barge drawn by two horses was coming slowly down the canal nearing its destination at Portobello Bridge, Dublin. There was no moon, but now and again glaring lights from the tramcars that rattled over the Bridge lit up the dark waters of the Canal, the grey bulk of the barge, the taut rope, the narrow gravel path and the two lean horses walking slowly in single file with their heads drooping.'

Liam's affinity with nature and action was spawned in his isolated Aran Islands birthplace. The first sounds he heard were of waves pounding the cliffs beside his Gort na gCapall home. Sometimes, the cottage shook in the gales which swept in from the Atlantic. Born on 28 August 1896 to Michael and Margaret O'Flaherty, Liam was the second surviving son of a family of fourteen. His parents were poor but a visiting priest arranged his enrolment at Rockwell College. Liam's way with words won a Gaelic essay competition. He moved to a Dublin seminary in 1914 and was given a scholarship to University College Dublin. First World War action proved more tempting than the priesthood. He joined the Irish Guards under an assumed name in February, 1916.

The following year, shortly after compatriot Tom Kettle was killed on the Somme, Liam became one of the war's victims. While fighting in the muddy wastes of Flanders, an exploding shell wounded him in the head. Lucky to have escaped death, he was discharged from the army. He was treated for shell-shock, which would affect him in later life. Future artist friend, Arthur Power was another Flanders casualty.

Liam survived on a small pension until he signed on a ship bound for Rio de Janeiro. It was the start of an odyssey which took him to Canada, the USA, Greece and Turkey. He returned to Dublin in time to see the installation of the first Free State government. By now, Liam was a member of the Communist Party and on 18 January 1922, he led a force of two hundred men to occupy the Rotunda. He told *The Irish Times*: 'The unemployed in Dublin have seized the concert room at the Rotunda, and they declare that they will hold that part of the building until they are removed, as a protest against the apathy of the authorities.'

The occupation lasted for four days, after which its leader evaded the police and escaped to England. Liam was now 25. He felt it was time that he concentrated on fulfilling his writing ambitions. Influenced by Guy de Maupassant, his first stories quickly found their way back to his Fitzroy Street garret. But, in 1923, the socialist weekly *New Leader* accepted his short story, 'The Sniper': 'Here and there through the city, machine guns and rifles broke the silence of the night, spasmodically, like dogs barking on lone farms. Republicans and Free Staters were waging civil war...'

Shortly afterwards, Jonathan Cape published his first novel, *Thy Neighbour's Wife*. It was followed by *Funny the Way Is* and *The Black Soul*, about a former soldier who seeks tranquillity on a remote western island. Comparing Liam to Dostoyevsky, George Russell described the book as: 'the most amazing thing in modern Irish literature, written with elemental energy from the first page to the last.' In 1925, Cape published Liam's most famous work, *The Informer*, about a revolutionary who betrayed a fellow-independence fighter. Like the subsequent *The Assassin*, *The Puritan* and *The Insurrection*, the book was set in Dublin.

The Informer won Liam the James Tait Black Memorial Prize for fiction. John Ford later adapted it as an Oscar-winning film. Subsequent novels included *Skerrett* and *Famine*, which dealt with the 1840s

Famine's effect on the individuals of a small community: 'Mary and the old man saw people looking over fences, just as they themselves were doing. These people had begun to wail. In this wailing there was a note of utter despair...'

Liam's work owed much to the influence of his native Irish language. But his work had international roots and appeal. Biographer Peter Costello noted: 'In his writings we can see the beginnings of much that is now being done in both Gaelic and Irish literature. Though often neglected in the sweep of modern Anglo-American criticism, he was widely appreciated on the continent: and his own love of France and admiration for Russian literature suggest that he was more truly a European writer.'

Liam embarked on a short-lived marriage with Margaret Barrington in 1926. But his social life continued unabated, with regular visits to Madame Toto Cogley's cabaret at 29 Harcourt Street, where he drank with Austin Clarke, F.R. Higgins and Harry Kernoff. He resumed his nomadic life, travelling to London and Moscow. In Paris, he met James Joyce, Ernest Hemingway, Sylvia Beach and fellow-Flanders survivor, Arthur Power. It was Power who pointed out to him that the young woman with whom he had made a date was Joyce's daughter, Lucia. Impressed by a mid-thirties visit to Hollywood, Liam revisited America. Like Oliver St John Gogarty and Padraic and Mary Colum, he remained there during the war with his new companion, Kitty Tailer. The couple returned to Ireland and settled in Court Apartments in 1952.

Like neighbours Frank O'Connor and Brendan Behan, Liam became a customer of nearby Parsons Bookshop. Manager Mary King frequently met him on the canal, where she once encountered him arguing loudly in Irish with local artist, Owen Walsh. Mary remembered: 'Unlike Frank, who was so friendly, Liam would collect his paper and depart with only a curt "Good Morning". We all got a big shock one day in the late seventies, when Liam marched into the shop. He had seen the window display of copies of Famine, which Wolfhound has just re-issued, and he offered to sign them for us. He was then in his eighties but, though he was a little deaf, he looked as if he was only about sixty.'

Liam O'Flaherty died on 7 September 1984 aged 88 and was cremated at Glasnevin Cemetery. Novelist John Broderick described him as 'one of the first of the modern revolutionary novelists, men like Hemingway and Malraux, who wrote about their experiences of rebellion and their own development as artists through it.'

Liam is commemorated in his native Gort na gCapall with a memorial garden and a plaque describing his life and work. His nephew, Breandan O'hEithir, continued the family writing tradition in both English and Gaelic until his death in 1990.

Scene from 1935 film of The Informer

25 Herbert Place

Brian O'Nolan/ Flann O'Brien
(1911-1966)

25 Herbert Place

Brian would refer to the Manichaean belief that the encounter between God and the rebel Lucifer had, despite all we were told, in fact gone the other way!
– Desmond MacNamara

Brian O'Nolan, Ireland's leading twentieth century satirist, was born in Strabane on 5 October 1911. He was third of the twelve children of Michael and Agnes O'Nolan, who moved twelve years later to 25 Herbert Place overlooking Dublin's Grand Canal. Brian first spoke and wrote in Irish, in which his parents were fluent. The family regularly visited the Donegal Gaeltacht, Brian once cycled there from Dublin with his brothers. The Irish language tradition enriched his later fiction and satire.

Educated at home until the age of twelve, Brian read most of his father's collection of books by Charles Dickens, Daniel Defoe, James Clarence Mangan and George A. Birmingham. He inherited his father's love of chess, an uncle taught him card tricks. Dublin brought the additional excitement of the stage. A gramophone played non-stop in the Herbert Place house, from which the family regularly set out to see John McCormack, Jan Paderewski and plays at the Abbey, Gaiety and Theatre Royal. The O'Nolan children staged their own dramas in the top floor front room, where Brian practised the violin and developed photographs. His journalist uncle George encouraged him to compile a 'newspaper', which he called *The Observer* and illustrated with his own drawings.

The city introduced Brian to the discipline of school. And what he perceived as the nightmare cramming institution of the Synge Street Christian Brothers. The punishment routine was a shock after his carefree home tutoring. Brian's only escape was physics and chemistry. His school experiences and the covering up of clerical excesses coloured his attitude to authority. Though it was unfashionable to criticise the religious orders, he later wrote: 'I remember a loutish teacher announcing that since it was only six weeks to the Inter Cert exam he was about to start a reign of terror. "I'll make ye dence," he said, with unintended pronunciational ambiguity.'

In 1927, when Brian was sixteen, his family moved to 4 Avoca Terrace, Blackrock. Brian enrolled at nearby Blackrock College. He concocted a series of letters to the Catholic *Standard* from parents concerned about the pressure of school homework. His satirical proclivities blossomed when he entered University College Dublin in 1929. He became a leading member of the Literary and Historical Society. His brother, Ciaran, recalled his unwillingness to concede anything in an argument. Brian's sideline interjections gained him the society's 1932 Impromptu Medal and launched his career as an observer and debunker. Nearby Grogan's initiated an equally enthusiastic association with drink.

Many students were disillusioned by the contrast between the original ideals and the mediocrity which had emerged from the fight for Irish independence. James Joyce added the ingredient of church criticism. Brian commenced his writing career with humorous and derisive stories in the students' *Comhthrom Feinne* paper. He also launched a satirical journal, *Blather*. But though he wrote every day, duty took precedence. The 23-year-old graduate brushed his suit and followed his father into the Civil Service in July 1935. His surrender to Custom House office routine was copperfastened two years later by his father's sudden death. Brian became the sole breadwinner for a family of twelve.

Despite family commitments, Brian gave his erudition full rein in *At Swim-Two-Birds*, which Longman's published in 1939 under the pen-name Flann O'Brien. Synthesizing themes and styles, it was a discursive romp which Graham Greene compared to *Tristram Shandy* and *Ulysses*: 'On all these, the author imposes the unity of his own humorous vigour, and the technique he employs is as efficient as it is original.' After receiving a copy from Samuel Beckett, James Joyce described Brian as: 'A real writer with the true comic spirit'.

In 1940, following stories in *The Bell* and a spate of spoof letters, editor Bertie Smyllie invited Brian to contribute a regular column to *The Irish Times*. Written originally in Irish over the pen-name, Myles na gCopaleen, Brian's targets included politicians, bureaucracy and various national absurdities. His column provided more joy than many books. The first port of call for readers, it brightened the lives of a whole generation. In 1941, Brian was between covers again with *An Beal Bocht*, an Irish-language parody of the fashionable Gaelic autobiographies, which Sean O'Casey hailed. *The Poor Mouth* translation, illustrated by Ralph Steadman, delighted a later audience.

Brian married Evelyn McDonnell in 1948. They lived at 81 Mount Merrion Avenue, Blackrock, before moving to 10 Belmont Avenue, Donnybrook. Of middle height, Brian remained an unobtrusive figure, hidden under his trademark hat. Reflecting his attire, his criticism of public figures and institutions demonstrated the sense of propriety which also dictated his attitude to vocabulary. Inevitably, politicians tired of his *Irish Times* rebukes. Criticism of his boss, the Minister for Local Government – the 'Yokel' Government – led to the 42-year-old columnist's 1953 retirement on a pension of £5 per week.

In June 1954, Brian organised the first Bloomsday celebration of *Ulysses* with *Envoy* editor John Ryan and Joyce's cousin, Tom Joyce. John maintained that Brian's writings did as much as Joyce's to preserve their beloved city: 'The Dubliner of the post-natal Free State and the subsequent Éire, as indeed the entire ethos of the Plain People of Ireland during the first heady morning of Nationhood, their manners and mores, vices and virtues, the incredible posturings and grotesque "patriotic" antics of the founding fathers, the proliferating tangle of bureaucracy that envelops the nouveau-Irish, are by him recorded as lovingly and faithfully as Joyce, a half century earlier, recalled his own post-Parnellite, Edwardian Dublin.'

At Swim-Two-Birds was acclaimed on its 1960 reprinting. *The Manchester Guardian* described it as: 'A book of ever-growing reputation which makes him a third musketeer along with Sterne and Joyce.' *The Hard Life* and *The Dalkey Archive* introduced Brian to a new generation. Published in 1967, *The Third Policeman* became his most widely read book. A murder thriller, it featured a surrealistic vision of eternity and an unrequited love affair between a man and his bicycle. And the much-quoted theory of the exchange of molecules between human and velocipede: 'The gross and net result of it is that people who spend most of their natural lives riding iron bicycles over rocky roadsteads of this parish get their personalities mixed up with the personalities of their bicycles as a result of the interchanging of the atoms of each of them and you would be surprised at the number of people in these parts who are nearly half people and half bicycle.'

A feeling of disappointment may have fuelled Brian's addiction to alcohol. James Joyce and Samuel Beckett flew the nets of language, nationality and religion. And the siren spell of Dublin's pubs. Brian never exhibited the duo's artistic zeal. Family responsibility and love of order were also sturdy brakes. What would he have achieved, had he also left? The miracle may be that he accomplished so much. His friends, Brendan Behan and Patrick Kavanagh, could devote all their time to writing. He endured a day's office toil before he could pen a creative word.

Brian died on 1 April 1966 of cancer of the pharynx, the result of smoking for most of his 54 years. Buried in Deansgrange Cemetery, he is commemorated by a bronze sculpture outside Fleet Street's Palace Bar. His Herbert Place eyrie was occupied until 1992 by one of his most enthusiastic fans, Mary King, legendary manageress of Parsons Bookshop.

Brian O'Nolan (centre) celebrating first Bloomsday with (l-r) John Ryan, Anthony Cronin, Patrick Kavanagh and Tom Joyce

Bath Street, Irishtown

JAMES PLUNKETT
(1920-2003)

20 Bath Street, Irishtown

Dublin was a good city to grow up in. The sea was at its feet, its Georgian buildings gave it nobility, its squares and its expanses of water made it a place of openness and light and air. – The Gems She Wore

Only one twentieth Dublin novel matched the scale and grandeur of James Joyce's *Ulysses*. Published in 1969, *Strumpet City* was universally lauded for its characterisation and integrity. Its sweep of subjects included deprived Dubliner, unlike Joyce's moderately middle class protagonists and those of Michael Farrell's *Thy Tears Might Cease*. Set between King Edward VII's 1907 visit and the outbreak of World War One, it traced the lives of a multitude of characters affected by the poverty and agitation of the tumultuous period. Its author was James Plunkett, who was born James Plunkett Kelly on 21 May 1920 at 20 Bath Street, Irishtown, to Cecilia and Patrick Kelly.

Patrick was a decorated Boer War and World War One veteran who worked as a chauffeur and mechanic. Reflecting the period's divisive politics, a cousin was killed in the Civil War shortly after James's birth. James witnessed nationalists snatching the poppies of Remembrance Sunday marchers. He was stirred by his father's tales of overseas adventure. Playing in the nearby sea afforded further opportunities to extend his imagination. Between tides, he walked the strand traversed by Joyce's alter ego, Stephen Dedalus. He observed the disparity between Sandymount's affluent villas and the cramped dwellings of adjacent Ringsend's dockers. When he was six, his family exchanged the sea air for the bustle of 26 Upper Pembroke Street, closer to the city centre.

Like Flann O'Brien, James was educated by the Synge Street Christian Brothers. He shared James Joyce's love of music and studied the violin in Camden Street's Municipal School of Music. Despite his slight build, he also played interprovincial football. In 1937, at the age of seventeen, he became a clerk with the Dublin Gas Company. He moved to 25 Richmond Hill to work in its Rathmines office. After marrying fellow music-lover, Valerie Koblitz, in 1945, he became an organiser with the Workers' Union of Ireland. Branch Secretary from 1946 until 1955, he worked beside veteran campaigner, Jim Larkin.

James had been writing poems and stories from his early teens. Concern for social justice was a recurring theme. In 1940, *The Bell* published the first of several stories, including 'Working Class', a precursor of *Strumpet City*. A decade later, the journal devoted an entire issue to his short stories. *The Bell*, ironically, was instrumental in James losing his job. Editor Peadar O'Donnell sent him on a cultural visit to the Soviet Union in 1955. Catholic church officials were outraged by this apparent endorsement of a communist country.

The religious *Standard* called for his dismissal from his trade union secretaryship. Petitions were signed, efforts were made to suppress a play he had written. The union supported James but, to avoid further controversy, he resigned voluntarily. One critic wondered what James could have learned about the Soviet Union in four weeks. The budding writer retorted: 'Not much – but I learned a hell of a lot about Ireland.'

The Dubliner also contributed stories and talks to Radio Eireann. The station transmitted three plays between 1952 and 1954, including *Dublin Fusilier*, based on a shell-shocked war veteran he had seen wandering the streets. In 1955, James was appointed assistant head of drama and variety. The 35-year-old writer celebrated with the play, *Big Jim*, set during the 1913 lockout of workers by Dublin employers. Labour leader Jim Larkin was his hero: 'James Joyce spoke of Dublin as the centre of paralysis, blinding conscience and soul. It remained to Jim Larkin to see the slum dweller as a human being – degraded, yet capable of nobility, perceptive, yet capable of living with dignity: capable, even, of music and literature – Jim Larkin's great task was to create a new social conscience.'

James made his Abbey Theatre debut in 1958 with *The Risen People*, which Sean O'Casey subsequently launched in London's Unity Theatre. Three years later, James became one of the first producer-directors of the country's national television service and was acclaimed for his early drama of the 1798 rebellion, *When Do You Die Friend?*

He continued his evening writing. In 1959, Hutchinson published his short story collection, *The Trusting and the Maimed*. Its variety of characters wrestled with religious guilt.

Unmarried pregnant Rita Kilshaw in the title story wanders by the Liffey: 'Gulls circled with sharp cries. Going home was out of the question. She could not sit down at table with the family in the drab loneliness of the kitchen to lie to them when she was asked why she had not been home to lunch. She could not sit listening to the radio in the front room with the holy pictures staring at her from the walls.'

The book's success led to the company's commission of *Strumpet City*. Working at night, it took James ten years to complete his 200,000-word odyssey. Each Christmas, Hutchinson director Robert Lusty sent a card: 'How's the novel coming along?' *Strumpet City* recorded the impact on a diversity of individuals of the landmark five-month lockout of 20,000 Dublin workers in 1913. Its author explained: 'Joyce wrote about the moderately middle class, and O'Casey about the slums of the period. I was concerned with finding a form in which all the elements could fit.'

Frank O'Connor hailed the book as a masterpiece, Anthony Burgess included it in his *Ninety-Nine Novels: The Best in English since 1939*. The book's colourful tramp, 'Rashers' Tierney, became a household name. Commending its integrity, Eileen Battersby of the *Irish Times* celebrated: 'If *Ulysses* is Dublin's odyssey, *Strumpet City* is Dublin's epic. James Plunkett's panoramic masterpiece is shaped by the Joyce of *Dubliners* but also by the social realism of Dickens and above all, Zola. There are no literary tricks, no displays of cleverness, little rhetoric and less sentimentality: it is full-hearted, astutely observed novel writing at its most cohesive.'

Hugh Leonard adapted *Strumpet City* for television. Starring Cyril Cusack, Donal McCann and David Kelly, it became one of Raidio Teilifís Eireann's most successful drama productions and was sold to thirty countries. Its triumph did not deflect James from his writing and television work. He scripted a joint BBC-RTÉ documentary, *Bird's Eye View*, which led to a 1972 travelogue, *The Gems She Wore: A Book Of Irish Places*. Set in the period following *Strumpet City*, the semi-autobiographical novel, *Farewell Companions*, was published in

1977. Thirteen years later, he published *The Circus Animals*, which considered the power of the Catholic clergy in the 1940s and 1950s.

In addition to his books and five radio plays, James wrote two short story collections and won awards for his television productions. A major achievement for a man who alleged he found writing difficult. Valerie Koblitz, died in 1986. James spent his final years in Kilmacanogue, Wicklow. He died on 28 May 2003 at the age of 83. He was cremated at Mount Jerome Cemetery and his ashes interred in the grave of his wife in Kilmacanogue.

James never lost his love of the city he had immortalised in *Strumpet City*. He paid a final tribute in *The Gems She Wore*: 'Despite its tensions and its tragedies, Dublin was a good city to grow up in. The sea was at its feet, its Georgian buildings gave it nobility, its squares and its expanses of water made it a place of openness and light and air.'

A contrast to Strumpet City – Beckett Bridge and modern Dublin

17 Rathgar Avenue

GEORGE RUSSELL (AE)
(1867-1935)

17 Rathgar Avenue

From the cool and dark-lipped furrows
Breathes a dim delight
Through the woodland's purple plumage
To the diamond night. – The Earth Breath

George Russell's redbrick villa at 17 Rathgar Avenue was the secular equivalent of a religious charity with the motto: 'We never turn anyone away.' From 1906 to 1933, it was a rendezvous for anyone interested in Ireland's artistic and economic future. A succession of artists, poets and writers climbed its welcoming steps. None left without books under their arms and encouragement ringing in their ears. Among them were James Stephens, Liam O'Flaherty and Frank O'Connor, who insisted that Russell was 'the father to three generations of Irish writers'. Twenty-six-year old

Patrick Kavanagh arrived in muddied boots after a three-day walk from Monaghan. He left weighed down with books he could never have afforded to buy.

Russell also bolstered a youthful James Joyce. Impressed with his poems but less so with the iconoclast's opinions, he recollected that Joyce, 'not only spoke slightingly of Yeats but of all others. His arrogance was colossal in one so young'. Nevertheless, Russell arranged the publication of his first short stories in the *Irish Homestead*. Russell's encouragement marked the genesis of Dubliners. Joyce, in turn, featured his mentor in *Ulysses*: 'His eyes followed the high figure in homespun, beard and bicycle...'

Renaissance figure, artist, poet and mystic, George Russell was born to a Protestant family in Lurgan, County Armagh, on 10 April 1867. They moved eleven years later to Dublin, living at 33 Emorville Avenue and, from 1885, at 67 Grosvenor Square. Russell excelled in English, French, mathematics and classics at Rathmines College and could quote long passages word-perfect from favourite books. His facility for drawing led him to the Metropolitan School of Art and the Hibernian Academy, where fellow-student W.B. Yeats shared his interest in spiritualism.

Russell adopted the pen-name 'AE' for Aeon, representing the lifelong quest of the human spirit. A vegetarian, he lived for seven years from 1891 at 3 Upper Ely Place with the Theosophical Society, whose beliefs incorporated aspects of Buddhism and Brahmanism. These energised his consciousness of Celtic myth and nature spirits, which he reflected in his visionary landscape pictures. After visiting Kilmashogue above Dublin, he wrote that the heart of the hills was opened to him: 'the winds were sparkling and diamond clear, yet full of colour as an opal, as they glittered through the valley, and I knew the Golden Age was all about me, and it was we who had been blind to it but that it had never passed away from the world.'

In 1898, Russell married Violet North. They lived at 25 Coulson Avenue, before settling in Rathgar Avenue eight years later. Equally adept at murals and friezes, Russell exhibited in 1905 at the RHA, the London Salon and the London Fine Arts Society. And, in 1908, with Auguste Rodin and the French Impressionists at Hugh Lane's newly-opened Municipal Gallery of Modern Art. He regularly painted Ireland's North West and Lissadell, home of the Gore-Booth family. His Otherworld paintings did not appeal to everyone. Despite having visited Neolithic sites together, George Moore dubbed him 'DD, the Donegal Dauber', after seeing his pictures of fairies painted on a northern holiday. Russell himself was similarly dismayed by modern art. He uncharitably described pioneering Mainie Jellett as 'a late victim to Cubism in some sub-section of this malaria'.

It was as a poet and writer that Russell achieved national fame. W.B. Yeats praised his first 1894 collection, *Homeward: Songs by the Way*. Russell encouraged the establishment of the Irish Literary Revival, writing to Yeats in 1896: 'Out of Ireland will arise a light to transform many ages and peoples.' In 1902, Frank Fay produced his play, *Deirdre*, at the Mechanic's Theatre, the future Abbey. Russell became friends with John Millington Synge and Lady Gregory, who invited him to Coole Park. She was one of his many Sunday evening guests, together with poets and writers Austin Clarke, Francis Ledwidge, James Stephens and Frank O'Connor. And Padraic and Mary Colum, who said that their host 'with his full brown beard, looked like the Celtic sea god Mananaun Mac Lir'.

In 1903, 36-year-old Russell was appointed Vice-President of the newly-founded Irish National Theatre Society. Yeats introduced him to Horace Plunkett, founder of the Irish Cooperative Movement. Russell edited the society's journal, *The Irish Homestead*, subsequently *The Irish Statesman*, from 1905 to 1930. Committed to improving the lives of farm labourers and small farmers, he directed the Irish Agricultural Organisation Society from an office at 84 Merrion

Square. Conspicuous in tweeds and steel-rimmed spectacles, he crisscrossed the country by bicycle, opening creameries and explaining the Cooperative Movement to farmers. He insisted: 'The decay of civilization comes from the neglect of agriculture. There is need to create, consciously, a rural civilization.'

Russell also supported the urban workers. During the 1913 Dublin Lock-Out he despatched an open letter asking employers to negotiate with their staff: 'Your insolence and ignorance of the rights conceded to workers universally in the modern world were incredible, and as great as your inhumanity – it is you who are the blind Samsons pulling down the pillars of the social order.'

The practical patriot did not neglect his writing. W.B. Yeats described him as 'the most spiritual and subtle poet of his generation, and a visionary who may find some room beside Swedenborg and Blake'. Russell published no fewer than twenty books, mainly poetry collections. Launched in 1918, *The Candle of Vision* was a series of essays on Celtic mysticism which recounted many of his divinations: 'I think of earth as the floor of a cathedral where altar and Presence are everywhere.'

Russell expressed his political idealism in two novels, *The Interpreters* and *The Avatars*. Published in 1922, *The Interpreters* advocated the theory of non-violence and resulted in an invitation to meet Mahatma Gandhi. Russell was shocked by the violence of the 1922-23 Civil War. He condemned republican extremists and also rejected the offer of a senatorship by the opposition Free State government.

Violet Russell died in 1932. Disillusioned with the independent Ireland he had helped to create, Russell sold his house, gave away his possessions and moved to London. Following a lecture tour of the USA, he died in Bournemouth on 17 July 1935, aged 68. He was buried in Mount Jerome cemetery, close to fellow-writers, John Millington Synge, William Carleton and Thomas Davis. Frank O'Connor delivered an oration and, as well as W.B. Yeats, the attendance included political arch-enemies Eamon de Valera and W.T. Cosgrave. Merrion Square Park features a bust of Russell, appropriately close to Jerome Connor's brooding Eire monument.

Russell's importance in the development of modern Ireland has yet to be properly acknowledged. Poet, editor, encourager and political thinker, he represented the conscience of the emerging nation. Calling him the practical mystic of his country, fellow-Northerner Robert Lynd wrote: 'Magnanimity is the rarest of the virtues, and AE contrived to distribute it to every one of the many controversies in which he took part. He was a champion of freedom, of freedom of mind no less than of political freedom, and a champion of the poor and defenceless at all times.'

33 Synge Street

GEORGE BERNARD SHAW
(1856-1950)

33 Synge Street

A life spent making mistakes is not only more honourable, but more useful than a life spent doing nothing.

Dublin taxi drivers will have you believe that Shaw was born in Synge Street and Synge was born in Shaw Street. They are half right. But it is difficult to believe that the cramped two-storey over basement redbrick at 33 Synge Street produced one of the early twentieth century's most famous iconoclasts. George Bernard Shaw became a novelist, playwright, social reformer and Nobel Prize winner. Born on 26 July 1856, he was one of a family of three. His mother was mezzo-soprano and piano teacher Lucinda Elizabeth Gurly. She performed at the Antient Concert Rooms and was fifteen years younger than her husband, George Carr Shaw, a grain merchant of Scottish origin.

George's fortunes mirrored those of another natural storyteller, John Stanislaus Joyce. Unsuccessful at business, he turned to drink, while masquerading as a teetotaler. Humour became an early defensive weapon for his disillusioned son who later wrote: 'If you cannot get rid of the family skeleton, you may as well make it dance'. Despite their reduced circumstances, Shaw's parents maintained an air of Protestant social superiority. Biographer Sally Peters noted: 'Although there was never enough money to allow the Shaws to live up to class expectations, the family was rich in pretension, the soil of satire.'

Shaw's governess was struck by his comprehension and reading ability. In 1865, he entered the Wesleyan School on Stephen's Green, before moving to the Central Model School, where he mixed with Catholic children for the first time. He concluded his education at the age of fifteen in an Aungier Street commercial college. As unhappy at school as Flann O'Brien, he later derided the standardized curricula as stifling the intellect. He described schools as 'prisons and turnkeys in which children are kept to prevent them disturbing and chaperoning their parents'.

Shaw enjoyed a more fruitful education at the National Gallery and the concerts of his mother's voice teacher, George Vandaleur Lee. Listening to works by Beethoven, Handel, Mozart and Verdi inspired a life-long passion for music, which he later turned to good use as a critic. A visit to Dublin's slums educated him on social injustice. He wrote of the poverty he witnessed: 'I saw it and smelt it and loathed it'. After a spell in Torca Cottage, Dalkey and 1 Hatch Street, Shaw moved in 1871 to 61 Harcourt Street. At the age of 15, he commenced working for an estate agent at 15 Molesworth Street in 'a stuffy little den counting another man's money'. His first published writing was an 1875 letter to *Public Opinion* on the influence of evangelist preachers. The following year, he moved to London, never to return home except for brief holidays.

The 20-year-old Dubliner earned a modest allowance by ghostwriting a music column for Vandeleur Lee. He devoted his remaining time to studying and writing in the British Museum. Evening lectures and debates educated him on issues of the day, he was soon converted to socialism and vegetarianism. Six feet tall, and distinguished by his brogue and red beard, he became a prominent member of the Fabian Society and wrote many of their pamphlets. In the 1880s, he achieved fame for his digressions as a reviewer and music critic for the *Dramatic Review* and the *Pall Mall Gazette*. He harnessed his polemical powers to a *Saturday Review* campaign for more vital theatre. Soon, he commenced writing his own plays.

Shaw's early novels including *Immaturity*, published in 1879, failed miserably. His theatre work, however, established him as Britain's most controversial and stimulating playwright. Like James Joyce, he was an early supporter of Henrik Ibsen's social realism. His plays lambasted social hypocrisy and the sentimentality of Victorian drama. Staged in 1892, *Widowers' Houses* criticized slum landlords. *Arms and the Man* considered the futility of war. *Mrs. Warren's Profession* concerned a well-bred woman who discovers that her mother's fortune was made in prostitution. Shaw's radicalism and irreverence did not endear him to the Establishment, *Mrs Warren* was refused a licence for almost a decade. But his forthright and ironic wit guaranteed provocative entertainment and Full House signs.

In 1898, at the age of 42, Shaw married Derry-born Charlotte Payne-Townshend and settled in Ayot St. Lawrence, Hertfordshire. Continuing Oscar Wilde's practice of portraying the English to themselves, he alluded to their occupation of Egypt in his next play, *Caesar and Cleopatra*. He postulated in *Major Barbara* that poverty was the cause of all evil, the medical profession was the butt of his irony in *The Doctor's Dilemma*.

Shaw's only play to be set in Ireland was *John Bull's Other Island*, in which he pleaded for Irish Home Rule: 'A healthy nation is as unconscious of its nationality as a healthy man of his bones. But if you break a nation's nationality it will think of nothing else but getting it set again.' British politicians flocked to see the play. King George VII laughed so much that he broke his chair. The class system of George's era was satirised in *Pygmalion*, about a speech professor's transformation of a Cockney girl into a lady. It subsequently became an Oscar-winning film and musical, *My Fair Lady*.

Shaw's pronouncements on religion and social issues ensured further recognition: 'The fact that a believer is happier than a sceptic is no more to the point than the fact that a drunken man is happier than a sober one.' He scolded public attitudes on corporal punishment, education, health care and religion. Campaigning for equal rights for men and women, and for public ownership of productive land, he co-founded the *New Statesman* and the London School of Economics. He appealed for a reprieve for Sir Roger Casement and supported Indian independence.

The Dubliner's zeal sometimes impaired his judgement. He supported Stalinism in the new USSR, unlike appalled fellow-visitor Bertrand Russell. Nevertheless, his opinions were courted by politicians and the media. Occasionally, his legendary wit met its match. He invited Winston Churchill to the opening of *Saint Joan*: 'Bring a friend – if you have one.' Churchill requested tickets for the second night – 'if there is one'.

Acknowledged as the foremost drama and music critic of his time, Shaw helped to shape modern theatre. The most trenchant pamphleteer since Swift, he also moulded political and social philosophy. His generations of acquaintances ranged from Oscar Wilde and Edward Elgar to Ingrid Bergman and Indian independence leader Mahatma Gandhi. The latter described him as 'a Puck-like spirit and a generous ever young heart, the Arch Jester of Europe'. Shaw was awarded the 1925 Nobel Prize for Literature – 'for his work which is marked by both idealism and humanity, its stimulating satire often being infused with a singular poetic beauty'.

Shaw died on 2 November 1950 at the age of 94. He left a legacy of sixty plays, five novels and countless essays. His ashes were mixed with those of his wife who had predeceased him and scattered in the flower beds at Ayot St Lawrence. Like Samuel Beckett, Shaw felt indebted to Ireland's premier art institution: 'I am one whose whole life was influenced by the Dublin National Gallery for I spent many hours of my boyhood wandering through it and so learned to care for art.' He bequeathed a third of the royalties of his estate to the gallery, which features a sculpture of the writer. Thanks to a campaign led by the late actress Nora Lever, his Synge Street birthplace is now a museum.

Shaw shortly before he died at Ayot St. Lawrence

5 Thomas Court, Thomas Street

JAMES STEPHENS
(1880-1950)

5 Thomas Court, Thomas Street

*In the centre of the pine wood, called Coilla Doraca,
there lived not long ago two philosophers...*
– The Crock of Gold

Humour and lyricism marked the work of James Stephens. Particularly, his exuberant and universally loved fantasy, *The Crock of Gold*. His early years were far from rhapsodic. He was born on 9 February 1880 to Francis and Charlotte Stephens. Poor Protestants, they lived in the shadow of St. Catherine's Church in 5 Thomas Court, off the high escarpment of Thomas Street. When James was two, his vanman father died. Four years later, James was found begging for food in the street. At the age of six, while living at 8 St Joseph's Road, Prussia Street, Charlotte committed him to Blackrock's Meath Industrial School for Boys. James never saw her again.

The institution provided James with a much-appreciated education. He learned to read and write during his ten years incarceration. In 1896, he followed in the footsteps of James Clarence Mangan to work for a solicitor at 9 Eustace Street, the first in a series of office jobs. His life improved when he was welcomed into the 30 York Street home of two friends, Tom and Dick Collins. He developed a love of literature and learned shorthand and typing. Equally determined to increase his height of four feet ten inches, he took up cycling and gymnastics. His height remained unchanged, but he was one of the club based at 8 Dawson Street which won the 1901 Irish Shield for gymnastics.

From composing on scraps of paper in Mecredy's office at 91 Merrion Square, James progressed to stories which he sent to newspapers. He studied Irish language and mythology and became friendly with nationalist leader, Arthur Griffith. In September 1905, Griffith published his first story, 'The Greatest Miracle', in *The United Irishman*. Publisher George Russell sought James out in Merrion Square, where 'A great head and two soft brown eyes looked at him over a typewriter'. Russell wrote to Katherine Tynan: 'I have discovered a new young poet in a fellow called James Stephens who has a real original note in him. He has had the devil of a time poor fellow. Works about fourteen hours a day for twenty shillings and is glad to get it.'

The discovery's soft eyes belied a hot temper. Tynan noted that, though James was a gentle genius, he was perfectly ready to shout down an opponent in a discussion. Soon, James met George Moore, Lady Gregory, W.B. Yeats and Oliver St John Gogarty, who noted: 'Poverty never got him down nor suffering either'. James joined the Bailey pub's coterie of scribes where, for the first time, he heard poetry 'spoken of with the assured carelessness with which a carpenter talks of his planks and of the chairs and tables and oddments he will make of them'.

George Russell encouraged the 1909 publication of James's first poetry collection, *Insurrections*, which railed against the conditions endured by Dublin's poor. Apart from his love for his fellow-man, James was also distinguished by his affection for nature and animals. 'The Snare' became a much-quoted poem:

> *I hear a sudden cry of pain!*
> *There is a rabbit in a snare:*
> *Now I hear the cry again,*
> *But I cannot tell from where.*

James's life took another turn for the better when he went to live with the Kavanagh family at 17 Great Brunswick Street (now Pearse Street). The Kavanaghs separated and James started a relationship with 'Cynthia' Millicent Kavanagh, with whom he had a son in 1909. Three years later, a thinly-disguised Cynthia was the day-dreaming heroine of his first novel, *The Charwoman's Daughter*. The year 1912 marked a turning point, when 32-year-old James abandoned office work to write full-time. He published a poetry collection, *The Hill of Vision*. And his most successful fantasy, *The Crock of Gold*, which critic Richard Fallis hailed as 'a profound and joyful account of our inner lives.'

Combining legend with parable and parody, *The Crock of Gold* revolves around two philosophers and their wives and children. In their quest for happiness, they encounter a host of characters from policemen to leprechauns and the god Pan. James's humour illuminates the pages as he describes his protagonists Aengus Og and Caitlin, who had descended on a mission of liberation from the Dublin hills, the home of the Gods: 'And they took the Philosopher from his prison, even the Intellect of Man they took from the hands of the doctors and lawyers, from the sly priests, from the professors whose mouths are gorged with sawdust, and the merchants who sell blades of grass – the awful people of the Fomor... and then they returned again, dancing and singing, to the country of the gods...'

The Crock of Gold was awarded the Edmund Polignac Prize of £100 and led to the London *Nation's* commission of a series of short stories. James and Cynthia moved in 1913 to Paris, where they would live until 1915. Two more novels followed, including the picaresque *The Demi-Gods*, before they returned to Dublin. James was appointed Registrar of the National Gallery and, for the first time, he lived in style in a spacious apartment at 42 Fitzwilliam Place. His play, *The Wooing of Julia Elizabeth*, was produced at the Abbey Theatre in 1920. Four years later, he won the Aonach Tailteann medal for fiction.

James, however, became disillusioned with life in Ireland. He moved permanently in 1925 to London. Oliver St. John Gogarty lamented his departure:

> *It's not as if you had no wit, and cared for recognition:*
> *A mind that lit the Liffey could emblazon all the Thames,*
> *But we're not ourselves without you, and we long for coalition:*
> *Oh, half of Erin's energy! What can have happened, James?*

In London, James became friends with Virginia and Leonard Woolf, Middleton Murry and Lady Ottoline Morrell. On a 1927 sojourn in Paris, he forged a close relationship with James Joyce, who shared his February 18 birthdate. So friendly did they become that the *Ulysses* author requested James to complete *Finnegans Wake*, should his sight deteriorate further. The Dublin exiles discussed the book when Joyce visited the Stephens' Kingsbury home in 1929. Joyce enjoyed his compatriot's humour, which Mary Colum described as 'the rainbow above the waterfall of his exuberant discourse'.

As well as regular US lecture tours, the BBC invited James to give a series of radio talks in the late 1920s. He proved a captivating storyteller, the series lasted for over two decades. James described his theory of art in *On Prose and Verse*: 'The function of the artist is to transform all that is sad, all that is ugly, all that is "real" into the one quality which reconciles the diversities that trouble us: into pure Poetry.'

James was awarded a British Civil List pension and an honorary degree from Trinity College Dublin. He died aged 70 on 26 December 1950 and was buried beside his wife, Cynthia, in the graveyard of St. Andrew's Church, Kingsbury. Literature had done more for his stature than gymnastics, he left over twenty novels, plays and poetry collections. He had travelled far from Thomas Court to become, as Oliver St. John Gogarty insisted, 'the most lyrical spirit of his time'.

James Stephens in Paris with James Joyce and tenor John Sullivan

15 Marino Crescent, Clontarf

BRAM STOKER
(1847-1912)

15 Marino Crescent, Clontarf

How blessed are some people, whose lives have no fears, no dreads: to whom sleep is a blessing that comes nightly, and brings nothing but sweet dreams.
– Dracula

Abraham 'Bram' Stoker was born on 8 November 1847 in three-storied 15 Marino Crescent, overlooking the sea at Clontarf. The third of seven children of Protestant civil servant Abraham Stoker and his feminist wife, Charlotte. Like James Joyce, young Bram was regularly carried out to the lawn in front of his house: 'If I lie on the grass, those days come back to me with never-ending freshness.' Indoors, he enjoyed the library of parents whose regular theatregoing awakened a lifelong love of the stage. From his bedroom window, he could observe the spire of Clontarf Church and the panorama of Dublin Bay. Steam-shrouded trains bustled northwards on the new railway embankment, tall-masted sailing ships battled wind and wave as they entered and exited port.

Bed-ridden for his first seven years, Bram would never forget the stories and fables he heard from his mother. Particularly, her accounts of the 1832 cholera epidemic which claimed thousands of lives. And the rumours of premature burials, which would later inform *Dracula*: 'By twos and threes our dead neighbours were carried away.' The Stoker home was within walking distance of the Ballybough plot for suicides, who originally were buried with a stake through their hearts to prevent their spirits from troubling the living. Bram afterwards confirmed, 'I was naturally thoughtful, and the leisure of long illness gave opportunity for many thoughts which were fruitful according to their kind in later years.'

Bram compensated for his childhood illness by throwing himself into physical activities from the age of eight. In 1864, he entered Trinity College, where he distinguished himself as a champion walker, oarsman, swimmer and rugby player. Like Oliver St John Gogarty, he was later awarded a Royal Humane Society bronze medal for rescuing a drowning man. Six feet four inches tall and red-bearded, he cut an impressive figure. Exploiting his knowledge of literature, he excelled in college debates. In 1867, he became president of the Philosophical Society, his first paper was 'Sensationalism in Fiction and Society'. Bram was also elected auditor of the Historical Society. His eloquence impressed Lady Wilde, who invited him to her soirees. He became friends with Oscar and Sir William Wilde, author of *Irish Popular Superstitions*, who was equally au fait with the legends of Transylvania.

In 1870, Bram graduated with an Honours degree in mathematics and joined the civil service.

His inherited love of the theatre was, however, his main preoccupation. In 1871, he commenced writing reviews for *The Dublin Eve-*

ning Mail, which was co-owned by Gothic novelist, Sheridan le Fanu. It was but a short step from the illusion of the stage to Bram's own fiction writing. In 1872, the *London Society* published his first ghostly story, 'The Crystal Cup'. This was followed by *The Shamrock*'s four-part horror sequence, 'The Chain of Destiny'.

Bram's first novel, *The Primrose Path*, was published in 1875, when he was 28. A moral fable, it centred on a Dublin theatre carpenter who emigrated to London and fell victim to alcohol. When his parents moved abroad, Bram rented a top-floor apartment at 30 Kildare Street, before moving in 1876 to 16 Harcourt Street. Now recognised as Dublin's most erudite critic, his reviewing was to change the course of his life. The celebrated Henry Irving was so impressed with Bram's review of his performance in *Hamlet*, that he visited him in Kildare Street and invited him to dine at the Shelbourne Hotel. Biographer, Barbara Belford, noted: 'They talked until daybreak, forging an almost sacred bond.'

Two years later, Irving took control of London's Lyceum Theatre and asked Bram to become his manager. In December 1878, before Bram left for London, he married Oscar Wilde's former girlfriend, Florence Balcombe. Wilde remained friendly with the couple and they met frequently in London. Managing Irving and his Lyceum Theatre for the following twenty seven years taxed Bram's stamina and patience. There were the compensations of world tours, invitations to the White House and meetings with Arthur Conan Doyle, Franz Liszt, Mark Twain and Walt Whitman. A supporter of Irish Home Rule, Bram also became a friend of British prime minister, William Gladstone.

Despite his theatrical work, the Dubliner found time to study law at London's Inner Temple, from which he graduated in 1890. He never practised but used the quiet library to write. His brother, George, published a book on Turkey and Transylvania, which intrigued Bram with its descriptions of virtually unknown regions of Europe. Bram himself travelled to France, Germany and Italy. He also holidayed in Whitby where, under the shadow of the ruined abbey, fishermen told him tales of shipwrecks and drownings. Here, he penned the first notes for the book that would become *Dracula*.

In 1890, Bram published his second novel, *The Snake's Pass*. Set in Mayo, it was the story of a romance between an English visitor and a local girl. But it was *Dracula*, published when he was 50 in 1897, which established his fame. One newspaper advised its readers: 'Persons of small courage and weak nerves should confine their reading of these gruesome pages strictly to the hours between dawn and sunset.' Reflecting Bram's interest in the occult, the main character, Dracula, a centuries-old vampire, attempts to relocate from Transylvania to England in search of fresh blood. A saga of the fight against evil, *Dracula* also features sexual overtones. The tension never falters: 'And so we remained till the red of the dawn began to fall through the snow-gloom. I was desolate and afraid, and full of woe and terror: but when that beautiful sun began to climb the horizon life was to me again. At the first coming of the dawn the horrid figures melted in the whirling mist and snow: the wreaths of transparent gloom moved away towards the castle, and were lost.'

Bram was a prolific writer. He also published a best-selling biography of Henry Irving, three collections of short stories and twelve other novels. These included *The Jewel of Seven Stars*, *The Shoulder of Shasta* and *The Lair of the White Worm*, about a worm that adopts a human form. Bram's works demonstrated his understanding of physics, chemistry and anthropology. Fascinated by medicine and science, he blended the Gothic with technological innovation. His second last novel in 1909, *The Lady of the Shroud*, is regarded by many as early science fiction. Bram died on 20 April 1912, aged 64. Like his wife, Florence, he was cremated at Golders Green Cemetery, where his ashes now rest.

It may be no coincidence that two of the earliest and most influential vampire novels were written by Irishmen, Bram's *Dracula* and le Fanu's *Carmilla*. Coleraine University lecturer Bob Curran suggested that Bram may have been inspired by the legend of a cruel sixth century Derry chieftain, Abhartach. Slain by the warrior Cathain, the chieftain became one of the *marbh beo*, the living dead, when he rose three times from the grave and demanded blood sacrifices. A druid instructed Cathain to kill him once more and bury him upside down under a large stone. Known as Cathain's Dolmen, Abhartach's alleged grave can still be seen near Garvagh, Co Derry.

Bram presented the 541-page manuscript of *Dracula* to an American who had helped with his research on vampires. When rediscovered in a Pennsylvania barn in the 1980s, the long lost manuscript bore Bram's original title, *The Un-Dead*.

Abbey at Whitby where Stoker commenced Dracula

St. Patrick's Cathedral where Jonathan Swift was Dean

JONATHAN SWIFT
(1667-1745)

7 Hoey's Court and St. Patrick's Cathedral

A young healthy child well nursed, is, at a year old, a most delicious nourishing and wholesome food, whether stewed, roasted, baked, or boiled: and I make no doubt that it will equally serve in a fricassee, or a ragoust. – A Modest Proposal

A year after the Great Fire of London, the equally incandescent polemicist Jonathan Swift was born on 30 November 1667 in a four-storey mansion at 7 Hoey's Court, Dublin. This was off Werburgh Street, close to the birthplace of poet, James Clarence Mangan. Now demolished, Hoey's Court is commemorated by a plaque at nearby Little Ship Street.

Few mixed as easily with the privileged, few were as charitable to the local poor. None matched the indignation with which Swift assailed church hypocrisy, civil corruption and English misrule in Ireland. He spent many years in England, where his friends included government leaders and writers Joseph Addison and Richard Steele. He returned in 1713 to act as Dean of St. Patrick's Cathedral for the next thirty years. St. Patrick's, Ireland's largest church where Swift was buried, features many links with the writer. These include his pulpit, death mask, a marble bust and the confirmation of the Freedom of Dublin granted to him in 1729.

Swift's parents had fled the English Civil War. His father died before he was born. When Swift was one, his mother left him in the care of a nurse who brought him to live with her family in England. His uncle, Godwin, rescued him and sent him in 1673 to Kilkenny Grammar School, where one of his schoolmates was future playwright, William Congreve. Better known for his pranks than scholastic interests, Swift boarded in Kilkenny until he was fourteen. There was no indication that the reluctant scholar would become the eighteenth century's most brilliant satirist.

He studied at Trinity College, Dublin from 1682 to 1689. Equipped with a BA degree, family contacts enabled him to secure a position as Secretary to Sir William Temple in Surrey. Temple introduced him to leading political figures and also to King William III. Swift made an equally significant contact, when he tutored young Esther Johnson, known as 'Stella', who later became one of the two great loves of his life.

The Dubliner composed his first poems at Moor Park. He later edited Temple's memoirs and wrote *The Battle of the Books*, a satire on critics of his former employer. When his hopes of progressing through Temple's patronage went unfulfilled, he was ordained in the Church of Ireland. He received his Doctor of Divinity from Trinity College and ministered at Laracor, near Trim, from 1700 to 1710. Religious fanaticism and the gulf between church practice and Christian ideals inspired his first major work in 1704 when he was 37. Distinguished by its clear style and sparkling wit, *A Tale of a Tub* attacked 'the Abuses and Corruptions in Learning and Religion' and writers who had sold themselves for money.

Swift's widely-read book did not enhance his chances of Church advancement. Missing the political excitement of London, he moved back there in 1710. He quickly achieved fame as an essayist and political journalist. He contributed to Richard Steele's *Tatler* and was a founder-member of the Scribblers Club with Alexander Pope and John Gay. Though rarely seen to smile, his wit and intellect ensured the attention of statesmen and social hostesses. He became one of the Tory party's inner circle and edited their paper, the *Examiner*. When the opposition Whigs regained power, a disappointed Swift returned to Ireland in 1713. He took up his appointment as Dean of St. Patrick's Cathedral and lived in the adjacent Deanery for the rest of his life.

His friend, John Sweetman, described him: 'At the period of his final settlement in this country he was forty-six years of age. His personal appearance was still attractive: his features were regular and striking: he had a high forehead and broad massive temples: heavy-lidded blue eyes, to which his dark complexion and bushy black eyebrows gave unusual capacity for sternness, as well as brilliance and kindliness: a slightly aquiline nose: a resolute mouth: a handsome, dimpled double chin, and over all the pride of a confident, calm superiority.'

Though opposed to the Catholic religion, Swift felt for the mainly Catholic victims of English injustice. He could claim to have preceded fellow-Protestant Wolfe Tone as the father of Irish separatism. Incensed by English misrule, he turned his pamphleteering skills to good use with a series of anti-colonial books. In his 1720 *A Proposal for Universal Use of Irish Manufacture*, he urged fellow-citizens to boycott English goods in response to laws which harmed Irish commerce: 'Burn everything from England but her coal.'

The government's unilateral decision to allow profiteer William Wood to make coins for Irish circulation outraged Swift and most of his compatriots. In 1724, Swift commenced *The Drapier Letters*, in which he denounced the coinage and insisted that all government without the consent of its citizens was slavery. He enquired: 'Were not the People of Ireland born as free as those of England? ... Am I a Free-man in England, and do I become a Slave in six Hours, by crossing the Channel?'

Swift became a national hero, medals were struck in his honour. The subsequent *A Modest Proposal* cemented his reputation as a passionate advocate for justice and the leading satirist of his time. It suggested that, having already devoured family breadwinners, absentee landlords should now consume their children. Two centuries later, Frank O'Connor described the *Proposal* as 'the first great masterpiece of literature written in English in this country'.

Abbreviated to an equally popular children's fable, Swift's most famous satire was *Travels into Several Remote Nations of the World*, which became known as *Gulliver's Travels*. Reflecting his political experiences, it was an anatomy of human nature and the pettiness of people and politics. *Gulliver* was an immediate success and was quickly translated into French and German.

His sermons and sometimes scatological poems were equally popular. In *Verses on the Death of Dr Swift*, he mused on the effect his death would have on friends and London Society. The Queen asks 'Is he gone? 'Tis time he should'. *Verses* concluded with the lines on his bequest to Dublin's first mental hospital:

> *And show'd by one satiric touch,*
> *No nation wanted it so much.*

Plagued all his life by Meniere's disease, Swift became increasingly quarrelsome in his declining years. Though nausea and vertigo ensured isolation, he enjoyed long relationships with his former pupil, Esther Johnson and Hester Vanhomrigh, better known as Vanessa, whom he had met in London. Swift died on 19 October 1745, aged 77. Crowds paid tribute, as he lay in his open coffin in the Deanery. He was buried beside Esther 'Stella' Johnson in St. Patrick's Cathedral. W.B. Yeats translated his Latin epitaph:

> *Swift has sailed into his rest:*
> *Savage indignation there*
> *Cannot lacerate his breast.*
> *Imitate him if you dare,*
> *World-besotted traveller: he*
> *Served human liberty.*

First edition of Gulliver's Travels

4 Orwell Park, Rathgar

JOHN MILLINGTON SYNGE
(1871-1909)

4 Orwell Park, Rathgar

I knew the stars, the flowers, and the birds,
The gray and wintry sides of many glens,
And did but half remember human words,
In converse with the mountains, moors, and fens.
– Prelude

John Millington Synge shared Samuel Beckett's view of the Dublin hills from 4 Orwell Park, where he spent half his short life. Born on 16 April 1871 at 2 Newtown Villas, Rathfarnham, his mother Kathleen moved here after her barrister husband, John Synge, died of smallpox the following year. The future playwright developed a life-long empathy with nature. Before he was old enough to tramp the beckoning heights, his happiest hours were spent exploring the greenery and wild life of the nearby Dodder river. With cousin Florence Ross, he studied and sketched the birds and collected their eggs. Summer holidays in Greystones cemented his addiction to the outdoors and his meditative character. Later, he adventured with an older brother to the foothills of Bohernabreena and Glenasmole, a precursor of future treks in the Wicklow mountains and abroad.

The teenager's interest in nature led to the loss of his Protestant faith. After joining the Dublin Naturalists' Field Club, he read Charles Darwin at the age of fourteen: 'It opened in my hands at a passage where he asks how can we explain the similarity between a man's hand and a bird's or bat's wings except by evolution... I lay down in an agony of doubt. Till then I had never doubted and never conceived that a sane and wise man or boy could doubt. I had of course heard of atheists but as vague monsters that I was unable to realize... Soon afterwards I turned my attention to works of Christian evidence, reading them at first with pleasure, soon with doubt, and at last in some cases with derision.'

Synge's disenchantment with religion resulted in family disharmony and girlfriend Cherrie Matheson's rejection of his marriage proposal. The Aran Islands and *The Playboy of the Western World* were a long remove from river walks and religious doubts. But it was his loss of faith which heightened Synge's appreciation of his country's history and antiquities: 'Soon after I had relinquished the kingdom of God I began to take up a real interest in the kingdom of Ireland. My politics went round ... to a temperate Nationalism.'

Like Bram Stoker, Synge was a sickly youth. His early education was haphazard, apart from a period at Herrick's School, 4 Upper Leeson Street and regular violin lessons at the Royal Irish Academy of Music. Nevertheless, he easily adapted to the regime of Trinity College, which he entered in 1889 at the age of 18. His first published work, a nature poem, appeared in the college *Kottabos* magazine. Awarded a Royal Irish Academy of Music scholarship, he played in its orchestra at the Antient Concert Rooms, where future friend James Joyce would sing. In 1890, Synge moved to 31 Crosthwaite Park West, Dún Laoghaire. Two years later, he graduated and left Ireland to pursue his musical studies in Germany.

He did not neglect his walking. The legends of mountain people above Wurzburg reminded him of those he had heard in Ireland. Literature replaced music, he wrote verse and a play in German. In January 1895, he moved to Paris. He studied French literature at the Sorbonne and suffered his first attack of Hodgkins' disease. He later encountered James Joyce but his most fateful meeting was in 1896 with W. B. Yeats. Impressed with his learning and knowledge of Breton culture, Yeats encouraged him to devote his life to creative work. To go to the Aran Islands and 'express a life that has never been expressed'.

Synge first visited Aran in 1898, when he was 27. He spent the next five summers there. His fiddle playing and Trinity-acquired Gaelic ensured his acceptance and a rare insight into the lives and culture of the islanders. He was captivated by the poetic speech of people who spoke English while thinking in their native language, and 'whose lives have the strange quality that is found in the oldest poetry and legend'. After writing about Aran life for the *New Ireland Review* in 1898, he completed a book, *The Aran Islands*, which was illustrated by Jack B. Yeats. He met Lady Gregory, Edward Martyn and George Moore, with whom he was to play a major role in the Irish Literary Revival.

In appearance, Synge was five feet eight inches tall and broad shouldered, with frank hazel eyes, dark hair, a luxuriant moustache and short beard. Oliver St John Gogarty met him at a rehearsal: 'He was silent, holding his stick between his knees, his chin resting on his hands. He spoke seldom. When he did, the voice came out in a short rush, as if he wished to get the talk over as soon as possible. A dour, but not forbidding, man... He never relaxed his mind from its burden.'

Synge's first play was rejected by Lady Gregory, but he achieved recognition with his 1903 black comedy, *In the Shadow of the Glen*. Set in an isolated Wicklow cottage, it featured a lonely and unhappily married woman and a tramp who offered her freedom. The first play directly based on his Aran experiences was *Riders to the Sea*, which depicted Inishmaan islanders' struggle with the harsh ocean which shaped their lives. *The Manchester Guardian* described it as: 'the tragic masterpiece of our language in our time'. Based on the drowning of an islander, the play concluded: 'Bartley will have a fine coffin out of the white boards, and a deep grave surely. What more can we want than that? No man at all can be living for ever, and we must be satisfied.'

In 1907, the new Abbey Theatre staged Synge's most famous play, *The Playboy of the Western World*: 'A daring fellow is the jewel of the world.' The comedy on an apparent patricide angered nationalists and puritans alike. Mention of a woman's underclothes drove *The Freeman's Journal* to describe the play as 'an unmitigated, protracted libel upon Irish peasant men, and worse still upon Irish girlhood'. George Moore defended the play and its author: 'There is no literary revival. There is only one man, Mr. Synge...'

The furore was an additional strain for Synge, fighting a losing battle against Hodgkin's disease. Now living at 47 York Road, Rathmines, he postponed plans to marry actress Molly Allgood. His mother died at the end of 1908. Shortly afterwards, Synge entered the Elphis Nursing Home at 19 Lower Mount Street. 'Have you heard any blackbirds singing yet?' he asked Edward Stephens, a few days before he passed away on 24 March 1909, aged 37.

Synge died before he could complete his final play, *Deirdre of the Sorrows*. His premature demise was a major loss to Irish Theatre. W.B. Yeats lamented: 'He was a drifting silent man full of hidden passion, and loved wild islands, because there, set out in the light of day, he saw what lay hidden in himself.'

The playwright's Protestant relatives, who had not read Darwin, forbade Catholic Molly Allgood to attend his funeral. The family headstone bears no mention of his playwriting. Synge was more at home with nature than with fundamentalism. Blackbirds, robins and sparrows now chant an eternal chorus around his grave in leafy Mount Jerome.

Irish actors Sara Allgood and J.M. Kerrigan in
Playboy of the Western World, *1911*

1 Merrion Square

Oscar Wilde and the Wilde Family
(1854-1900)

1 Merrion Square

Life is much too important a thing ever to talk seriously about it. – Lady Windermere's Fan

Merrion Square will forever be associated with playwright Oscar Wilde and his parents, Lady Jane Francesca and Sir William. The family resided at the number one corner house from 1855 until 1879. Oscar was born on 16 October 1854 at nearby 21 Westland Row, two years after his brother, Willie. In Merrion Square, Oscar learned to read and write, and recited for guests. His much-travelled father completed his books on archaeology, folklore and medicine. His mother penned nationalistic articles in an upstairs study and also established Dublin's most famous literary salon.

Boasting an Italian great-grandfather, Lady Jane Wilde was born in 1821 to a conservative Wexford Protestant family. She was a niece by marriage of Gothic writer, Charles Maturin. Author, poet, linguist and wit, her translations and Irish folk-tales influenced the pre-Raphaelites and W.B. Yeats. She campaigned for better education and women's rights: 'We have now traced the history of women from Paradise to the nineteenth century and have heard nothing through the long roll of the ages but the clank of their fetters.'

The carriages of academics, barristers, politicians and writers queued around the lilac-bordered square on the Saturdays of Lady Wilde's salon. Guests included painter George Petrie, writers Charles Lever and Samuel Ferguson, mathematician Sir Rowan Hamilton and Home Rule party leader, Sir Isaac Butt. Closed shutters, flickering candles and classical busts ensured a dramatic atmosphere. Lady Jane invariably wore a towering head-dress and velvet gown, long gold ear-rings, bracelets of turquoise and gold, and rings on every finger. *The Athenaeum* wrote that her guests included all those 'whom prudish Dublin had hitherto carefully kept apart. Hers was the first, and for a long time, the only "Bohemian" house in Dublin.'

William Wilde matched his wife's erudition, eccentricity and generosity. While treating his rich patients, he also established a dispensary for the poor, the precursor of Dublin's Eye and Ear Hospital. Knighted in 1864, he was appointed Surgeon Occulist to Queen Victoria and also decorated by King Karl XV of Sweden. Happy to be addressed as 'Chevalier', he frequently wore the uniform and Order of the Polar Star.

Literature was the family's staple diet. Oscar's favourites were historical romances. He spoke French and German and was a prodigious reader by the age of ten. He told a friend: 'I would for a wager, read a three-volume in half an hour so closely as to be able to give an accurate resume of the plot of the story: by one hour's reading I was enabled to give a fair narrative of the incidental scenes and the most pertinent dialogue.'

Tragedy, sadly, fuelled the Wilde fantasies. Sir William's illegitimate daughters, Emily and Mary Wilde, perished in a fire. When Oscar was twelve, he experienced his first major personal tragedy. His nine-year-old sister Isola, 'the radiant angel of our home', died in February 1867. Heartbroken, Oscar regularly visited her grave until he left for England. He wrote 'Requiescat' in her memory:

Peace, peace, she cannot hear
Lyre or sonnet,
All my life's buried here,
Heap earth upon it.

Oscar later lost the second great love of his life when he was 23. The beautiful Florence Balcombe, whom he met when she was 17 and he 20. He did not have the means to marry and she became the wife of author Bram Stoker. Oscar subsequently wrote of their time together: 'the two sweet years - the sweetest years of all my youth.'

One of Trinity College's most outstanding students, Oscar was awarded the Berkeley Gold Medal for Greek and a scholarship in 1874 to Oxford University. Here, his poem, 'Ravenna', won him the prestigious Newdigate Prize. He graduated in 1878, met Walter Pater and John Ruskin and established himself as a leading light of the aesthetic movement. A tall and imposing figure, his charisma, striking dress and scintillating conversation made him an essential invitee to London cultural and social events.

Oscar had written verse and features while at Trinity College. In 1881, he published his first book, *Poems*. Three years later, he married Constance Lloyd, with whom he had two sons. He wrote the children's tales, *The Happy Prince and Other Stories*, which was followed by two informed works of criticism, *The Decay of Lying* and *The Critic as an Artist*. In 1891, he published *The Picture of Dorian Gray*, which outraged staid Victorians. The hedonistic Dorian sold his soul to ensure that his excesses would cause his portrait to decay, rather than himself.

It was Oscar's irreverent and satirical plays such as *Lady Windermere's Fan*, *An Ideal Husband*, and *The Importance of Being Earnest*, which established him as a master of paradox and the most famous playwright of the period. 'She who hesitates is won': audiences hailed his literary inversions, without realising their subversiveness. His 1895 trial on homosexuality charges represented a spectacular fall. He was ostracised by most of his Society acquaintances, his plays were removed from the theatres in which they had previously been acclaimed. His refusal to flee to France moved W.B. Yeats to see him as a man of honour. Only a few friends remained loyal, notably Ada Leverson, the author and confidante of George Moore.

Ada had frequently noted his generosity. A trait that did not desert him in prison. He wrote to a warder requesting 'the names of the children who are in for the rabbits and the amount of the fine. Can I pay this and get them out? If so I will get them out tomorrow. Please. Dear friend, do this for me.' Oscar served two years in Reading prison. Constance came to tell him of his mother's death. Separated by metal grills, she recorded: 'I could not see him and I could not touch him'. Constance died shortly afterwards at the age of 39.

On his release in May 1897, Oscar travelled to France, under the pseudonym, Sebastian Melmoth. Here, he published his last work, *The Ballad of Reading Gaol*: 'But each man kills the thing he loves'. Now destitute, he was not allowed to see his two sons. He died in Paris of cerebral meningitis on 30 November 1900, aged 46. He had earlier told a friend: 'My wallpaper and I are fighting a duel to the death. One of us has to go.'

Among Oscar's few possessions was a lock of 'My Isola's Hair', enclosed in a hand-coloured envelope with their interlinked initials. The Dubliner's grave, under a monument designed by Jacob Epstein, is one of the most-visited in Pere Lachaise Cemetery.

Oscar was the last of the family which had enlivened Merrion Square and enriched Irish literature and history. He is commemorated by sculptures in Merrion Square and London's Adelaide Street, Charing Cross. Sixty one-year old Sir William Wilde died in 1876 and was buried in Mount Jerome Cemetery. Journalist Willie Wilde, 46, died in 1899. A monument in Kensal Green Cemetery commemorates Lady Wilde, who passed away in 1896, aged 74. Appropriately for a woman noted for the diversity of her salon, her neighbours include writers Samuel Lover and Anthony Trollope, artist William Mulready, mathematician Charles Babbage, Chartist leader Feargus O'Connor and HRH Princess Sophie.

82 Merrion Square

W.B. Yeats
(1865-1939)

82 Merrion Square

Hope and Memory have one daughter and her name is Art, and she has built her dwelling far from the desperate field where men hang out their garments upon forked boughs to be banners of battle. O beloved daughter of Hope and Memory, be with me for a little. – The Celtic Twilight

But for the plaque at 82 Merrion Square, one could pass by without realising that this was once home to a pivotal figure of twentieth century literature. Thanks to money earned on an American lecture tour, W.B. Yeats bought the house early in 1922. The residence had a special significance in his life. It was the first

Irish family home of the 57-year old poet and his 29-year old wife, George, and their two young children.

Here, after an apprenticeship of over three decades, honours finally arrived. The 1923 Nobel Prize for Literature and Yeats's appointment as a senator by the new national government. The £7,000 Nobel money helped to carpet and furnish the mansion, and purchase reference books. And, it was rumoured, a gilded cage for the canaries who enlivened his study. Yeats did not easily shed his former absentmindedness. Novelist V.S. Pritchett was taken aback when the poet emptied a cold teapot out the front window.

Merrion Square marked a rounding of the circle for the peripatetic Yeats, the grandson of a Banbridge Protestant rector. Two years after his birth at 5 Sandymount Avenue on 13 June 1865, he was taken to London by his artist father, John B. Yeats. He did not distinguish himself in Hammersmith's Godolphin School. An early report described his spelling as 'very poor'. But, thanks to his father's readings, he grew up on a rich diet of Chaucer, Dante, Shelley and Shakespeare. *The Lays of Ancient Rome* and similar examples of the individual spirit in action influenced him more than any formal education. Biographer William M. Murphy acknowledged John Yeats's influence: 'It was his insistence to his children on the supremacy of the artistic over the material that encouraged the manifestation of their own unique qualities.'

The family returned to Dublin for six years in 1880, when Yeats was fifteen. They lived in Howth, before moving to what is now 418 Harold's Cross Road. Yeats continued his education at Harcourt Street High School and the Metropolitan School of Art. Here, he met George Russell, one of the first to hear the verse he had been writing since he was sixteen.

Yeats's first published poems appeared in the *Dublin University Review* in 1885. His verse-play *Mosada, a Dramatic Poem* was printed privately the following year.

The aspiring poet met Katherine Tynan and other leading literati. But the person who most shaped his future life was John O'Leary. The former Fenian prisoner introduced him to Gaelic and recent Anglo-Irish literature and lent him books on Irish myth and legend. Yeats acknowledged that O'Leary provided one of the sparks which ignited the Irish Literary Revival: 'From these debates, from O'Leary's conversation, and from the Irish books he lent or gave me has come all I have set my hand to since.'

In 1887, the Yeats family moved back to London. The aspiring poet met George Bernard Shaw. And Oscar Wilde, his senior by twenty years: 'I never before heard a man talking with perfect sentences, as if he had written them all over night with labour and yet all spontaneous.' Yeats was equally smitten by English-born actress Edith Maud Gonne, mistress of a right-wing French politician. Though she inspired his poetry, his ardour was unreciprocated. He published the mystical saga, *The Wanderings of Oisin and other Poems* in 1889, and founded the Rhymers' Club with Ernest Rhys. Frequently homesick for Sligo, where he had holidayed with his maternal grandparents, the 25-year old poet published the much-quoted 'Lake Isle of Innisfree' in 1890:

> *I will arise and go now, for always night and day*
> *I hear lake water lapping with low sounds by the shore:*
> *While I stand on the roadway, or on the pavements grey,*
> *I hear it in the deep heart's core.*

The Dubliner also wrote drama based on Irish legends. In 1892, he published *The Countess Kathleen* and, two years later, *The Land of Heart's Desire*. In 1896, playwright Edward Martyn introduced him to Lady Gregory, who shared his cultural nationalism. This meeting and George Moore's collaboration led to the 1899 founding of the Irish Literary Theatre, a platform for Celtic and Irish drama. Yeats wrote three of its earliest plays, *Cathleen Ni Houlihan*, *The King's Threshold* and *Deirdre*. The initiative spawned the Abbey Theatre, a nursery for playwrights such as John Millington Synge and Sean O'Casey. In 1902, Yeats supported his sister, Elizabeth's launch of the Dun Emer Press, which published works associated with the Literary Revival.

Yeats married George Hyde Lees on 20 October 1917. They lived in Oxford before returning to Dublin and purchasing their Merrion Square house in 1922. One night two months after their arrival, Oliver St John Gogarty inscribed 'Senator Yeats' on their dewy doorplate. The first intimation of Yeats's appointment as a senator. Fellow-poet Maurice Bowra described him at this time: 'He was tall and quite heavily built. His hair was turning grey: he had a fine straight nose, and dark eyes, which had that look of peering into infinity which is the privilege of the short-sighted.'

Like his wife, Yeats had a life-long interest in mysticism and spiritualism and he co-founded the Dublin Hermetic Society. But the contemplator was also a man of action. He defied Abbey Theatre agitators who protested John Millington Synge's *Playboy of the Western World*. And in 1926, he confronted rioters who interrupted a play by Sean O'Casey. He was equally fearless in senate debates on censorship and divorce: 'If you show that this country... is going to be governed by Roman Catholic ideas and by Catholic ideas alone, you will never get the North ... You will put a wedge in the midst of this nation.'

Yeats's work included two volumes of autobiography, *Reveries over Childhood and Youth* and *The Trembling of the Veil*. His 1923 Nobel Prize provided a major boost for fledgling independent Ireland. The Nobel committee described his work as 'inspired poetry, which in a highly artistic form gives expression to the spirit of a whole nation'. Unlike many Nobel recipients, Yeats continued to develop. He wrote much of his best work after the award, including 'The Second Coming', which featured some of literature's most potent images of the twentieth century:

Things fall apart: the centre cannot hold:
Mere anarchy is loosed upon the world...

The poet bought a riverside Norman tower, Thoor Ballylee near Gort, where he stayed periodically with his family between 1921 and 1929. In 1934, the family moved to Riversdale House, Rathfarnham. Yeats had affairs in the 1930s with novelist Ethel Mannin and the poet, Margot Ruddock. He hoped that the south of France would provide respite from increasing breathing and heart problems. But he suffered a heart attack in the Hotel Ideal Sejour at Menton, and died there on 28 January 1939 at the age of 73.

Yeats was re-interred in Drumcliffe churchyard in 1948. In addition to a bust on Sandymount Green, he is commemorated in a Stephen's Green sylvan sanctuary by Henry Moore's 'Knife Edge' sculpture.

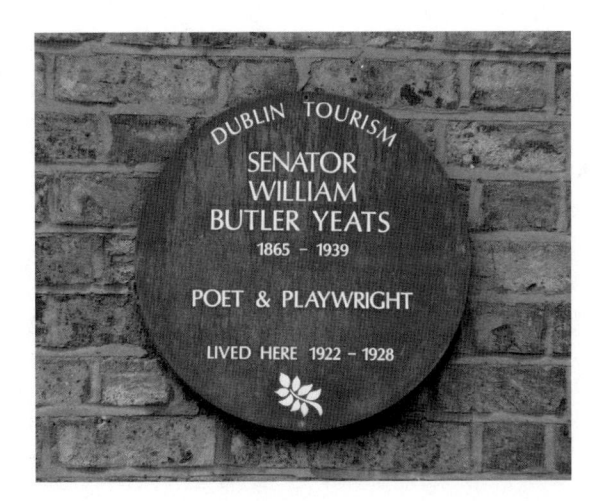

Baggot Street Bridge

PARSONS BOOKSHOP
(1949-1989)

Baggot Street Bridge

Parsons, where one met as many interesting writers on the floor of the shop as on the shelves!
– Mary Lavin

Where there are writers, there are bookshops. One of Europe's most famous bookshops graced Baggot Street Bridge from 1949 to 1989. It was at the heart of the literary and artistic quarter which *Envoy* editor John Ryan christened Baggotonia. Rivalling Sylvia Beach's Shakespeare and Company, Parsons attracted the country's leading writers and artists. From Brendan Behan, John Broderick, Patrick Kavanagh and Brian O'Nolan to Nobel Prizewinner, Seamus Heaney and Pulitzer

Prizewinner, Theodore Roethke. And fellow-visitors Nelson Algren, John Berryman and Laurie Lee. Prominent academics, clerics and politicians were regulars, including Taoisigh (Prime Ministers) Jack Lynch and Garrett Fitzgerald.

Like its Paris counterpart, Parsons boasted an all-female staff. Proprietor May O'Flaherty, manager Mary King and colleagues, Carmel Leahy, Mary O'Riordan and Patricia Ronan. But it was far from books that Parsons Bookshop started life. Father Aidan Lehane, nephew of May O'Flaherty who bought Parsons hardware store in 1948, explained: 'My aunt originally had absolutely no idea of opening a bookshop, she just wanted to be her own boss and run her own business. She fell for Parsons, she liked its situation on the crest of the canal bridge, with its view out the door and the broad windows on the passing street life.'

May – or Miss O'Flaherty, as she was known to her customers – was content with her *Irish Times* round and with selling hardware, stamp collections and nets for children who fished in the canal. But, after a spring clean, she left some books on a table outside the door. They sold immediately. Poet Patrick Kavanagh suggested that there might be a market for literature: 'Contact the Oxford University Press.'

When the first OUP rep banged his bowler hat against a hanging bucket, May thought that would be the end of her bookselling dreams. But, once recovered from the shock of finding a hardware rather than a book shop, the salesman fell victim to May's enthusiasm. A cup of tea later, he took orders for dictionaries, *The Letters of Samuel Johnson* and titles by former Merrion Square resident, Sheridan le Fanu. May conscripted Father Lehane to ferry further volumes from quayside publishers, Burns Oates. Gradually, books and periodicals encroached on the window display of hardware and stamps.

Like a beacon of culture, the elevated shop marked the confluence of flat-land Bohemia and the affluent Ballsbridge suburbs. Garrett

Fitzgerald remembered: 'There were few bookshops around when I first visited Parsons. My wife Joan and I lived in Eglinton Road nearby, and it was great not to have to go into town to buy a book.' The affordable Penguin paperbacks attracted university students. *Envoy* and literary magazines drew canalside residents, Thomas Kinsella, James Liddy, Frank O'Connor and Liam O'Flaherty. Artists John Behan, Brian Bourke, Michael Kane, Elizabeth Rivers and Owen Walsh were also lured from their flats and mews. Their presence consolidated the shop's reputation and attracted further customers. The OUP man returned in 1953. 'Where are the buckets?' he enquired.

May O'Flaherty built extra shelves for art and architectural tomes. New customers included Maeve Binchy, Ben Kiely, James Plunkett, UCD president, Dr. Michael Tierney and Archbishop George Simms. Novelist Mary Lavin remarked: 'One met as many interesting writers on the floor of the shop as on the shelves!' Parsons also appeared in books. Including David Hanley's *In Guilt and in Glory* and *Balcony of Europe* by Aidan Higgins: 'The ghost of Teilhard de Chardin stalked along the Grand Canal and peered through the windows of Parsons Bookshop near Baggot Street bridge, saw the reflection of his own austere countenance superimposed on many volumes of his own works.'

Booklover Mary King from Moyard in Connemara was the perfect manageress. Her down to earth manner balanced May O'Flaherty's natural aloofness. Mary read every book which passed through the shop. She had fond memories of Brendan Behan and Patrick Kavanagh: 'Brendan was a showman who loved an audience. He'd march into the shop, maybe say something funny or outrageous, then glance around to see how listeners reacted. Patrick could be irascible and touchy at times, and would easily take offence. But behind the gruffness was a sensitive thoughtful individual with a great underlying vein of wisdom, spirituality and depth of vision.'

May O'Flaherty's favourite was Patrick Kavanagh. She frequently stood by the door to watch his ascent from Pembroke Road, arms folded, his hat at its customary quizzical angle. Patrick treated the shop as a village store: 'He would stroll in and perch himself on a little stool. He would go through the papers, maybe say something about the weather and then he was off again, usually across the road to Mrs. Murray, whose bet he would take to the bookies.'

Patricia Ronan, a true-Blue Dublin fan of Brendan Behan, did not share May's regard for Patrick: 'God forgive me, but he was a rude ignorant bogman. He was always spitting – and you should see the way he searched the papers for racing tips, and then scattered their pages all around the place as he finished with them!'

Parsons' wooden counter and creaking floorboards remained unvarnished for its four decades. May O'Flaherty presided by the cash till, under her portrait by Owen Walsh and a ledge, on which a small bottle of brandy gathered dust: 'For emergencies, in case anyone falls ill in the shop.' A clearing house for local gossip, Parsons' open door tempted passers-by and locals marooned by family and social change. Two regulars were Sir Anthony Houghton and heiress, Miss Brown. Sir Anthony, allegedly a cashiered RAF officer, sometimes wore only a sack, while he sipped wine at the counter. Miss Brown was rarely out of her fur coat, even in summer.

May O'Flaherty, a devout Catholic, ensured the wholesomeness of the window display. But Mary King insinuated the latest avant-garde works. John Banville described the shop as 'A wonderful institution, a haven of civilization in a barbarous little country'. Nobel Prizewinner Seamus Heaney sensed a controlling spirit: 'Because of the decorum and general propriety of the ladies, not to mention a certain natural grandeur in Miss O'Flaherty, the shop felt a little bit like a domestic establishment. It was an emporium, of course, but it wasn't entirely a public house. Something told you that this was a slightly privileged zone.'

Parsons boasted an international clientele. Mary King recalled: 'There were also Joycean scholars from Japan. Owen Walsh said they were probably the only ones who could make sense of *Finnegans Wake!*' Brendan Kennelly, Paul Durcan and Richard Murphy represented a new generation of poets. Like Patrick Kavanagh, some used the shop as a poste restante. Parsons staff kept in touch with exiled James Liddy and Peter Kavanagh. When John Montague settled in Paris, Mary King regularly sent him books and newspapers.

The arrival of computerisation and chain bookstores spelt the end of the casual chaos of Parsons. May O'Flaherty switched off its lights at 6pm on Tuesday, 31 May 1989. She died two years later at the age of 86 and was buried in Glasnevin cemetery, close to Brendan and Beatrice Behan. US poet Ben Howard eulogised her as the creator 'who made a temple of a common shop'.

Mary King passed away aged 83 in 1995. She was buried in Ballinakill Cemetery, Galway, beside one of her favourites, Oliver St John Gogarty. In Milwaukee, James Liddy lamented: 'The loss of Parsons signalled the shut down of Dublin as a literary city.'

Patrick Kavanagh checks the Parsons window display

Some Literary Walks, Pubs and Cemeteries

1. Fitzwilliam Square to Merrion Square, Kildare Street and Ely Place

This largely Georgian area is Dublin's most majestic quarter. Start at the corner of Leeson Street and Fitzwilliam Place, just before the canal bridge. This leads you into spacious and elegant Fitzwilliam and Merrion Squares. Sentried by silver swan-neck lamps and awash with ornate balconies, railings, doors and delicate fanlights. In the 1940s and 50s, the basement of number 13 on the right-hand side hosted the indelicate Catacombs drinking den, frequented by Brendan Behan, Anthony Cronin, J.P. Donleavy, 'Ginger man' Gainor Crist and poet, Pearse Hutchinson. And by artists Irene Broe, Des MacNamara and Tom Nisbet, and actors Dan O'Herlihy and Godfrey Quigley.

After being gassed in Flanders, artist and writer Arthur Power stayed at 21 Fitzwilliam Place, before moving Paris in 1920. Five years earlier on his return from Paris, James Stephens lived across the street at number 42. Jack B. Yeats lived from 1929 to 1957 at the end of the street in the 18 Fitzwilliam Square South corner house. His visitors included Samuel Beckett, Oscar Kokoschka, Louis MacNeice and Thomas MacGreevy.

Turn left into the square and you will pass number 19, where naturalist and historian, Robert Lloyd Praeger, lived for many years.

Novelist Kate O'Brien frequently stayed with her elder sister, May at 13. Left at the end of the square leads into Upper Pembroke Street. James Plunkett moved to number 26 in 1926. Further up on the left is Pembroke Lane, where Deirdre O'Connell and Luke Kelly of The Dubliners founded the Focus Theatre at number 6 in 1967.

Retrace your steps and you will reach 36 Fitzwilliam Square West, where artist Mainie Jellett was born in 1897. Turn right into Fitzwilliam Square North, where Polish patriot and philosopher, Jan Lukasiewicz lived at 57 from 1946 until his death in 1956. Turn left into Fitzwilliam Street Upper and you will reach number 3, the Dublin United Arts Club. Writers and artists from W.B. Yeats, Oliver St. John Gogarty, Tom Kettle and Percy French to Sean Keating, Harry Kernoff and Arthur Power traversed its steps. Continue straight on, crossing Baggot Street, to Merrion Square. On the corner of Baggot Street, look out for Larry Murphy's pub, which boasts a mural by

Merrion Square

1950s artist, Owen Walsh. A friend of Liam O'Flaherty, Owen lived opposite the pub at 108 Lower Baggot Street.

Turn left from Fitzwilliam Street Upper into Merrion Square South. Catholic Emancipation advocate Daniel O'Connell bought number 58 in 1809. Nobel Prize-winning Austrian physicist, Erwin Schrödinger, lived at 65 in the 1940s. Joseph Sheridan le Fanu died at number 70 in 1873 and sculptor Andrew O'Connor at number 77 in 1941. W.B. Yeats lived at number 82 from 1922 to 1928. George Russell worked in number 84 for many years from 1908, his body lay in state here after his 1935 death in Bournemouth.

Turn right to the National Gallery, where Samuel Beckett and George Bernard Shaw regularly sought refuge and inspiration. At the end of the road, on the opposite side, is 1 Merrion Square, home of the Wilde Family. A sculpture of Oscar faces the house from the park.

Turn left into Clare Street. Greene's Bookshop stood at number 16. Opposite, Samuel Beckett wrote his first book in number 6. Poet, physician and Feis Ceoil co-founder George Sigerson, who studied with Sigmund Freud, lived at number 3 from 1877 until his demise in 1925. Katherine Tynan and W.B. Yeats visited regularly, John O'Leary dined here every Sunday until his death in 1907.

At end of street, turn right into Lincoln Place. Continue right around until, on the righthand side by traffic lights, you meet Sweny's Chemists, immortalised in *Ulysses*. Opposite Sweny's is Kennedy's pub. 'Conway's Corner' in *Ulysses*, it was frequented by both Beckett and James Joyce. Further down Westland Row on the left, Oscar Wilde was born at number 22 in 1854. John Stanislaus Joyce worked as an accountant at number 13 in 1879.

Retrace your steps back along Lincoln Place. George Russell produced *The Irish Homestead* and *The Irish Statesman* at number 22, where he published James Joyce's first stories, *The Sisters* and *Eveline* in 1904. Brendan Behan sang outside the nearby Lincoln Inn pub on his way to Paris with Beatrice after their 1955 marriage. Nora Barnacle, who married Joyce, was a chambermaid a few doors away at Finn's Hotel, 1 and 2 Leinster Street South. Beside Trinity College Park, where Patrick Kavanagh once played cricket and Oliver St John Gogarty competed in the Irish cycling championships.

Continue along Nassau Street and take first left into Kildare Street. Lady Morgan lived on the righthand side at number 39, opposite the National Library which was frequented by every major Irish writer from Joyce and Gogarty to Beckett and Behan. Joyce's daughter, Lucia, stayed at Buswell's Hotel on the corner of Molesworth Street in 1935.

Charles Lever lodged in the 1820s at 33 Molesworth Street, Lisle House, which also featured as Mrs. Clanfrizzle's boarding house in his book, *Harry Lorrequer*. Across the street, George Bernard Shaw worked in 1871 at number 15. Turn left into Dawson Street to St

National Library of Ireland

Ann's Church, where Lafcadio Hearn's great grandfather was Rector in the early 1700s and where Bram Stoker married in 1878. Poet Felicity Hemans was buried here in 1835, after her death at number 21, further up on the left.

Retrace your steps to Kildare Street. On the right, you will find number 30, where Bram Stoker lived in the 1870s. Turn left at the Shelbourne Hotel, where George Moore wrote *A Drama in Muslin* and corresponded with Emile Zola. Rudyard Kipling and William Thackeray stayed here, as well as Elizabeth Bowen and novelist, Brian Moore. Oliver St John Gogarty had consulting rooms next door at 27 St Stephen's Green.

Continue along Merrion Row, past the Huguenot Cemetery, and take first right into Ely Place. Oscar Wilde proposed to Constance Lloyd at number one on the left. At the top of the street, on the same side, George Moore lived at number 4. Opposite was Oliver St John Gogarty's balconied home at number 15, which has been replaced by the RHA oblong.

2. Stephen's Green to Trinity College, St. Patrick's Cathedral and York Street

Start in flower-bordered St Stephen's Green. Its statuary includes Henry Moore's apposite 'Knife Edge' tribute to W.B. Yeats. And busts of James Clarence Mangan and James Joyce and his friend, Tom Kettle.

Exit by the Boer War Dublin Fusiliers Arch, whose list of victims includes Private J. Behan, an uncle of Brendan Behan. Cross the road towards Grafton Street. On the right is number 9 St. Stephen's Green, where crowds cheered Sir Walter Scott, on his 1825 visit to Maria Edgeworth. Number 7 housed the studio of three of Ireland's most famous artists, Walter Osborne, John B. Yeats and, in the 1950s, Sean O'Sullivan.

Heading down Grafton Street, novelist Samuel Lover was born a few doors away at number 60 (now, Disney) on the left. Number 39 on the right (now a hamburger emporium) housed John Ryan's *Envoy* magazine. Brendan Behan, J P Donleavy, Ernie Gebler, Patrick Kavanagh, Nobel Prize-winning physicist, Erwin Schrodinger and the Pike Theatre's Alan and Carolyn Simpson were among the many visitors to the top-floor studio and salon of sculptor Des MacNamara and his wife, Bevelie.

Henry Moore's tribute to W.B. Yeats

Many went across the road to Harry Street on the left and established McDaid's as a leading literary bar. Left at the end of Harry Street is Balfe Street, where composer William Balfe was born in 1808 at number 10 on the left, now a restaurant.

Back on Grafton Street, Percy Bysshe Shelley stayed at the corner number 17 (now Marks and Spencer), on his 1812 visit. Number 79, opposite, housed Samuel Whyte's Academy. Established in 1758, its students included Lover, Tom Moore, Richard Brinsley Sheridan, Robert Emmet and the Duke of Wellington. Bewley's opened a cafe there in 1927, which boasts six stained glass windows by artist Harry Clarke and customers including Patrick Kavanagh and Maeve Binchy.

On the left off Grafton Street is Andrew Street. In the graveyard of its church on the left (now the Failte Ireland office) Jonathan Swift's friend, Hester 'Vanessa' Vanhomrigh, was buried in

1723. Continuing down Grafton Street, number 116 was the meeting place of the late nineteenth century Contemporary Club. Its debaters included Stephen Gwynn, Douglas Hyde, George Sigerson, John B. and W.B. Yeats, Michael Davitt and John O'Leary.

Trinity College is on the right at the end of Grafton Street. Its roll-call ranges from Oliver Goldsmith, Edmund Burke, Charles Lever, Samuel Lover, Bram Stoker and Oscar Wilde to John Millington Synge, Samuel Beckett, Eavan Boland, J. P. Donleavy, Anne Enright and Brendan Kennelly.

Oliver Goldsmith, one of Trinity College's best-loved writers

Facing Trinity is Dame Street and, on the right, the former Irish parliament, which Thomas De Quincey visited in 1800. Half way up on the right at the junction with Eustace Street in number 60, Sydney Lady Morgan's first home in 1777.

Continuing up Dame Street past the City Hall on the left (well worth a visit), one reaches the higher ground of the original city. Turn left on its summit into Christ Church Place, opposite the Cathedral, and you will find the pub which occupies the site of James Clarence Mangan's birthplace.

Continue down into Werburgh Street (in whose church composer John Field was baptised in 1782) and you will find cobbled Little Ship Street on the left. On the left, just before the Dublin Castle gateway, you will find high up on the wall a stone plaque pointing to the site of 7 Hoey's Court, where Jonathan Swift was born in 1667.

Back on Werburgh Street, continue downhill. Second turn on the right is Bride Road. Half way down on the left is the Iveagh Hostel, where Patrick Kavanagh and Liam O'Flaherty briefly lodged. At the end of Bride Road, turn left and you will find St Patrick's Park and its memorial plaques to writers from Wilde to Behan. Overlooking the parade of plaques, a granite stone marks the 1782 birthplace of John Field at the junction of Bride Street and Golden Lane.

Jonathan Swift was Dean of Patrick's Cathedral, where one can see his pulpit, death mask and grave, beside that of his friend, Esther 'Stella' Johnson. Also, a rush lamp, by whose light Stella and he are said to have read. Opposite the cathedral in St. Patrick's Close is the deanery where Swift died in 1745.

On the left, where the Close bends, is Marsh's Library, Ireland's first public library built in 1701. Its wide timber stairs and book-filled alcoves provide a breathtaking step back into the eighteenth century. Some of its treasures were smuggled out of France by its first librarian, Dr. Elias Bouhereau, one of the 10,000 Huguenots who found

St. Patrick's Park features plaques of Dublin writers

refuge in Ireland. Many writers studied and wrote in Marsh's, including William Carleton, James Joyce, James Clarence Mangan, Charles Maturin, Thomas Moore, Bram Stoker, and, possibly, Oliver Goldsmith. At the end of the St. Patrick's Close, turn left into Kevin Street.

After 250 yards, you will reach the junction with Camden Street. Turn right and on the right at number 37 is the birthplace of Robert Noonan aka Tressell, author of *The Ragged Trousered Philanthropists*. Continue up Camden Street a short distance to the Art Deco Camden De Luxe Cinema, now a hotel, where Ernie Gebler worked as a projectionist in the 1940s. Returning towards Kevin Street, on the left is Camden Row, where poet Tom Moore's parents are buried a few yards up on the right, in the tiny oasis of St. Kevin's Churchyard. Continue along Camden Street, across Kevin Street, into Aungier Street. After the church, you will reach the birthplace of Tom Moore at number 12 on the right.

Retrace your steps once more and, after a few yards, turn left into York Street. Imagination is required, thanks to the depredations of developers, but the College of Surgeons complex on the left includes the site of number 7, where Gothic novelist Charles Maturin lived from 1804 until his death in 1824. Also, next-door number 6, where poet James Clarence Mangan started work as a scrivener in 1818. James Stephens lodged in the 1890s at number 30, across the street. At the end of York Street, you will find your original Stephen's Green starting point.

Thomas Moore, The Bard of Erin

*Generations of writers from Swift and Mangan to Carleton and Joyce
traversed these stairs to Marsh's Library*

3. Grand Canal – Grand Canal Street to Herbert Place and Portobello

Greeny banks, reflected light and sparkling cascades illuminate the very literary Grand Canal. Among those who traversed or wrote about it were Nelson Algren, Elizabeth Bowen, Paul Durcan, Michael Hartnett, Aidan Higgins, Nevill Johnson, James Joyce, Patrick Kavanagh, Brendan Kennelly, Thomas Kinsella, Charles Lever, James Liddy, John Montague, Liam O'Flaherty, George Moore, William Trollope and artist and writer, Jack B. Yeats.

Start at Macquay's Bridge on Grand Canal Street. The adjacent canal basin houses the *Naomh Eanna* Aran islands ferry, whose distinguished passengers included Liam O'Flaherty, Brendan Behan and artist Paul Hogarth. Look down Grand Canal Street towards the city centre and you will see on the left Sir Patrick Dun's Hospital, where Charles Lever and Sir William Wilde studied. In 1828, Lever launched a canoe in the canal which he had brought back from Canada.

Walk west towards McKenny's Bridge in Lower Mount Street and you will traverse the stretch on which Stephen Dedalus, aka James Joyce, discussed his theories of art with his friend, Lynch. Look right along Lower Mount Street. One hundred metres down on the left, is the projecting canopy of the Elphis Nursing Home, number 19, where J.M. Synge died in 1909.

Continuing west along the canal, you will pass the sites of the former temporary homes of Sheridan le Fanu at numbers 1 and 15. And once-book-lined number 11, where W.B. Yeats's mentor, John O'Leary lived. Poet Thomas Kinsella lived on the opposite bank at 47 Percy Place, overlooking the canal's most beautiful crossing, Huband Bridge.

St. Stephen's Church, The Peppercannister

Edward Bunting was once organist in St Stephen's Church, The Peppercannister, on the right, which Elizabeth Bowen attended as a child. Percy French married here in 1890, and Jack Yeats's funeral was held at the church in 1957. The church faces Mount Street Upper, where many 1950s artists lived and where, at number 23, Liam Millar launched the Dolmen Press, which published Frank O'Connor and leading writers. John Betjeman was wartime British Press Attache at number 50. Anne Yeats lived at 39 after her uncle Jack's death, while Patrick Kavanagh stayed at number 37 in 1963.

To the left of the rear of The Peppercannister is Herbert Lane, where sculptor John Behan once lived and where, at number 18, the Pike Theatre staged the 1954 premiere of Brendan Behan's *The Quare Fellow*. Reginald Gray, best man at Behan's wedding, designed the sets for the theatre's 1957 *Rose Tattoo* production, which resulted in Alan Simpson's arrest in Herbert Lane. Herbert Street is on the left of the church entrance. Samuel Beckett's mother and poet Patrick Kavanagh died at number 21, originally the Merrion Nursing Home. Brendan Behan lived at 15, John Montague at number 6.

Back on the canal, turn right and you will pass Brian O'Nolan's lofty former residence 25 Herbert Place. Elizabeth Bowen was born at 15 in 1899. Further on, Macartney Bridge crosses Baggot Street. George Moore remembered: 'Gill and I leaned over Baggot Street Bridge, watching the canal-boat rising up in the lock, the opening of the gates to allow the boat to go through, and the hitching on of the rope to the cross-bar...'

A typewriter wobbling in his handlebars' basket, legendary editor Bertie Smylie daily cycled across the bridge in the 1940s and 1950s en route to his *Irish Times* office. Patrick Kavanagh and artists Nevill Johnson and Michael Kane were among those who savoured its canal

Harry Kernoff's atmospheric Tram Over Leeson Street Bridge

views. Parsons Bookshop, now a cafe, stood beside the bridge's junction with Mespil Road. Its clientele was a Who's Who of 1950s Irish writers and artists.

South, down Pembroke Road, past Patrick Kavanagh's favourite pubs, Searson's and the Waterloo, the poet lived on the left side at number 62. Maeve Binchy taught at Miss Meredith's School, number 1, on the opposite side at the junction with Waterloo Road. North of the bridge, descending into Dublin, is Lower Baggot Street. Thomas Davis died at number 67 on the right in 1845 and artist Francis Bacon was born at 63 in 1909.

Continuing along the canal, you reach the memorial seats to Patrick Kavanagh and Percy French, who lived on the opposite bank at 35 Mespil Road. On the right is Wilton Place and Court Apartments, where Frank O'Connor and Liam O'Flaherty lived their final years. Harry Kernoff, Liam C. Martin, Bunch Moran, Tom Nisbet, Owen Walsh and Sunny Apinchapong are among the artists who painted this stretch. Nelson Algren walked here with John Montague, while fellow-American Thomas Flanagan discoursed with Frank O'Connor and Ben Kiely.

Around 1909, Mainie Jellett made some of her earliest drawings here, where, fourteen years later, Brian O'Nolan trudged to Synge Street School. Late after a date, J.P. Donleavy's *Ginger Man* walked here, wondering what excuses to make to his long-suffering wife. On the right, just before the next bridge, is 11 Upper Lad Lane, where Mary Lavin lived in the 1950s.

Eustace Bridge straddles the canal between Lower and Upper Leeson Street. On the western side is the lock in which Brendan Behan joined frolicking children one hot day in 1950. J.M. Synge attended school at nearby 4 Upper Leeson Street, on the bridge's south side. In the late 1850s, Lafcadio Hearn lived two hundred metres further down (same side) at number 73. Artist Nuala O'Donel lived across Eustace Bridge in 1899 at 47 Lower Leeson Street before moving to

Paris, where she committed suicide out of unrequited love for sculptor Auguste Rodin.

Charlemont Bridge is the next bridge at the junction of Charlemont Street and Ranelagh Road. Samuel Beckett walked along here in the 1950s when visiting Jack B. Yeats in the Portobello Nursing Home. Charlemont is followed by La Touche Bridge at Portobello Harbour. Jack B. Yeats died in 1957 in the adjacent Portobello Nursing Home, now a college. Novelist Katherine Tynan was born in 1859 at 25 South Richmond Street, which runs down from the bridge towards the city centre. Turn left into Lennox Street, and the first right will bring you to George Bernard Shaw's 1856 birthplace at number 33, now a museum. Right at the end of the street into South Circular Road, and left into Camden Street, will bring you back to Dame Street and the city centre.

4. Lower Gardiner Street to North Circular Road and Parnell Square

Start at Beresford Place, behind the Custom House, and turn into Lower Gardiner Street. On the left side is number 47, where playwright Dion Boucicault was born in 1820. Continue for 300 metres up the slope, turn right into Mountjoy Square South and left into Mountjoy Square East. At the end, across the traffic lights is 2 Belvedere Place, home of the cultured Sheehy family in the early 1900s. James Joyce visited and sang here to his mother's piano accompaniment. His friends Tom Kettle and the pacifist Francis Skeffington were also regular guests. Hannah Sheehy married Francis Skeffington, Mary married Tom Kettle. Both men perished in 1916, Skeffington in Dublin, Kettle on the Somme.

Retrace your steps along the square and, at the end Mountjoy Square East, turn left into Great Charles Street. James Clarence

Mangan and scholar John O'Donovan worked on the right side of the street at number 21, the Ordnance Survey Office. Between 1835 and 1850, it was also the home of one of Ireland's most unsung Men of Letters, the artist, antiquary and music collector, George Petrie.

Continue down and turn right into North Circular Road (NCR). After the school on the opposite side, turn left into North Richmond Street. The Joyce family lived at number 17 on the right, from which James Joyce walked to Belvedere College (mentioned later) in the mid-1890s. Turn back and left into NCR. On the left you will reach number 617, James Joyce's last Dublin address. He lodged here in August-September 1912 and then left Ireland, never to return.

Retrace your steps and after North Richmond Street, you will find O'Connell's School, whose pupils included Tom Kettle, poet Thomas Kinsella, singer Luke Kelly and WWII Spitfire ace, Brendan 'Paddy' Finnucane. Brendan Behan attended St. Canice's School at number 575. With his left-wing credentials, he would no doubt be pleased that it is now the Communications Workers' Union headquarters, named William Norton House after his contemporary, Labour Party leader, Bill Norton. Second road on the right is Russell Street. The yarns in Brendan's *Hold Your Hour and Have Another* – a rare record of Dublin wit - were mainly based on characters in Gill's corner pub. Brendan spent his youth at number 14 on the left side, now demolished. Luca's adjacent Asti restaurant dispenses cheer and good coffee for thirsty walkers.

Retrace your steps and turn right into NCR. After crossing Sherrard Street Lower, veer right into Belvedere Road. Cross busy Dorset Street into Innisfallen Parade. Sean O'Casey lived on the right at number 9, where his father died in 1886. Take first turn left into Synnott Row. Walk to the junction with NCR and, on the opposite side, is number 422. Here, Sean O'Casey wrote his first three plays between 1923 and 1926, *The Shadow of a Gunman, Juno and the Paycock* and *The Plough and the Stars*.

Walk down the slope to the left and turn right into Upper Dorset Street. After about 200 metres, on the righthand side junction with St. Joseph's Place, you will find number 85, where Sean O'Casey was born in 1880. Retrace your steps along Dorset Street and take the second left turn into Eccles Street. Larry O'Rourke's corner pub, now the Aurora, and St. George's Church on the opposite side of Dorset Street, both feature in *Ulysses*. Its protagonist, Leopold Bloom, lived on the right side at now demolished 7 Eccles Street, the real-life home of Joyce's loyal friend, J.F. Byrne.

Continue up Eccles Street and take first left into Nelson Street. Sheridan le Fanu lived briefly on the left at number 2 after his marriage in 1844. Nelson Street is also the setting for Brendan Behan's play, *The Hostage*. Veer left and across into downhill Mountjoy Street. Take the fourth right into Fontenoy Street. Number 44 was one of the final addresses of the impoverished Joyce family. James Joyce stayed here with his son Giorgio in 1909. And between October 1909 and June 1910, while trying to set up the Volta Cinema.

Return to Mountjoy Street. Turn right and on the opposite side beside the boarded-up shop is the site of number 15, where Austin Clarke lived from 1899 until 1910. The adjacent island Black Church features in his work and also in *Ulysses*.

St. Mary's Chapel of Ease, known as the Black Church, featured in Joyce's Ulysses

Turn left by the side of the church and descend the short

distance to Dorset Street. A few metres down Dorset Street to the right is the site of Richard Brinsley Sheridan's 1751 birthplace at number 12. Retrace your steps and turn right into Granby Row. Turn left into Parnell Square North and you will find the Dublin Writers Museum on the left. Turn right and down Parnell Square East, almost opposite the Gate Theatre, is Oliver St. John Gogarty's 1878 birthplace, number 5.

Beside the Gate are the Rotunda Rooms, where Charles Dickens gave a reading from his works in 1858 and over which Liam O'Flaherty hoisted the red Flag in 1922. After Gogarty's house, turn left into Parnell Street. Take the second left into North Great Georges Street. Sir Samuel Ferguson kept open house for all interested in literature and art at number 20, on the left. Opposite at number 35 is the James Joyce Cultural Centre, product of the dream and dedication of Senator David Norris and Ken Monaghan, the writer's nephew.

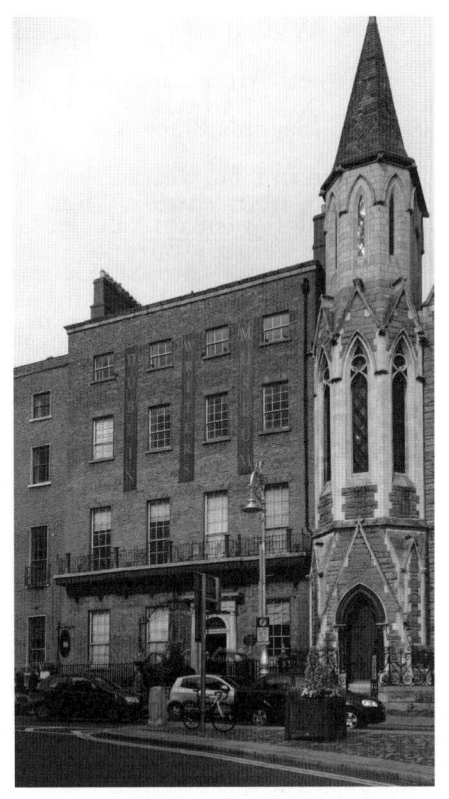

Dublin Writers Museum is well worth a visit

On the same side, Oscar Wilde's Trinity College mentor, John Pentland Mahaffy, lived at 38. Belvedere College closes the top of the street. Austin Clarke, Denis Devlin, Conal O'Riordan and Mervyn Wall studied here. And, between 1894 and 1896, James Joyce. The atmospheric Cobalt Cafe and Gallery, on the left side, at 16 North Great Georges Street, provides a convenient resting place.

5. Literary Pubs – Fleet Street to Duke Street and Westland Row

Dublin's literary hostelries were among the liveliest in twentieth century Europe. Start in Fleet Street, off Westmoreland Street, which features two famous establishments. The Pearl Bar was situated on the east side. The Palace Bar, which still stands, on the west.

Cyril Connolly enjoyed a 1940s Dublin visit: 'The Palace Bar is perhaps the last place of its kind in Europe. A Café Literaire, where one can walk in to have an intelligent discussion with a stranger, listen to Sean O'Sullivan on the early days of James Joyce, or discuss the national problem with the giant Hemingway-esque editor of the *Irish Times*.'

The Palace features the original of Dublin's most famous pub scene. The cartoon by Alan Reeve which captured such writers and artists as Austin Clarke, Padraic Fallon, Brinsley MacNamara, Ewart Milne, Brian O'Nolan and Sean O'Sullivan. Con Houlihan, Dylan Thomas and William Saroyan visited later. The pub was immortalised in Patrick Kavanagh's 'The Battle of the Palace Bar', about a fight which erupted after Louis MacNeice was allegedly insulted: 'They fought like barbarians, these highbrow grammarians...'

A short walk via Westmoreland Street to Grafton Street leads to Duke Street, on the left, and the Joycean strongholds of Davy Byrne's and the Bailey. Their roll-call included Oliver St John Gogarty, Tom Kettle, Sir William Orpen and James Stephens. Also frequented by Samuel Beckett, Brendan Behan and J.P. Donleavy, Davy Byrne's was immortalised in *Ulysses*: 'Moral pub. He doesn't chat. Stands a drink now and then. But in leapyear once in four. Cashed a cheque for me once.'

Cecil Salkeld painted the *Bacchanalia* murals which illuminate the bar's wall. George Bernard Shaw and other literati disport them-

Alan Reeve's cartoon of The Palace Bar

selves on an eternally sunny beach. A plaque at Duke Street's junction with Dawson Street marks the spot where Leopold Bloom asked a blind man if he wanted to cross the road.

Oliver St. John Gogarty described the Bailey as: 'the true museum of Dublin because it is the House of the Muses.' Impecunious Padraic O'Conaire visited, to the discomfiture of literary editor, Seamus O'Sullivan: 'Here comes O'Conaire who will soon be drinking beyond our means.' Owned in the 1950s by *Envoy*'s John Ryan, the Bailey welcomed actors and writers from Cyril Cusack and Michael Hartnett to Richard Murphy, Ted Hughes and Sylvia Plath. J.P. Donleavy drowned his sorrows here with Brendan Behan, Des MacNamara and actor Richard Harris after *The Ginger Man* play was banned in 1959.

Across the laneway from the Bailey is the Duke, originally Tobins, where Parnell's Land League supporters regularly supped. Brendan Behan and Patrick Kavanagh also visited. It was also the pub to which James Joyce brought James Stephens, a fortnight before he left Dublin for good in September, 1912. Stephens remembered that, after Joyce had disparaged his writing: 'I confided to him that I had never read a word of his, and that, if heaven preserved to me my protective wits, I never would read a word of his unless I was asked to review it destructively.' Joyce mellowed and sang 'The Yellow Ale' for Stephens and the pair subsequently became close friends in Paris. Duke proprietor, Tom Gilligan, insists: 'I am always conscious of those giants who came through our door.'

Tom Gilligan, proprietor of The Duke

Retrace your steps to Grafton Street and the next left, South Anne Street, features Kehoe's. Brendan and Beatrice Behan frequently sought the solitude of its cosy snug. Back on the opposite side of Grafton Street, is Harry Street and McDaid's. Its earliest literary association was a visit by James Joyce's father, John Stanislaus, who fell down the stairs. A mishap later attributed to Tom Kernan in the short story, 'Grace'.

As well as Brendan Behan, Patrick Kavanagh, J.P. Donleavy, 'Ginger Man' Gainor Crist and Brian O'Nolan, McDaid's attracted younger literati Pearse Hutchinson, Val Iremonger and John Jordan. Louis MacNeice, Theodore Roethke and Stephen Spender also visited. McDaid's success owed much to manager, Paddy O'Brien who, according to novelist Leland Bardwell acted 'as bank and nursemaid to all and sundry.'

When Paddy was employed by Grogan's Castle Lounge, McDaid's clientele immediately followed him across to South William Street. A shortcut through Westbury Mall to Coppinger Row will bring you to Grogan's, whose regulars included Michael Hartnett, John Jordan, Des MacNamara, Macdara Woods and artists Brian Bourke, Charlie Brady and Owen Walsh.

Walk southwards along South William Street and take the first left into Chatham Row, which leads to Chatham Street. Near its junction with Grafton Street, a pair of upraised lanterns welcome you to happily television-less

Paddy O'Brien in McDaid's

Neary's. It was a favourite of Stephen and Kathleen Behan. Brendan and Beatrice Behan also drank here, as did Brian O'Nolan and actors Cyril Cusack, Jimmy O'Dea and Michael Caine.

John Ryan recalled the day he left Neary's for a betting shop with myopic English poet John Heath-Stubbs: 'Never having even seen a bookie's shop, but dimly comprehending a counter, assistants and noisy, beery customers, Heath-Stubbs, thinking that we were in yet another bar, called for a fresh round for the whole company!'

Turn right from Neary's into Grafton Street and then left at the top along Stephen's Green. First left is Dawson Street and a few doors down on the left, you will find the entrance to Dublin's smallest pub, the Dawson Lounge. Its owner, Arthur Gilligan, once had to bail out Brendan Behan. After closing time, Sean O'Sullivan, who painted James Joyce, would often carry on his arguments with Behan in the middle of the traffic-free street.

Continue along Stephen's Green to the Shelbourne Hotel, whose bar welcomed writers from George Moore and Elizabeth Bowen to J.P. Donleavy and Brian Friel. The street leads into Merrion Row. Past O'Donoghue's, where the Dubliners group exploded into life, you will find Doheny and Nesbitt's on the left. A haunt of politicians, it was frequented by artists such as Nevill Johnson and Owen Walsh and later writers, David Hanly, Neil Jordan and Joseph O'Connor.

Merrion Row becomes Baggot Street. On the left, beside the next junction, Larry Murphy's features a long-hidden mural by Owen Walsh. A few doors away, also on the left, a banking oblong occupies the site of Phil Ryan's landmark *Lampshades* lounge. Its imbibers included publisher Liam Miller, poet John Montague, novelist Kate O'Brien, theatre owner, Madame Toto Cogley and actors Milo O'Shea, Marie Conmee and Marie Keane.

The Pike Theatre's Alan and Carolyn Simpson retreated here in 1957, after their indecency prosecution for staging Tennessee Williams' *The Rose Tattoo*. Former barman Peter Keogh remembered: 'We gave them what support we could – as well as a great send-off, when they all marched down together to the court on the quays.'

Continue up Baggot Street and over the canal bridge. Patrick Kavanagh and Brendan Behan set their watches by the clock which hangs over the Mespil Road junction. Opposite Parsons Bookshop, the financial building was formerly Mooney's pub, where Behan regularly entertained visiting journalists. Continue down the slope and you will find two of Kavanagh's haunts, Searsons and the Waterloo.

Retrace your steps and, after recrossing the bridge, turn right. A pleasant canal walk will bring you to Mount Street Lower. Turn left and walk to the end of Merrion Square. Turn right at Oscar Wilde's house and at the junction with Westland Row, you will find Kennedy's, a convenient place to rest your feet.

Kennedy's was well known to Brendan Behan, James Joyce and Samuel Beckett. The latter celebrated pub life in the days before television and the conversation-killing mobile phone: 'The bottles drawn and emptied in a twinkling, the casks responding to the slightest pressure on their joysticks, the weary proletarians at rest on arse and elbow, the cash-register that never complains, the graceful curates flying from customer to customer... a pleasant instance of machinery decently subservient to appetite.'

6. Glasnevin Cemetery

Having retraced writers' footsteps, readers may wish to visit the final resting places of those buried in Dublin. Glasnevin and Mount Jerome CemeteriesI are each within fifteen minutes of the city centre.

Northside Glasnevin Cemetery features the graves of writers from Brendan Behan to Patricia Lynch and James Clarence Mangan. And James Joyce's parents, John Stanislaus and Mary Jane Joyce.

Turn right at the entrance and immediately left down by the circle. Just after the junction with the fifth pathway, you will see on the left the slim granite stone to Labour leader, James Larkin. Shortly after the junction with the sixth pathway, on the right, a white marble Virgin on a plinth overlooks the grave of *Envoy* editor John Ryan. With his well-thumbed copy of *Ulysses,* he was buried here in 1992, beside his film star sister, Kathleen.

Retrace your steps and turn left at the road just before the entrance. After one hundred metres, take the second-last turn on the left. On the right, another hundred metres down, you will find the grave of Brendan and Beatrice Behan, together with poet Blanaid Salkeld and artist Cecil Salkeld. Opposite, is the grave of Francis Sheehy-Skeffington and his Suffragette wife, Hanna, friends of James Joyce.

Commemorated by John Coll's sculpture seat, Brendan Behan is buried in Glasnevin

Continue down this road and turn left. Twenty metres forward on the right side is a square grave enclosed by railings. Turn right on to the grass and you will find James Clarence Mangan's grave two thirds of the way down, just before the next road. It is one of a pair of identical head-high granite monuments with low conical crowns.

Continue straight down and cross the road and – beside a lofty urn - you will find the plain cross on two granite blocks which marks the grave of John Cornelius O'Callaghan, who wrote the history of the Irish Brigades in France. A few yards to the right and in about twenty rows, is the grave, topped by a raised sarcophagus, of William John Fitzpatrick, who wrote biographies of Lady Morgan and Samuel Lover.

Back on the road, almost directly opposite to the right, you will see a pair of imposing Celtic crosses, one of which is over the grave of novelist Rosa Gilbert. Beside her, is the grave of biographer Sarah Atkinson. Nearby, one row in, after Alice McCann's monument, a tall cross marks the grave of poet Denis Florence MacCarthy.

Return to the road and head back towards the centre of the cemetery. Ignore the fork to the left, and take the third smaller path to the left (which features the Borza plot). Up on the left is the broken column over nationalist leader, Arthur Griffith. On the right of the path, a few rows in, is the grave of novelist Maura Laverty.

Continue up the path and turn right onto the road which leads to the huge stone which marks the grave of Charles Stewart Parnell on the left. One of his admirers was James Joyce and, almost opposite, three rows in, on the right of the road, is the vertical white stone which marks the grave of the writer's parents, John Stanislaus and Mary Jane Joyce.

Continue along this road and take the first right. After the next crossroads, you will find the grave of former President Sean T. O'Kelly under an ornate Celtic cross on the left. Midway between the next two paths to the left, close to the religious Horan statue, is the dark vertical slab which marks the graves of storyteller Patricia Lynch and her journalist husband, R.M. Fox. Further down this road, on the left after crossing the third pathway to the left, is the grave of novelist, Kate Cruise O'Brien, under a tall slim stone.

Retrace your steps and head up the slope. On the right, just before you reach the boundary wall, poet Gerard Manley Hopkins is buried in the enclosed Jesuit Plot. May O'Flaherty of Parsons Bookshop, who died on 27 March, 1991, is buried further up on the right, the cemetery office will provide the best route to her Lehane family grave. Novelists Christy Brown, Seamus O'Kelly and singer Luke Kelly are buried in St. Paul's Cemetery on the other side of busy Finglas Road.

7. Mount Jerome, Harold's Cross Road

An oasis of space and bird-song like Glasnevin, Mount Jerome cemetery to the south-west of the city contains the graves of William Carleton, Thomas Davis, Sheridan le Fanu, George Russell and John Millington Synge.

Walk up The Avenue from the entrance to the church. On the right, just past the righthand Low Walk, you will find three steps which lead to William Carleton's mini obelisk Sir William Wilde rests on the left of the Avenue, opposite the church.

Keep to left of church on Guinness Walk. Behind the first gap in the righthand shrubbery is the grave of Gate Theatre owner Lord Longford and his playwright wife, Christine. A few metres in, on the opposite side of Guinness Walk, is the canopied monument to Martha Magee, philanthropist and founder of Derry's Magee College.

Retrace your steps to the chapel and turn at the top of the Avenue into Hawthorn Walk. Twelve metres after the junction with Long Walk, take the path on the left by the Hudson headstone. Thirty metres up, take the right path (by the Wingfield Figgis headstone) and, twelve spaces down, you will find John Millington Synge's grave.

Turn left into Nevill's Walk, which leads into Archbishop's Walk. Turn right onto Consecration Walk. Twenty seven plots up, on the right, you will find the graves of Thompson and O'Rorke. George Russell (AE) is buried five rows in, behind Thompson's grave.

Turn right into Drummond Walk. Cross North East Walk onto a small path which leads (five rows in) to the grave of Brendan Behan's friend, the composer Freddie May. Back on North East Walk, turn right towards the boundary wall and right again into Nun's Way. Joseph le Fanu is buried in the large flat Bennett family tomb on the left, where the road curves (beside headstone to Kathleen Keane). Opposite, on the right, lies artist Sarah Purser.

Continue down Nun's Walk and turn right into the Long Walk. Seventy metres up (opposite monument of a lady leaning on an urn), turn left onto a small path. Twenty metres in, a high Celtic cross marks the grave of poet Thomas Davis. Continue up Long Walk and turn left into Hawthorn Walk, which leads back to the church.

With over 300,000 burials, Mount Jerome requires a more detailed signpost. Roy Bateson's pocket-size *Dead and Buried in Dublin* (Irish Graves Publications) provides the most comprehensive and rewarding guide to it and all Dublin's cemeteries. Marvellously researched and illustrated, it boasts detailed directions and maps.

The book's Glasnevin notables range from poet George Sigerson, scholar Eugene O'Curry, John O'Leary, legendary book publisher, James Duffy, sculptors John Hogan and Christopher Moore to singers Josef Locke and Margaret Burke Sheridan, Conor Cruise O'Brien and a host of political figures Its Mount Jerome writers, artists and architects include Edward Dowden, George Fitzmaurice, William Edward Lecky, Mairtin O'Cadhain, Walter Osborne, Thomas Kirk, Thomas and John Skipton Mulvany, George Petrie and George Carr Shaw, father of George Bernard, and Jack B. Yeats.

Bateson's guide also covers Dean's Grange Cemetery, near Blackrock, six miles south of Dublin. The final resting place of writers Donal Foley, Francis MacManus, Frank O'Connor, Brian O'Nolan, Arts Club stalwart Tom Casement, actors Barry Fitzgerald and Anew McMaster, and singers Delia Murphy and John McCormack.

Mount Jerome Cemetery includes the graves of Sheridan le Fanu, George Russell and John Millington Synge, among others

Recommended Reading

Samuel Beckett:
Murphy. Molloy. Watt. More Pricks than Kicks. Waiting for Godot. Krapp's Last Tape. Selected Poems 1930–1989. Samuel Beckett: A Biography, Deirdre Bair. *Samuel Beckett: The Last Modernist*, Anthony Cronin.

Brendan Behan:
Borstal Boy. Hold Your Hour and Have Another. The Quare Fellow. The Hostage. Poems and a Play in Irish. My Life with Brendan, Beatrice Behan. *Brendan Behan*, Ulick O'Connor. *Brendan Behan - A Life*, Michael O'Sullivan.

Maeve Binchy:
Light a Penny Candle. Echoes. Firefly Summer. Circle of Friends. Tara Road.

Dion Boucicault:
London Assurance, The Colleen Bawn, Arrah-na-Pogue, The Shaughraun. *Dion Boucicault*, Richard Fawkes.

Elizabeth Bowen:
Encounters. The House in Paris. The Death of the Heart. The Heat of the Day. The Last September. Elizabeth Bowen: Portrait of a Writer, Victoria Glendenning.

Christy Brown:
My Left Foot. Down All the Days. The Collected Poems of Christy Brown. Christy Brown. The Life that Inspired My Left Foot, Georgina Louise Hambleton.

William Carleton:
Traits and Stories of the Irish Peasantry. Autobiography. Tales of Ireland. William Carleton: The Authentic Voice, Gordon Brand. *Poor Scholar*, Ben Kiely

Austin Clarke:
Collected Poems, Twice Around the Black Church. A Penny in the Clouds. Austin Clarke Remembered: Essays, Poems and Reminiscences to Mark the Centenary of His Birth, edited by R. Dardis Clarke.

Padraic Colum:
Wild Earth. Collected Poems. Castle Conquer. The Flying Swans. Our Friend James Joyce (Co-writer, Mary Colum). *Life and the Dream* by Mary Colum.

J P Donleavy:
The Ginger Man. A Singular Man. A Fairy Tale of New York. The Beastly Beatitudes of Balthazar B. The History of the Ginger Man. J P Donleavy's Ireland.

Ernest Gebler:
The Plymouth Adventure. Hoffman. He Had My Heart Scalded. The Love Investigator.

Recommended Reading

Oliver St. John Gogarty:
As I was Going Down Sackville Street. Intimations. Rolling Down the Lea. Tumbling in the Hay. Collected Poems. Oliver St. John Gogarty, Ulick O'Connor. *Surpassing Wit: Oliver St. John Gogarty, His Poetry and His Prose*, James F. Carens.

Lafcadio Hearn:
One of Cleopatra's Nights and Other Fantastic Romances. Kwaidan: Stories and Studies of Strange Things. The Romance of the Milky Way and other studies and stories. Japanese Lyrics. Out of the East. Reveries and Studies in New Japan. The Life and Letters of Lafcadio Hearn, Elizabeth Bisland. *Lafcadio Hearn*, Nina H. Kennard.

James Joyce:
A Portrait of the Artist as a Young Man. Dubliners. Ulysses. Collected Poems. James Joyce, A Biography, Gordon Bowker. *James Joyce: The Years of Growth, 1882-1915*, Peter Costello. *James Joyce*, Richard Ellmann.

Patrick Kavanagh:
Collected Poems. Collected Pruse. The Green Fool. Tarry Flynn. *Patrick Kavanagh, A Biography*, Antoinette Quinn. *Sacred Keeper*, Peter Kavanagh.

Ben Kiely:
Nothing Happens in Carmincross. Proxopera: A Tale of Modern Ireland. Land Without Star. A Letter to Peachtree. Drink to the Bird. The Waves Beneath Us.
Mary Lavin: *Tales from Bective Bridge. The House at Clewe Street. The Stories of Mary Lavin* (2 volumes). *The Four Seasons of Mary Lavin*, Leah Levenson.

Joseph Sheridan le Fanu:
The House by the Churchyard. Uncle Silas. In a Glass Darkly. Carmilla. Sheridan Le Fanu, Nelson Browne. *Joseph Sheridan Le Fanu*, Michael H. Begnal.

Charles Lever:
The Confessions of Harry Lorrequer. Charles O'Malley. Davenport Dunn. Lord Kilgobbin: A Tale of Ireland in our Own Time. Life of Charles Lever, W. J. Fitzpatrick. *Charles Lever, The Lost Victorian*, S.P Haddelsey (Foreword, Ben Kiely).

Literary Pubs:
The Dublin Literary Pub Crawl, Peter Costello. *Dead as Doornails*, Anthony Cronin. *Remembering How We Stood*, John Ryan.

Mary Lavin:
Tales from Bective Bridge. The House at Clewe Street. The Stories of Mary Lavin (2 volumes). *The Four Seasons of Mary Lavin*, Leah Levenson.

Samuel Lover:
Handy Andy. Rory O'More, A National Romance. Legends and Stories of Ireland. Poems of Ireland. The Life of S. Lover, RHA, Artistic, Literary and Musical, W. B. Bernard. *Samuel Lover*, A. J. Symington.

Patricia Lynch:
The Turf-Cutter's Donkey. King of the Tinkers. The Bookshop on the Quay. The Grey Goose of Kilnevin. The Brogeen Stories. Patricia Lynch, Storyteller, Phil Young.

James Clarence Mangan:
The Collected Poems of James Clarence Mangan. James Clarence Mangan, Selected Writings, Sean Ryder. *James Clarence Mangan*, Ellen Shannon-Mangan.

Charles Robert Maturin:
Melmoth the Wanderer. The Fatal Revenge. Women. The Universe (poems). *Charles Maturin. Authorship, Authenticity and the Nation*, Jim Kelly.

George Moore:
Esther Waters. A Mummer's Wife. The Lake. Confessions of a Young Man. Hail and Farewell. Conversations in Ebury Street. George Moore 1852-1933, Adrian Frazier. *G.M.: Memories of George Moore*, Nancy Cunard.

Thomas Moore:
The Poetical Works of Thomas Moore. Irish Melodies and Songs. Lalla Rookh, an Oriental Romance. Memoirs, Journal, and Correspondence of Thomas Moore. The Life of Thomas Moore, Ronan Kelly.

Sydney Lady Morgan:
The Wild Irish Girl. The Missionary: An Indian Tale. Florence Macarthy: An Irish Tale. Lady Morgan's Memoirs: Autobiography, Diaries and Correspondence. Lady Morgan: the Life and Times of Sydney Owenson, Mary Campbell.

Flann O'Brien:
At Swim-Two-Birds. The Hard Life. The Third Policeman. The Dalkey Archive. An Beal Bocht (The Poor Mouth). The Best of Myles: A Selection from 'Cruiskeen Lawn'. No Laughing Matter: The Life and Times of Flann O'Brien, Anthony Cronin.

Seán O'Casey:
The Shadow of a Gunman. Juno and the Paycock. The Plough and the Stars. The Silver Tassie. Autobiographies. Seán O'Casey and his World, David Krause.

Frank O'Connor:
The Stories of Frank O'Connor. The Best of Frank O'Connor. An Only Child. My Father's Son. The Midnight Court. The Little Monasteries. A Life of Frank O'Connor, James Matthews

Sean O'Faolain:
Bird Alone. A Nest of Simple Folk. The Collected Stories of Sean O'Faolain. Vive Moi. Sean O'Faolain, A Life, Maurice Harmon.

Liam O'Flaherty:
Famine. The Informer. Land. Skerrett. The Pedlar's Revenge and Other Stories. Shame the Devil. Liam O'Flaherty's Ireland, Peter Costello.

Parsons Bookshop:
Parsons Bookshop. At the Heart of Bohemian Dublin 1949-1989, Brendan Lynch.

James Plunkett:
Strumpet City. The Trusting and the Maimed. Farewell Companions. The Gems She Wore.

Recommended Reading

George Russell:
Collected Poems. Writings on Literature and Art, Politics, Society and Nationhood. The Descent of the Gods: The Mystical Writings. George Russell (AE) and the New Ireland 1905-30, Nicholas Allan. *That Myriad-Minded Man*, Henry Summerfield

George Bernard Shaw:
Collected Plays. The Complete Prefaces. The Selected Prose of Bernard Shaw. Bernard Shaw, Michael Holroyd.

James Stephens:
The Crock of Gold. The Charwoman's Daughter. Deirdre, The Hill of Vision, Irish Fairy Tales. The Poems of James Stephens. James Stephens, His Work and an Account of His Life, Hilary Pyle

Bram Stoker:
Dracula. The Judge's House. The Lady of the Shroud. The Mystery of the Sea. The Shoulder of Shasta. Bram Stoker: A Biography of the Author of 'Dracula', Barbara Bedford. *Jonathan Swift: A Tale of a Tub. The Battle of the Books. The Drapier's Letters. A Modest Proposal. Gulliver's Travels. Complete Poems. Jonathan Swift*, Victoria Glendenning.

Jonathan Swift:
A Tale of a Tub. The Battle of the Books. The Drapier's Letters. A Modest Proposal. Gulliver's Travels. Complete Poems. Jonathan Swift, Victoria Glendenning.

John Millington Synge:
Collected Works of John Millington Synge (4 vols). *J.M. Synge 1871-1909*, David H. Greene and Edward M. Stephens.

Oscar Wilde:
The Importance of Being Earnest and Other Plays. Complete Short Fiction. The Ballad of Reading Gaol. Oscar Wilde, Richard Ellmann. *Son of Oscar Wilde*, Vyvyan Holland. Lady Jane Wilde: *Poems. Ancient Legends. Speranza: A Biography*, Horace Wyndham. Sir William Wilde: *Lough Corrib. its Shores and Islands. The Narrative of a Voyage to Madeira, Teneriffe, and Along the Shores of the Mediterranean. The Wildes of Merrion Square*, Terence de Vere White.

W.B. Yeats:
Collected Poems. Collected Plays. Reveries over Childhood and Youth. The Trembling of the Veil. W. B. Yeats, A Life (2 vols), R.F. Foster.

Bibliography

Bair, Deirdre, *Samuel Beckett: A Biography*, Jonathan Cape, London, 1978.

Bardwell, Leland, *A Restless Life*, Liberties Press, Dublin, 2008.

Bateson, Ray, *The End, Graves of Irish Writers*, Irish Graves Publications, Warrenstown, 2004.

Beckett, Samuel, *More Pricks than Kicks*, Calder and Boyars, London, 1970.

Behan, Beatrice with Hickey, Des and Smith, Gus, *My Life with Brendan*, Leslie Frewin, London, 1973.

Belford, Barbara, *Bram Stoker: A Biography of the Author of 'Dracula'*, Weidenfeld & Nicolson, London, 1996.

Bourke, Marcus, *John O'Leary*, Geography Publications, Dublin, 2009.

Bowen, Elizabeth, *Seven Winters: Memories of a Dublin Childhood*, Longmans, Green and Co., London, 1943.

Bowker, Gordon, *James Joyce, A Biography*, Weidenfeld and Nicolson, London, 2011.

Boylan, Patricia, *All Cultivated People: A History of the United Arts Club*, Dublin, Colin Smythe, Gerrards Cross, 1988.

Bulfin, William, *Rambles in Eirinn*, M. H. Gill, Dublin, 1908.

Campbell, Mary, *Lady Morgan: the Life and Times of Sydney Owenson*, Pandora Press, London, 1988.

Colum, Mary, *Life and the Dream*, Macmillan & Co, London, 1947.

Cooper, Artemis. *Patrick Leigh Fermor*, John Murray, London, 2012.

Costello, Peter, *The Dublin Literary Pub Crawl*, A & A Farmer, Dublin, 1996.

Costello, Peter, *James Joyce, The Years of Growth, 1882-1915*, Kyle Cathie, London, 1992.

Costello, Peter, *Liam O'Flaherty's Ireland*, Wolfhound Press, 1996.

Costello, Peter and Jackson, John Wyse, *John Stanislaus Joyce*, Fourth Estate, London, 1997.

Bibliography

Cowell, John, *Where They Lived in Dublin*, The O'Brien Press, Dublin, 1980.

Cronin, Anthony, *Dead as Doornails*, Dolmen Press, Dublin, 1976.

Cronin, Anthony, *No Laughing Matter, The Life and Times of Flann O'Brien*, Grafton Books, London, 1989.

Cunard, Nancy, GM, *Memories of George Moore*, Rupert Hart-Davis, London, 1956.

Donleavy, J.P., *The Ginger Man*, Penguin Books, London, 1968.

Donleavy, J.P., *The History of the Ginger Man*, Viking, London, 1994.

Donleavy, J.P., *Ireland in All her Sins and in Some of her Graces*, Michael Joseph, London, 1986.

Downey, Edmund, *Charles Lever, His Life in His Letters*, Blackwood, London, 1906.

Ellmann, Richard, *James Joyce*, Oxford University Press, 1983.

Ellmann, Richard, *Oscar Wilde*, Hamish Hamilton, 1987.

Fallis, Richard, *The Irish Renaissance*, Gill and Macmillan, Dublin, 1978.

Fawkes, Richard, *Dion Boucicault*, Quartet Books, London 2011.

Fitzpatrick W. J., *The Life of Charles Lever*, Chapman and Hall, London, 1879.

Flanagan, Thomas, *The Irish Novelists 1800-1850*, Columbia University Press, 1959.

Foster, R. F., *W. B. Yeats: A Life. The Apprentice Mage, 1865-1914*, Oxford University Press, 1997.

Foster, R. F., *W. B. Yeats: A Life. The Arch Poet, 1915-1939*, Oxford University Press, 2003.

Frazier, Adrian, *George Moore*, Yale University Press, New Haven, 2000.

Glendenning, Victoria, *Jonathan Swift, A Portrait*, Henry Holt, London, 1999.

Gogarty, Oliver St John, *As I Was Going Down Sackville Street*, Sphere Books, London, 1988.

Gogarty, Oliver St John, *Intimations*, Sphere Books, London, 1985.

Greene, David H. and Stephens, Edward M., *J. M. Synge*, New York University Press, 1989.

Harmon, Maurice, *Sean O'Faolain, A Life*, Constable, London, 1994.

Harrison, Wilmot, *Memorable London Houses*, Reprint Press, London, 1971.

Healy, Elizabeth, *Literary Tour of Ireland*, Wolfhound Press, Dublin, 1995.

Hill, Judith, *Lady Gregory, An Irish Life*, Sutton Publishing, Thrupp, 2003.

Holland, Merlyn, *The Wilde Album*, Fourth Estate, London, 1997.

Igoe, Vivien, *A Literary Guide to Dublin*, Methuen, London, 1994.

Jackson, John Wyse and Bernard McGinley, *James Joyce's Dubliners: An Annotated Edition*, Sinclair-Stevenson, London, 1993.

Jeffares, A. Norman and van de Kamp, Peter, *Irish Literature. The Nineteenth Century*, Irish Academic press, Dublin, 2006.

Johnson, Nevill, *The Other Side of Six*, The Academy Press, Dublin, 1983.

Joyce, James, *A Portrait of the Artist as a Young Man*, Penguin Books, London, 1960.

Joyce, James. *Ulysses*, Penguin Books, London, 1969.

Kavanagh, Patrick, *Collected Poems*, edited by Antoinette Quinn, Allen Lane, London, 2004.

Kavanagh, Peter, *Patrick Kavanagh: A Life Chronicle*, The Peter Kavanagh Hand Press, New York, 2000.

Kearney, Colbert, *The Writings of Brendan Behan*, Gill and Macmillan, Dublin, 1977.

Kennard, Nina H., *Lafcadio Hearn*, Appleton, New York, 1912.

Kiely, Benedict, *The Waves Behind Us*, Methuen Publishing, London, 1999.

Kiely, David M., *John Millington Synge, A Biography*, Gill and Macmillan, Dublin, 1994.

Krause, David, *Sean O'Casey and His World*, Thames and Hudson, London, 1976.

Lalor, Brian (Editor), *The Encyclopedia of Ireland*, Gill and Macmillan, Dublin, 2003.

Lennon, Sean, *Dublin Writers and Their Haunts*, Fingal County Council, Dublin, 2003.

Levenson, Leah, *The Four Seasons of Mary Lavin*, Marino Books, Dublin, 1998.

Lynch, Brendan, *Parsons Bookshop, At the Heart of Bohemian Dublin 1949-1989*, Liffey Press, Dublin, 2006.

Lynch, Brendan, *Prodigals and Geniuses. The Writers and Artists of Dublin's Baggotonia*, Liffey Press, Dublin, 2011.

Lyons, J. B., *The Enigma of Tom Kettle*, Glendale Press, Dublin, 1983.

Bibliography

McCall, John, *The Life of James Clarence Mangan*, Carraig Chapbooks, Dublin, 1975.

McCarthy, Muriel, *All Graduates and Gentlemen, Marsh's Library*, O'Brien Press, Dublin, 1980.

Matthews, James, *Voices: A Life of Frank O'Connor*, Gill and Macmillan, Dublin, 1983.

Montague, John, *Company: A Chosen Life*, Duckworth, London, 2001.

Moore, George, *Hail and Farewell*, Heinemann, London, 1933.

Murphy, William M., *Prodigal Father: The Life of John Butler Yeats*, Cornell University Press, Ithaca, 1979.

Norris, David, *A Kick Against the Pricks*, Transworld Ireland, 2012.

O'Brien, Eoin, *The Beckett Country*, The Black Cat Press/Faber and Faber, Dublin, 1986.

O'Brien, Flann, *The Third Policeman*, McGibbon and Kee, London, 1967.

O'Connor, Ulick, *Brendan Behan*, Hamish Hamilton, London, 1970.

O'Connor, Ulick, *Oliver St John Gogarty*, Jonathan Cape, London, 1965.

O'Nolan, Kevin (editor), *The Best of Myles*, McGibbon and Kee, London, 1968.

O'Nuallain, Ciaran, *The Early years of Brian O'Nolan*, Lilliput Press, Dublin, 1998

O'Sullivan, Michael, *Brendan Behan: A Life*, Blackwater Press, Dublin, 1997.

Peters, Sally, *George Bernard Shaw. The Ascent of the Superman*, Yale University Press, 1996.

Pyle Hilary, *James Stephens, His Work and an Account of His Life*, Routledge & Kegan Paul, London, 1965.

Quinn, Antoinette, *Patrick Kavanagh: A Biography*, Gill and Macmillan, Dublin, 2001.

Ryan, John, *Remembering How We Stood*, Gill and Macmillan, Dublin, 1975.

Ryder, Sean, Editor, *James Clarence Mangan, Selected Wtritings*, University College Dublin Press, 2004.

Stephens, James, *The Crock of Gold*, Gill and Macmillan, Dublin, 1980.

Thomas, Edward, *Lafcadio Hearn*, Houghton Mifflin Co., New York, 1912.

Tomedi. John, *Bloom's Literary Guide to Dublin*, Chelsea House, New York, 2005.

Tynan, Katherine, *Twenty-five Years: Reminiscences*, Smith, Elder, London, 1913.

Walsh, Caroline, *The Homes of Irish Writers*, Anvil Books, 1982.

de Vere White, Terence, *The Parents of Oscar Wilde*, Hodder and Stoughton, 1967.

Williams, George, *Guide to Literary London*, Batsford, London, 1973.

Yeats, W. B., *The Collected Poems*, Macmillan, 1976.

Young, Phil, *Patricia Lynch: Storyteller*, Liberties Press, Dublin, 2005.

Newspapers and Periodicals
- The Chicago Tribune
- The Guardian
- The Irish Independent
- The Irish Press
- The Irish Times
- The Bell
- Envoy
- The Paris Review